A Book Of

MANAGING FOR SUSTAINABILITY

For
M.B.A. (Semester - IV)
And Other Allied Courses
As Per Revised Syllabus
Effective from June 2014

Dr. Nachiket M. Vechalekar
Associate Dean - Post Graduate Programmes
IndSearch, PUNE

MANAGING FOR SUSTAINABILITY   ISBN 978-93-5164-257-2

Second Edition : January 2016
© : Author

The text of this publication, or any part thereof, should not be reproduced or transmitted in any form or stored in any computer storage system or device for distribution including photocopy, recording, taping or information retrieval system or reproduced on any disc, tape, perforated media or other information storage device etc., without the written permission of Author with whom the rights are reserved. Breach of this condition is liable for legal action.

Every effort has been made to avoid errors or omissions in this publication. In spite of this, errors may have crept in. Any mistake, error or discrepancy so noted and shall be brought to our notice shall be taken care of in the next edition. It is notified that neither the publisher nor the author or seller shall be responsible for any damage or loss of action to any one, of any kind, in any manner, therefrom.

Published By :
NIRALI PRAKASHAN
Abhyudaya Pragati, 1312, Shivaji Nagar
Off J.M. Road, PUNE – 411005
Tel - (020) 25512336/37/39, Fax - (020) 25511379
Email : niralipune@pragationline.com

Printed By :
Repro Knowledgecast Limited,
Thane

☞ DISTRIBUTION CENTRES

PUNE
Nirali Prakashan : 119, Budhwar Peth, Jogeshwari Mandir Lane, Pune 411002, Maharashtra
Tel : (020) 2445 2044, 66022708, Fax : (020) 2445 1538
Email : bookorder@pragationline.com, niralilocal@pragationline.com
Nirali Prakashan : S. No. 28/27, Dhyari, Near Pari Company, Pune 411041
Tel : (020) 24690204 Fax : (020) 24690316
Email : dhyari@pragationline.com, bookorder@pragationline.com

MUMBAI
Nirali Prakashan : 385, S.V.P. Road, Rasdhara Co-op. Hsg. Society Ltd.,
Girgaum, Mumbai 400004, Maharashtra
Tel : (022) 2385 6339 / 2386 9976, Fax : (022) 2386 9976
Email : niralimumbai@pragationline.com

☞ DISTRIBUTION BRANCHES

JALGAON
Nirali Prakashan : 34, V. V. Golani Market, Navi Peth, Jalgaon 425001,
Maharashtra, Tel : (0257) 222 0395, Mob : 94234 91860

KOLHAPUR
Nirali Prakashan : New Mahadvar Road, Kedar Plaza, 1st Floor Opp. IDBI Bank
Kolhapur 416 012, Maharashtra. Mob : 9850046155

NAGPUR
Pratibha Book Distributors : Above Maratha Mandir, Shop No. 3, First Floor,
Rani Jhanshi Square, Sitabuldi, Nagpur 440012, Maharashtra
Tel : (0712) 254 7129

DELHI
Nirali Prakashan : 4593/21, Basement, Aggarwal Lane 15, Ansari Road, Daryaganj
Near Times of India Building, New Delhi 110002
Mob : 08505972553

BENGALURU
Pragati Book House : House No. 1, Sanjeevappa Lane, Avenue Road Cross,
Opp. Rice Church, Bengaluru – 560002.
Tel : (080) 64513344, 64513355,Mob : 9880582331, 9845021552
Email:bharatsavla@yahoo.com

CHENNAI
Pragati Books : 9/1, Montieth Road, Behind Taas Mahal, Egmore,
Chennai 600008 Tamil Nadu, Tel : (044) 6518 3535,
Mob : 94440 01782 / 98450 21552 / 98805 82331,
Email : bharatsavla@yahoo.com

niralipune@pragationline.com | www.pragationline.com
Also find us on www.facebook.com/niralibooks

Preface

Sustainability is one of the primary challenges facing humanity in the 21st century. All corporations, from businesses to governments to community organisations, seek to generate value with limited resources. More and more businesses are working progressively toward sustainable operations, with the end goal of doing no harm.

Sustainability is being able to survive and endure in an environment into the future. In terms of business, sustainability management is about incorporating social, economic and environmental factors into the business decisions. It involves emphasising on future, long term goals for the business rather than focusing on short term profits.

There are many benefits that result from incorporating social, economic and environmental factors into the decision making process in the business. It can help the managers to identify and avoid future costs associated with unsustainable business practices, such as dumping industrial waste into the environment. It can also help the managers to plan for changes in consumer expectations and allow them to capitalise on emerging markets and industries.

Sustainable management involves concepts such as corporate social responsibility and business ethics. A socially responsible business is one that aims to decrease its negative impact on society and enhance its positive influence.

In this book 'Managing for Sustainability', we foster a learning aptitude where students gain the capacity to think holistically, live their values, and invent and build an alternative future in which everyone prospers: people, organisations, and the planet.

I am thankful to my friends and long time publisher Shri Dineshbhai Furia, Shri Jignesh Furia and the entire staff of Nirali Prakashan, Pune without whose unerring support and sustained efforts, this book would not have seen the light of the day.

I am grateful to my family for their cooperation and full support at every stage of this book.

It is hoped that the book will be of great help to the students. Both my publisher and I will be thankful for any suggestions for the improvement of the book. We are confident that this text book will receive the patronage of all for whom it is intended.

Author

Syllabus ...

Number of Sessions

1. **Corporate Social Responsibility :** (7 + 2)
   Concept, The Nature of Corporate responsibility and Corporate Citizenship, Relevance in the present day Business Environment.
   Corporate Social Responsibility and Stakeholders: Internal and External Stakeholders, Responsibility to various Stakeholder Groups, Interest and Influence of various Stakeholder Groups, Formulating and Implementing a Policy for Corporate Social Responsibility.
   Bottom of the Pyramid Opportunities: Issues and Opportunities for business in Socially and Environmentally Sensitive World, Social and Environmental Problems and how they Shape Markets.

2. **Sustainable Development:** (7 + 2)
   Concept, Definition of Sustainable Development, Need, Importance, Education, Philosophical Development, Gandhian Thought on Sustainable Development, Sustainable Development and Social Framework, Equitable Distribution, Difference between Sustainable Development and Green Development, Criticism.
   Stakeholder Impact: Stakeholders and the Power they Wield, Reducing Socio-environmental Costs and Risks: Managing the Downside, Driving Revenues and creating Intangible Value: Managing the Upside.

3. **3.1 Business Case for Sustainable Development:** (7 + 2)
   Three dimensions of Sustainable Development
   1. **Environmental:** Atmosphere, Fresh Water and Oceans, Land use, Management of Human Consumption, Energy, Food, Waste Management, Understanding Ecological "Footprint": Eco-tracking, Carbon marketing, Carbon credits, Economics of Sustainability, Designing for the Environment and "Greening' the Supply Chain, Regulation, Case Studies.
   2. **Economic:** Environment Degradation and Economic Growth, Nature as an Economic Externality, Economic Opportunity.
   3. **Social:** Peace, Security, Social Justice, Sustainability and Poverty, Human Relationship to nature, Human Settlements.

   3.2 Study of Business Models for Sustainable Development: Indian and Global Perspectives.

   3.3 Sustainability Reporting: Triple Bottom Line Reports - The Content of Sustainability Reports (also CSR reports, ESG Reports, Social and Environmental Reports).

   3.4 Social Accountability Standard - ISO 26000: Social Responsibility Guidance Standard, Global Compact Principles, Environmental Impact Assessment, Life Cycle Analysis, Social Impact Assessment.

4. **4.1 Corporate Governance:** (7 + 2)
   Meaning - OECD Principles, Difference between Governance and Management, Purpose of Good Governance, Potential Consequences of Poor Corporate Governance, Business Failure and the Contribution of Poor Governance.
   4.2 Relevant Theories: Agency Theory, Transaction Cost Theory, Stakeholder Theory, Friedman's Theory of CSR.
   4.3 Stakeholder Value Approach: Stakeholder Value Approach, Enlightened Stakeholder Approach, Stakeholder Approach to Governance, Risk and Financial Stability. The Balancing of Conflicting Objectives.
   4.4 Key issues in Corporate Governance: Role and Composition of the Board, Remuneration of Directors and Senior Executives, Accounting and Audit, Internal Controls, Checks and Governance, Relations with Shareholders and other Stakeholders, Clause 49 of Listing Agreement and Corporate Governance Code, CEO, CFC Certification. Role of regulators - SEBI, IRDA, RBI, ED, etc.
   4.5 Applying Best Practice in Governance: Voluntary and Regulatory Approaches, Rules or Principles, Concept of 'Comply or Explain'. Governance Problems for Global Companies and Groups. Governance issues in the Public Sector. Governance issues in the Voluntary Sector (NGOs and Charitable Organizations)
   4.6 Governance Aspects: Sarbanes-Oxley Act 2002: Section 302: CEO/CFO Certifications, Section 404(a): Internal Control Report, Governance and Role of Auditors and Audit Committee.
   4.7 Case Studies on Corporate Governance: Satyam, Infosys, Tata, Wipro.
5. **Corporate Ethics:** (7 + 2)
   5.1 The Ethical Value System: Universalism, Utilitarianism, Distributive Justice, Social Contracts, Individual Freedom of Choice, Professional Code.
   5.2 Values: Importance, Sources of Value Systems, Values across Cultures.
   5.3 Indian Values and Ethics: Respect for Elders, Hierarchy and Status, Need for Security, Non - Violence, Cooperation, Simple Living high Thinking, Rights and Duties, Ethics in Work life, Holistic relationship between Man and Nature, Attitudes and Beliefs.
   5.4 Business Ethics: Nature, Characteristics and Needs, Ethical Practices in Management, Ethical Values in different Cultures, Culture and Individual Ethics, Relationship between Law and Ethics, Impact of Laws on Business Ethics.
   5.5 Ethics and Corporate Excellence: Code of Ethics in Business Houses, Strategies o1 Organizational Culture Building, Total Quality, Customer Care, Care of the Employees as per Statutes, Objective and Optimistic Approach.
   5.6 Indian and Global Case Studies.

Contents ...

1. Corporate Social Responsibility — 1.1 – 1.50

2. Sustainable Development — 2.1 – 2.30

3. Business Case for Sustainable Development — 3.1 – 3.58

4. Corporate Governance — 4.1 – 4.70

5. Corporate Ethics — 5.1 – 5.52

Question Paper : April 2015 — P.1 – P.1

Chapter 1...

Corporate Social Responsibility

Contents ...

1.1 Corporate Social Responsibility
- 1.1.1 Introduction
- 1.1.2 The Concept of Corporate Social Responsibility
- 1.1.3 Nature of Corporate Social Responsibility
- 1.1.4 Aspects of CSR
- 1.1.5 Forces for Corporate Social Responsibility
- 1.1.6 Relevance of Corporate Social Responsibility in the Present Day Business Environment
- 1.1.7 Criticism of Corporate Social Responsibility
- 1.1.8 Limits to Corporate Social Responsibilities
- 1.1.9 Measures for Enforcing Corporate Social Responsibilities
- 1.1.10 Barriers to Corporate Social Responsibility
- 1.1.11 Formulating and Implementing a Policy for Corporate Social Responsibility

1.2 Corporate Citizenship
- 1.2.1 Meaning and Definitions
- 1.2.2 Difference between Concept of Global Corporate Citizen and Other Allied Concepts
- 1.2.3 Nature of Corporate Citizenship
- 1.2.4 Benefits of Corporate Citizenship
- 1.2.5 Stages of Corporate Citizenship

1.3 Corporate Social Responsibility and Stakeholders
- 1.3.1 Meaning of Stakeholder
- 1.3.2 Types of Stakeholder: Internal and External Stakeholders
- 1.3.3 Responsibilities of Business towards Different Stakeholders
- 1.3.4 Stakeholder's Interests
- 1.3.5 Influence of Various Stakeholder Groups

1.4 Bottom of the Pyramid Opportunities: Issues and Opportunities for Business in Socially and Environmentally Sensitive World
- 1.4.1 Four Consumer Tiers
- 1.4.2 The Invisible Opportunity
- 1.4.3 Tier 4 Pioneers
- 1.4.4 Creating Buying Power
- 1.4.5 Shaping Aspirations
- 1.4.6 Improving Access
- 1.4.7 Tailoring Local Solutions
- 1.4.8 Putting it all Together

1.5 Environmental and Social Issues and How they Shape Market
- Points to Remember
- Questions for Discussion
- Multiple Choice Questions
- Project Questions

Learning Objectives ...
- To understand the concept, nature and relevance of corporate social responsibility
- To study the concept of corporate citizenship
- To learn the types and influence of stakeholders in business
- To be able to explain the formulation and implementation of CSR policy
- To study the concept of Bottom of Pyramid in CSR

1.1 Corporate Social Responsibility

1.1.1 Introduction

There is an increasing awareness of the inter-dependence between business and its environment in the society. Business organisations are no longer viewed as totally private bodies free to pursue their own goals. They are also expected to contribute to the welfare of society. The Managers are no longer considered to have responsibility only to the owners. Managers today are increasingly held accountable for the social effects of their actions. The operators of business enterprises affect a wide spectrum. The shareholders, the suppliers of resources, the consumers, the local community and society at large are affected by the way an enterprise functions. Hence, a business enterprise has to be socially very responsible, so that a social balance may be struck between the opposing interests of these groups. Several forces have led to the development of the concept of social responsibility.

Kenneth and *Andrews* explain the concept as follows: "By social responsibility, we mean the intelligent and objective concern for the welfare of society that restrains individual and corporate behaviour from ultimately destructive activities, no matter how immediately profitable, and leads in the direction of positive contributions to human betterment".

1.1.2 The Concept of Corporate Social Responsibility

The term social responsibility has been termed in various ways. Some people define it as the responsibility of business to perform its basic economic functions of producing and supplying products and services in the most efficient manner so as to maximise profits; others define it as the obligation to consider the interests of society while performing its economic function; still others view it as the philanthropic and charitable activities to promote education, health, employment, rural development and other social issues. 'Social responsibility implies responsibility to society beyond the basic economic responsibility of efficiency and profitability. As an economic agent of the society, a business enterprise must use its economic power to protect and promote social values and public interest.'

The social responsibility transcends legal obligations and it is on a voluntary basis for the genuine benefit of the society. In the words of *Peter Drucker*, social responsibility requires managers.

"To consider whether their action is likely to promote the public goal, to advance the basic beliefs of our society, to contribute to its stability, strength and harmony".

H. R. Bowen has defined social responsibility as, *"obligation (of manager) to pursue those policies, to make those decisions, or to follow those lines of action which are desirable in terms of objectives and values of our society"*.

The concept 'Social Responsibility' is required to be differentiated from social obligations and social responsiveness. 'Social obligations' indicate the typical activities of an organisation directed in response to market forces and internal aspirations. Such behaviour has been criticised as being too narrow and insufficient for long-term success and survival of most organisations. 'Social responsibility' is much broader as it requires an organisation to meet the expectations, norms and values of the society. Social responsibility is concerned with current issues whereas 'Social responsiveness' is anticipatory in nature. A socially responsive organisation has to anticipate changing or emerging social problems and respond to them.

1.1.3 Nature of Corporate Social Responsibility

Increasing the shareholders' value is considered to be the main objective of any corporate strategy. In fact this has been the backbone of various strategies followed by leading corporate houses across the globe. However if the recent failures of some leading business houses across the globe is any indication, it seems that maximising the shareholders' value alone is not sufficient. It has been proved that only maximising the value of shareholders has created an unprecedented greed in the minds of some of the leaders of prominent business houses and ultimately has resulted into the downfall of them. On the other hand there are examples of several business houses who have responded to the needs of the society and are prospering even in adverse situations. A question that naturally arises is that why some business houses fail miserably while some business houses continue to progress in spite of difficult environment? If we try to find out the answer for this, it is realised that there are some important aspects of a business which are beyond just maximising the shareholders' value. A business has to be sustainable and for this profit maximisation alone will not be sufficient. It has to be understood that apart from the shareholders there are several other stakeholders and maximising value of all these stakeholders only will make the business sustainable.

A business has to look beyond profit maximisation otherwise the progress will not be permanent. A business has several stakeholders like society, environment, suppliers, Government, employees and shareholders. If the interests of these stakeholders are not protected, the business cannot be sustainable. The need of the hour is to be sensitive to the interests of all these stakeholders for a sustainable progress. This line of thinking is increasingly gaining ground across the world and the concept of 'Corporate Social Responsibility' is becoming the important aspect of business strategy.

It has been realised that a business cannot remain insensitive to the aspirations of stakeholders like the society, environment, employees, Government, suppliers and the shareholders. Creating and sustaining value for all these stakeholders has become the key for a sustainable business. Though the concept of Corporate Social Responsibility has gained much importance in the past two decades as such, the concept is not new to India. In fact, it is embedded in the Indian culture itself. As per the ancient Indian literature, it is expected that some portion of the income earned by either an individual or by an enterprise, should be devoted for social cause. The reason behind this is that any enterprise is using the resources of the society and hence it has an obligation to fulfill for the society. Therefore some portion of the income earned should be spent for social cause, for the upliftment of the society. It has been observed that there is an unequal distribution of wealth in several developing countries like India. This inequality creates lots of problems like acute poverty, terrorism, civil wars and so on. It should be remembered that the efforts of Government alone are not sufficient to meet this onerous challenge. The corporate sector has to come forward to assist the Government in removing the inequality of income in the society.

Ultimately a corporate organisation is working in a society and hence can't remain aloof to the various problems faced by the society. This feeling is gaining lot of ground today and there is growing awareness among the leading corporate houses that they have a role to be played in the social welfare and ensure that the dream of 'Inclusive Growth' is fulfilled. They cannot ignore the needs of the society as well as its welfare and it is of paramount importance from their sustainability point of view. Any business cannot sustain by offering harmful products, ignoring the interests of its stakeholders and thus ignoring the society as a whole. Therefore the corporate social responsibility is also connected with the sustainability of the enterprise. Corporate Social Responsibility is becoming an increasingly a prominent issue in the entire world especially due to the following reasons.

1. Globalisation and the rapid advances in information technologies.
2. The greater importance of citizen-driven activities, best seen in the work performed by the Non Government Organisations. [NGOs]
3. Greater social awareness among consumers.
4. Increased competition among business organisations.

1.1.4 ASPECTS OF CSR

There are different approaches to Corporate Social Responsibility concept. However CSR is not restricted to any one of them. It is a combination of all these approaches. These approaches, also known as models of CSR, are discussed below.

1. **Business Ethics:** The mention of Business Ethics is found in ancient Indian literature as well as in ancient Greece literature. The striking similarity between the two is that there has been a mention about the rules of conduct for the King and the business community as well. The role of business in society has been debated since then. Fieser describes that, 'business ethics examines moral controversies that commonly arise in the business world'. The application of ethics in business is reflected in the formulation of core values, stakeholders' interactions, social audit and other forms of social performance measurement and reporting. It has been observed that a business venture is more sustainable if ethical values are followed. There are several examples of corporate failures due to non-ethical behaviour. However there is a misconception that ethics and business do not go together and one has to compromise with ethics to run business successfully. This needs to be corrected if the concept of CSR is to be made deep rooted in the corporate culture. A leading example of an ethically driven business is that of an Indian company, Polyhydron Pvt Ltd, which is situated at Belgam, in the State of Karnataka. The company proves that a business can not only survive but also prosper by following ethical practices in every aspect of its business and thus there is no need to follow unethical practices to make profits.

2. **Philanthropic Approach:** This approach to CSR is humanitarian which implies that the philosophy behind CSR should be giving back to the society. This approach also means that corporate houses should donate money to development activities from the profits they earn.

3. **Strategic CSR:** The more broad approach to CSR is that it should be embedded in the strategy itself. This approach envisages that the CSR goes far beyond the old philanthropy of the past – donating money to good causes at the end of the financial year and is instead an all year round responsibility that companies accept for the environment around them, for the best working practices, for their engagement in their local communities and for their recognition that brand names not only depend on quality, price and uniqueness, but on how, cumulatively, they interact with companies workforce, community and environment. Now we need to move towards a challenging measure of corporate responsibility, where we judge results not just by the input but by its outcomes, the difference we make to the world in which we live, and the contribution we make to poverty reduction.

4. **Social Contract:** A social contract, with implicit and explicit terms, is conceived to exist between the organisation and the public at large and not just merely its shareholders.
5. **Stakeholder Theory:** Foreman, in 1984 focused on the view of the stakeholders and advocated that there are six stakeholders to a business and the business owes them certain responsibilities. These stakeholders are owners, employees, customers, suppliers, communities and governments. In addition to these stakeholders there are environmental factors also, which is an important stakeholder.
6. **Environmental Aspects:** It has been realised that the CSR extends to the environment protection aspect in a big way. A business cannot sustain its progress by inflicting damages to the environment. The Government, on its part has made various laws to protect the environment. However the responsibility of the business houses is not only to comply with the law but go beyond that and ensure that there is no harm to the environment. Similarly it should be realised that depletion and pollution of the Earth's natural resources at the current rate would eventually, lead to severe economic fallouts and thus make a business unsustainable. It is heartening to note that awareness on the global level of this very important aspect is increasing and is clear from the following examples.
    (a) A paper manufacturing company manufactures paper from waste cloth to reduce the use of pulp from trees.
    (b) A chemical manufacturer has protected the largest stretch of mangroves along Mumbai's coast.
    (c) A software company has developed a special cell receiving software for 1098 Childline, India's national helpline for children in distress.
    (d) An FMCG company is working to protect and conserve endangered plant species in India through re-forestation programs
    (e) 'Berger Paints', a leading company, having a broad range of paints, strongly feels that green paints is the future of the industry and the company is looking at newer technologies to develop the same. The carbon footprints of paint is very high as the chemicals evaporates quickly. Hence, the recent focus is on water based paints where only the water will evaporate. Similarly the company has switched its entire formulation in synthetic enamel to non-lead formulations. The focus is also on ways to reduce a building's energy cost which paints. The company, very soon will be launching a paint that will insulate the building from the heat of the sun, thereby reducing energy cost of the air conditioning. All these steps show the environmental awareness and efforts to control the environment pollution.[1]

---

[1] The Economic Times, dated 7th June 2010

(f) ITC, a leading company in India, which is a conglomerate of consumer goods and agri business has placed the 'Triple Bottom Line' methodologies at the heart of its business. This strategic initiative has slashed the group's dependency on natural resources, whilst maximising the returns to the stakeholders and local communities, which include subsistence farmers in some of the world's most remote areas. The initiatives include,
- Internationally benchmarked specific consumption of water, dedicated pursuit of the goal of zero discharge and scaling up of rainwater harvesting in several moisture stressed districts of India have enabled ITC retain its enviable position as a 'water positive' company for the forth successive year. The water harvesting potential created so far is over four times the company's net water consumption.
- Becoming 'carbon positive' during 2007 on the back of several energy conservation measures, usage of carbon-neutral fuels and carbon sequestration through large scale agro forestry programs.
- Making rapid strides towards attaining 'zero solid water' status.
- Providing direct employment to 20000 people and indirect employment across the value chain to nearly 5 million.

Danish company Novozymes, the world leader in 'green chemicals' was this year for the fifth time named one of Sustainable Business's 20 most sustainably innovative companies.[2] The company's work in reducing energy use and the release of toxic materials with biological enzymes in a host of industries has made it a recognised world leader in sustainability driven innovation. The company whose tagline is 'Rethink Tomorrow' places sustainability at the very heart of its structures and decision making process. Sustainability is a fixed agenda item at every board meeting. The company has a sustainability development strategy group, comprising vice presidents from different lines of business and geographical entities, which sets direction and monitors implementation on sustainability.

1.1.5 Forces for Corporate Social Responsibility

Some of the forces can be stated as under:
1. **Consumerism:** Growing consciousness among consumers about their rights, establishment of consumer groups and enactment of consumer protection laws has given rise to the dictum 'consumer is the king'. The businessmen have been forced to care for the interests of consumers and for their protection.
2. **Enlightened Self-interest:** The spread of education has led businessmen to concern themselves with the quality of life. Many of them recognise that business is a reflection of social objectives and values and an agent for promoting them.

---
[2] Sustainability Business, July 19, 2007

3. **Trade Unionism:** Growing power of trade unions and labour laws have led to business growth concerned with labour welfare.
4. **Public Opinion and Government Control:** Public opinion and the threat of government control have made businessmen realise that responsible behaviour is essential for preservation of free enterprise. If a business does not accept social responsibilities it would be forced upon it by the Government.
5. **Trusteeship:** The trusteeship principle indicates that business managers should be caretakers of the business property holding it in trust for the society as a whole. The more fortunate members of society should assist less fortunate ones.
6. **Professionalisation:** The separation of ownership from management in large enterprises has replaced the 'owner-manager' with the 'paid manager'. Ownership has become diffused in large companies. The managers having no stake in ownership tend to take a long-term and more responsible view of their role.

1.1.6 Relevance of Corporate Social Responsibility in the Present Day Business Environment

The rationale for assuming social responsibility lies in the following arguments.

1. **Business is a Creation of Society:** Business is a sub-system of society. It draws support and sustenance from society in the form of inputs. Socially responsible behaviour is essential to sustain this relationship between business and society.
2. **Work for the Interest of all Enterprise:** A business enterprise is a coalition of several interest groups or stakeholders, e.g., shareholders, employees, suppliers, customers etc. Hence business should work for the interest of all of them rather than only for the benefit of shareholders/owners.
3. **Improving Public Image:** The objective is to adopt social responsibility which will help to improve the public image of business. A good public image is a valuable asset for business. It may gain more customers, better employees, more responsive money markets and other benefits.
4. **Social Power:** Giant organisations have acquired tremendous social power through their multifarious operations. Social power may be misused in the absence of social responsibility. Social power and social responsibility should properly counter-balance. When an institution's power grows, its responsibility grows accordingly. *Keith Davis* states "in the long run those who fail to use power in a manner that society considers responsible will lose it. This is the iron law of responsibility."
5. **Competence and Leadership:** Business organisations and their managers have proved their competence and leadership in solving economic problems. Society expects them to use their competence to solve social problems by playing the role of a leader.

6. **Promotion of Economic Objectives:** Social responsibility 'legitimises' and promotes the economic objectives of business. By improving social life, business can obtain better customers, employees and neighbours. Social responsibility is thus good citizenship as well as good business.
7. **Professional Demand of Managers:** Professional managers are required to display a keen social sensitivity and serve the society as a whole. Social responsibility is one of the professional demands of managers in business organisations.
8. **Free Enterprise and Avoidance of Government Control:** If business does not voluntarily' assume social responsibilities, government may compel it to do so through regulations and control. If the responsibility is not discharged it will eventually result in the death of private enterprise. It is better to behave in a socially responsible manner and thereby avoid government control.
9. **Social Impact:** A business enterprise makes several decisions and actions during the course of its functioning. Its activities exercise a strong influence on the interests and values of society. The business should fulfill social obligations as compensation—for accidental or unavoidable undermining of the legitimate interests of society.

1.1.7 Criticism of Corporate Social Responsibility

Critics of the social responsibility concept present the following arguments:

1. **Dilution of Economic Goals:** The business will have to compromise its economic objectives by accepting social responsibility. Business is an economic institution and it is its responsibility to make maximum possible profits for its owners. It would endanger its economic viability by accepting any other responsibility. Social responsibility of business is regarded as a 'subversive' doctrine.
2. **Vague Concept Hence Risky:** The concept of social responsibility is very vague and amenable to different interpretations. There is no consensus on its meaning and scope. It would be futile and risky to accept social responsibility in such a situation.
3. **Burden on Consumers:** The cost of doing business would increase if business deals with social problems. These costs will have to be borne by the consumers in the form of higher prices or will have to be borne by the owners. This amounts to taxation without proper representation.
4. **Lack of Social Skill:** The managers are unfamiliar with social affairs. There are specialist social service organisations such as the Government which can better deal with social problems.
5. **Misdirection of Corporate Resources:** Acceptance of social responsibilities will involve diversion of precious managerial time and talent on social action programmes. It may result in misdirection of valuable corporate resources.

6. **Responsibility without Power:** A business organisation possesses only economic power and not social power. It is unfair to impose social responsibilities without social power. If business is allowed to intervene in social affairs it may perpetuate its own value system to the detriment of society.
7. **Unjust Overburden:** The business enterprises are already serving society by providing goods and services, generating employment, developing technology and contributing to public exchequer through tax payments. It would be unjust to overburden them with further responsibilities of any kind.
8. **No Measurements:** Decision-making in business profitability is common criteria. Tempering it with social responsibility would make the decision making process quite complex and controversial.
9. **Improper Role:** The proper role of business is to use its resources and energies efficiently so as to earn the best possible return on investment within the confines of law and ethics. It is essential for business to concentrate on economic performance leaving social service to other organisations.

The assumption of social responsibilities is favoured by the public. The question today is not whether to accept responsibilities, but how much of the responsibilities to assume.

1.1.8 Limits to Corporate Social Responsibilities

The managers must clearly recognise and understand that there are inevitable constraints on the acceptance of social responsibility. The major constraints are as follows:

1. **Ensuring Profitability and Viability:** While assuming social responsibility, a business enterprise must ensure its profitability and viability. A losing or a non-viable enterprise cannot discharge its social responsibilities successfully. Socially responsible behaviour should not endanger the economic survival of the enterprise. This does not imply that the enterprise should be allowed to earn profits at the cost of the society. It is essential to maintain a proper balance between social responsibility and economic viability.
2. **No Encroachment on Government Authority:** Socially responsible behaviour should be confined to the areas in which management has legitimate authority. Otherwise social action may result in usurpation of authority. Indiscriminate social responsibility may amount to undue corporate authority which may be unacceptable to society. Business management should not encroach upon authority of the Government and other social institutions.
3. **Confining to its Areas of Competence Only:** In the pursuit of social responsibilities management should confine itself to the areas of its competence. If incompetent managers start involving with social action programmes, the organisation will have to face dire consequences.

4. **Social Responsibility is Reciprocal:** The concept of social responsibility is reciprocal. Just as business owes responsibility to various interest groups, these groups owe responsibility to support and assist business.
5. **Balance with the Social Economic Power:** Social responsibility should be balanced with the socio-economic power of business. A large enterprise or enterprise supplying drugs for example, has a greater responsibility than a small enterprise or an enterprise supplying plastic items.
6. **Essential to Conduct Social Cost Benefit Analysis:** It is essential for the management to make social cost benefit analysis before undertaking any social action programme. If the social costs exceed social benefits then the programme may prove unprofitable and futile.

1.1.9 Measures for Enforcing Corporate Social Responsibilities

The following steps may be taken to make the Indian business discharge its social responsibilities:

1. Legislative Measures

The Corporate Social Responsibility was a voluntary measure to be undertaken from the social responsibility point of view. However as per The Companies Act 2013, the CSR has been made mandatory to certain types of companies. The provisions of the Companies Act 2013 regarding the CSR are given below.

Section 135 of The Companies Act 2013 provides that,

1. Every company having net worth of rupees five hundred crore or more, or turnover of rupees one thousand crore or more or a net profit of rupees five crore or more during any financial year shall constitute a Corporate Social Responsibility Committee of the Board consisting of three or more directors, out of which at least one director shall be an independent director.
2. The Board's report under sub-section (3) of section 134 shall disclose the composition of the Corporate Social Responsibility Committee.
3. The Corporate Social Responsibility Committee shall:
    (a) formulate and recommend to the Board, a Corporate Social Responsibility Policy which shall indicate the activities to be undertaken by the company as specified in Schedule VII;
    (b) recommend the amount of expenditure to be incurred on the activities referred to in clause (a); and
    (c) monitor the Corporate Social Responsibility Policy of the company from time to time.

4. The Board of every company referred to in sub-section (1) shall,—
   (a) after taking into account the recommendations made by the Corporate Social Responsibility Committee, approve the Corporate Social Responsibility Policy for the company and disclose contents of such Policy in its report and also place it on the company's website, if any, in such manner as may be prescribed; and
   (b) ensure that the activities as are included in Corporate Social Responsibility Policy of the company are undertaken by the company.
5. The Board of every company referred to in sub-section (1), shall ensure that the company spends, in every financial year, at least two percent of the average net profits of the company made during the three immediately preceding financial years, in pursuance of its Corporate Social Responsibility Policy: Provided that the company shall give preference to the local area and areas around it where it operates, for spending the amount earmarked for Corporate Social Responsibility activities:

   Provided further that if the company fails to spend such amount, the Board shall, in its report made under clause (o) of sub-section (3) of section 134, specify the reasons for not spending the amount.

   Explanation: For the purposes of this section "average net profit" shall be calculated in accordance with the provisions of section 198.

   Thus it can be seen from the above mentioned provisions of the Act, that the CSR has been made mandatory for certain category of companies. It remains to be seen as to what will be the impact of these compulsions on the CSR activities undertaken by different companies.

   (i) **Representation of Social Groups:** Representation of the social groups on the Board of Directors and at the Annual General Meeting of a company.
   (ii) **Social Audit to Judge Social Welfare:** A social audit to judge the contribution of a company towards the social welfare should be undertaken periodically.
   (iii) **Social Responsibilities Clause in the Memorandum:** The social responsibilities clause is to be specified by every giant company in its Memorandum and Articles of Association.

2. **Voluntary Measures**

   Enforcement through Law alone cannot make businessmen socially responsible. The following voluntary measures may also be adopted for this purpose:
   (i) **Establishment of Organisation to Compel Businessmen:** The Consumers should establish their organisations to compel businessmen to discharge their obligations towards community.
   (ii) **Exercising Effective Control:** Trade Associations and Chambers of Commerce should exercise effective control in order to prevent the anti-social practices among businessmen.

(iii) **Control over Management:** The shareholders should establish their associations/organisations to exercise effective control over the management of the company particularly in connection with their social responsibilities.

(iv) **Development of Organisational Control:** The business enterprises should develop an organisational culture conducive to the assumption and discharging of social responsibilities.

1.1.10 Barriers to Corporate Social Responsibility

At every level of the organisation, practical problems arise whenever efforts are undertaken to a quite greater social responsibility. If there is awareness regarding these problems it proves useful in order to take steps to overcome them.

1. **The Organisation:** The greatest barrier at the organisational level is the focus on profits. Social action projects should be evolved in terms of net cost. The shareholders have to decide whether the profits should be distributed in the form of dividends or the company's profits should be invested in order to expand production. The employees expect more remuneration and better working conditions. Thus, social programmes have remote opportunities against these competing claims.

2. **The Division:** The division is a part of organisation. A division should make effects to maintain itself as a centre of profit. Any social responsibility decision which results in the reduction in the profit level might threaten the viability of the division. Thus, unless and until the top management issues clear directions, the divisions are slow in initiating socially responsible programmes.

3. **The Individual Manager:** In order to carry out the social action programme of any organisation, the individual manager is the person who is ultimately held responsible. The successful implementation of the programme becomes possible due to him. The managers have to be careful while proposing significant changes in the organisation. They should take employees into confidence before making any such proposal.

4. **The Industry:** The competitors in the same industry may not extend their co-operation/support for social action programmes and thus, it may pose a barrier to acquitting social responsibility.

1.1.11 Formulating and Implementing a Policy for Corporate Social Responsibility

Implementation refers to the daily decisions, processes, practices and activities that make sure the firm fulfills the spirit and letter of its CSR commitments and thus carry out its CSR strategy. If CSR commitments can be called "talking the talk," then implementation is "walking the talk."

It is well known by business organisations that living up to the promises play a significant role in its success. Organisations which are not able to meet CSR promises can face problems like dissatisfied employees, shareholders, business partners, customers, communities and others. Organisations which meet their CSR commitments well are less likely to run into troubles. Such organisations are more positively looked upon by their stakeholders.

Different strategies for CSR implementation are adopted by different organisations. Following are the steps of one of the strategies to implement CSR commitments.

1. Develop an integrated CSR decision-making structure.
2. Plan and execute a CSR business plan.
3. Set measurable targets and make out performance measures.
4. Engage employees and others to whom CSR commitments apply.
5. Design and conduct CSR training.
6. Create mechanisms for addressing problematic behaviour.
7. Build internal and external communications plans.

1. Develop an Integrated CSR Decision-making Structure

Every firm has a decision-making structure in order to meet its commitments and needs of its customer. Firm's CSR goals and objectives should be aligned with its overall goals and strategies, so that the customer's perspectives are taken into account automatically while taking corporate decisions. There are different CSR decision-making structures adopted by firms like centralised, de-centralised and hybrid CSR decision-making structures, depending on their operating features and management style.

CSR is basically concerned with transparency, accountability and performance. CSR decision-making structure should be an integral component of the firm's governance activities and should be noticeable. CSR responsibilities are assigned to board members to make sure that CSR issues will get the consideration they deserve, and as a consequence form a strong foundation for an effective chain of CSR accountability within the organisation —all of which supports the board's corporate governance function.

There are number of alternatives for board participation such as assigning a sitting board member with broad responsibility for CSR activities; appointing a new member who has specific CSR expertise; add CSR responsibilities to the work of existing board committees; forming a new CSR board committee; or involve the entire board in CSR decisions.

A senior officer or committee should be appointed for overall CSR implementation within the firm to look after particular departments having CSR responsibilities such as environment, health and safety protection, worker relations, supplier relations, community relations, customer relations.

2. Plan and Execute a CSR Business Plan

The decision-making structure identifies who is accountable for CSR decision-making and action within the firm. These people play important roles in developing and implementing the CSR business plan, which should flow from the CSR strategy and commitments. The CSR business plan may be independently explained or incorporated as part of the company's existing overall business plan.

The CSR business plan makes certain that words are transformed into effective action. For example, a CSR commitment may be that the firm will not bribe any official for getting its work done. Below are the steps that can be followed to execute the CSR business plan:

- The **first step** might be to form a training course on distinction between appropriate and inappropriate payments, with an online version that includes frequently asked questions.
- A **second step** might be to assess the organisation's incentive and disincentive structure (e.g. commissions).
- A **third step** might involve setting up a hotline.
- A **fourth step** could be creating whistle-blower protection measures.

In the CSR business plan, each of these tasks could be further broken down into smaller components, with time lines and resource requirements for each. These duties should be put together into the job description and performance objectives of each lead person.

3. Set Measurable Targets and Make out Performance Measures

A firm needs to set measurable targets for effective implementations of the commitments. There are intermediate targets that guide to reach the ultimate goal, providing a measure of progress and an opportunity. Targets can help build momentum when achieved.

A broadly used approach to measure the success of a firm is to make out the objectives underlying a CSR commitment, build up key performance indicators, work out the measurement method and then measure the results. In spite of the accurate approach taken, it should follow the SMART guidelines:

- simple
- measurable
- achievable
- reliable
- time-bound

For example, making a commitment to reduce the quantity of waste a facility generates, there might be an objective to reduce solid waste by 25 percent by the end of the calendar year. The amount of waste sent to the landfill can be the key performance indicator. The measurement method might be the kilograms of garbage produced each month, which would be recorded.

A firm can modify its objectives by regular review of the commitments, objectives, indicators and measurement methods.

4. Engage Employees and others to whom CSR Commitments Apply

Following the approach set out in this guide, the input of employees and other key stakeholders has been solicited at every stage, from preliminary assessment, through strategy development and articulation of commitments. In CSR implementation employees play a vital role.

The success of CSR depends first on senior leadership and finally CSR implementation mainly lies in the hands of employees and, in some cases, suppliers. If employees and suppliers are not properly engaged, then they could be a source of problems for all concerned. Hence, good communication between top management and employees, employee representatives and suppliers about CSR strategy and commitment implementation is very important. All parties would be interested in implementing a firm's CSR commitments only when the senior management takes CSR issues seriously and acts in a manner that reflects the spirit of the commitments. Nothing will dissolve a firm's progress faster than a CSR approach that is perceived as being just "hot air."

The act of engaging employees, employee representatives and suppliers in implement-tation means focusing on awareness. By Involving stakeholders like employees, employee representatives and suppliers in discussions regarding strategies for implementing CSR commitments is a way to build a sense of ownership and pride in the firm's CSR activities to these stakeholders. CSR related messages should be conveyed to the stakeholders as they are in the best position to understand the matter and answer questions.

Employee support for CSR implementation can be maintained in a number of ways:

- CSR performance elements should be incorporated into job descriptions and performance evaluations.
- Regular updates on progress should be provided (in meetings or the company newsletter).
- Incentives such as rewards for best suggestions should be developed.
- Disincentives should be removed or reduced, for example, competing interests such as premature deadlines that encourage employees to choose non-CSR options.

5. Design and Conduct CSR Training

Employees who are directly involved in CSR activities should be trained by the firm. Training employees is an ongoing process as training needs will vary with the rise of different CSR issues. IKEA is one such comprehensive approach to training that ensures employees have information on the firm's CSR commitments, programmes and implementation. While preparing training modules, languages of a firm's employees and their cultural orientation must be considered.

There are five steps to establishing a successful training program:
- Conducting a needs analysis
- Setting learning objectives
- Designing the programme (i.e. content, format, logistics, timing, duration)
- Implementing the programme
- Evaluating the programme against the learning objectives.

6. Create Mechanisms for Addressing Problematic Behaviour

The success of a firm depends upon early detection of actions that are against CSR principles and commitments. Auditing and monitoring are the best way to detect such actions.

This is probably one of the most sensitive of CSR activities. In a perfect world, there would be no need to develop mechanisms for reporting problematic behaviour. However, people and organisations are imperfect. In the best-managed organisations, there should be no fear of retaliation when approaching one's superior to talk about a trouble. However, until such time when this is a reality in all workplaces, mechanisms for reporting and resolving problems are helpful.

Firms should create approaches that are sensitive to the susceptible position of employees who see illegal behavior or the possibility for disobedience. Firms should think about unspecified hotlines, e-mail boxes and ombudspersons to clear communications on the consequences of reporting breaches of CSR commitments. Care must be taken to ensure that not only are the mechanisms for dealing with the problems designed well, but also that they are the option of last resort. A senior manager should be assigned responsibility for investigating and reporting compliance on these issues.

7. Build Internal and External Communications Plans

Information about CSR commitments, activities and performance reporting through newsletters, annual reports, Intranet communication, meetings, training or informal mechanisms must be communicated visibly and frequently to all employees. Up to date information on CSR should be put on the agenda of meetings at all levels of the company.

A fine communications plan is essential for external audiences. It should make out the individuals and groups that are required to be aware of a particular CSR initiative and those who should receive hard copies of CSR documents, as well as how those individuals and groups are to be reached. The communications activities comprise of an awareness campaign, featuring advertising and speeches. Firms may wish to avoid creating CSR reports that, through their utter size, can scare potential readers. Website design can help to ensure that parties can easily access CSR information of interest to them. It is quite possible that communications might be customised for various audiences (e.g. communications to investors are likely to be quite different from those addressed to communities).

1.2 Corporate Citizenship

1.2.1 Meaning and Definitions

The term "corporate citizenship" (CC) has been used increasingly by companies consultants and scholars to echo, underscore, extend, or re-orient certain aspects of corporate social responsibility. While Corporate Social Responsibility according to Archie Carroll (1979), a business management professor at the University of Georgia is, "The social responsibility of business encompasses the economic, legal, ethical, and discretionary expectations that society has of organisations at a given point in time", Corporate Citizenship is about companies taking into account their complete impact on the economy and environment and not just their impact on the economy. The issue of corporate citizenship and the role of corporations in society have been debated for centuries. Corporate citizenship really means developing mutually beneficial, interactive and trusting relationships between the company and its many stakeholders—employees, customers, communities, suppliers, governments, investors and even nongovernmental organisations (NGOs) and activists, through the implementation of the company's strategies and operating practices. In this sense, being a good corporate citizen means treating all of a company's stakeholders [and the natural environment] with dignity and respect, being aware of the company's impacts on stakeholders and working collaboratively with them when appropriate to achieve mutually desired results. Thus the global corporate citizenship covers a wide array of activities that cover the triple bottom line concept of people, planet and profit.

Thus Corporate citizenship refers to the degree to which businesses are socially responsible for meeting legal, ethical and Economic responsibilities placed on them by shareholders. The aim of businesses is to provide higher standards of living and quality of life in the communities in which they run while still safeguarding profitability for stakeholders.

Due to increase in demand for socially responsible corporations, investors, consumers and employees use their individual power to punish companies that do not share their morals and standards. For example, investors refuse to invest in a company which follows negative corporate citizenship practices.

- *It involves the act of proactively addressing business and society issues, while building stakeholders partnerships.* **(Post et. al, 2002)**
- *Good corporate citizenship integrates social, ethical, environmental, economic and philanthropic values in the core decision-making processes of a business. Corporate citizenship has supporters and detractors; corporate citizenship is defined as the act of 'business taking greater account of its social, environmental and financial footprints.* **(Gianni Zappala, 2003)**
- *Corporate citizenship is the management of organisation's wider influences within the society for the mutual benefit of the company and the society.* **(Marsden and Andriof, 1998)**

1.2.2 Difference between Concept of Global Corporate Citizen and Other Allied Concepts

Five core concepts -- corporate governance, corporate philanthropy, corporate social responsibility, corporate social entrepreneurship, and global corporate citizenship -- define the different types of business engagement. Corporate governance is the governance pattern of a company. It means that a company complies with local and international laws, transparency and accountability requirements, ethical norms, and environmental and social codes of conduct. Every company is subject to some form of governance; otherwise, it would not have the basic license to operate. The central issue is the quality of this governance. An enterprise either complies or does not comply with the laws and standards that apply to it. Good corporate governance means that the company's conduct meets or exceeds what is required on paper -- not doing any harm because it is following the rules and possibly even doing good by going beyond the mandated minimum. Corporate governance is how a company behaves when nobody is looking. Without good corporate governance, no other form of corporate engagement is credible. Good corporate governance should not be seen as only a compliance issue. Companies should be actively involved in the development of standards and practices, adapting them continuously to the requirements of global markets and public expectations.

1. **Corporate Philanthropy**: Corporate philanthropy has been on the rise in many countries in recent years. It includes cash contributions; grants; donations, including salary-sacrifice programs and the giving of products; services; and investments. Thus, Corporate philanthropy does not go beyond writing a check or handing out donated goods. However, investment in social projects is a special form of corporate philanthropy, in which a company invests in organisations or programs that have broad social appeal, such as low cost housing projects or water supply scheme for villages.

2. **Corporate Social Responsibility:** Corporate Social Responsibility is a concept whereby companies integrate social and environmental concerns in their business operations and in their interaction with their stakeholders on a voluntary basis. It is about enterprises deciding to go beyond minimum legal requirements and obligations stemming from collective agreements in order to address societal needs. The basic idea behind corporate social responsibility is to give back to the society in return for the use of resources. Though earlier it was totally voluntary, now as per the provisions of Companies Act 2013, it has become mandatory for certain types of companies.

3. **Corporate Social Entrepreneurship**: Corporate social entrepreneurship is strictly defined as the transformation of socially and environmentally responsible ideas into products or services. The last decade has seen many individuals come up with innovative ideas to address the specific social and environmental needs of the communities in which they are living. The role model of these social entrepreneurs, Muhammad Yunus, the inventor of microcredit, received the Nobel Peace Prize in 2006. Today, pioneering enterprises integrate social entrepreneurship into their core activities by actively channelling their research-and-development capabilities in the direction of socially innovative products and services. Examples of corporate social entrepreneurship include Deutsche Bank offering innovative microfinance schemes or socially responsible investment products, the Toyota Motor Corporation producing a hybrid car, or Unilever empowering women to become entrepreneurs in rural India while at the same time raising awareness on the importance of hygiene and nutrition.

4. **Global Corporate Citizenship**: Global corporate citizenship goes beyond the concepts of corporate governance, corporate philanthropy, including social investing; corporate social responsibility; and corporate social entrepreneurship in that it entails focusing on "the global approach," which is increasingly shaped by forces beyond the control of nation-states. Global companies have not only a license to operate in this arena but also a civic duty to contribute to sustaining the world's well-being in cooperation with governments and civil society. Global corporate citizenship means engagement at the macro level on issues of importance to the world: it contributes to enhancing the sustainability of the global marketplace.

Global corporate citizenship refers to a company's role in addressing issues that have a dramatic impact on the future of the globe, such as climate change, water shortages, infectious diseases, and terrorism. Other challenges include providing access to food, education, and information technology; extreme poverty; transnational crime; corruption; failed states; and disaster response and relief. Each of these problems is global in scope, even if the solutions may be locally focused.

While practicing the global corporate citizenships, companies are expected to participate in the well being of the society as much as possible. Even though it is admitted that the primary responsibility for meeting the global challenges still is on the Government of respective countries, companies can assist these authorities in their own way, thus reducing the burden of the Government machinery up to certain extent.

1.2.3 Nature of Corporate Citizenship

1. Universal in nature (it applies to all business types)
2. Adopts strategic focus

3. Fulfillment of social responsibility (economic, legal, ethical and philanthropic)
4. Stakeholder oriented (responsibility to Government, customer, community, employee, investors etc.)
5. Global nature (due to globalisation of business)

1.2.4 Benefits of Corporate Citizenship

1. It improves the environment in which the company operates.
2. It builds good will and good relations with stakeholders.
3. It sharpens understanding of what the company is all about.
4. It improves morale, recruitment, retention.
5. It promotes development.

1.2.5 Stages of Corporate Citizenship

Like development of individuals, companies develop and grow in their maturity for dealing with corporate citizenship issues. A major contribution to how this growth occurs has been presented by Philip Mirvis and Bradley Googins at the Center for Corporate Citizenship at Boston College. The centre explains the significance of corporate citizenship is how companies convey their core values in a way that reduces harm, capitalise on benefits, is accountable and responsive to key stakeholders and supports strong financial results.

The development of the corporate citizenship model reflects a stage-by-stage process. The companies move through five stages and constitute of seven dimensions (citizenship concept, strategic intent, leadership, structure, issues management, stakeholder relationships and transparency). The Stage 1 of corporate citizenship model is elementary and growing towards Stage 5 which is transforming.

As seen in Fig. 1.1, the citizenship concept states with an emphasis on "jobs, profits and taxes" in Stage 1 and progresses through several emphases such as "philanthropy, environmental protection", "stakeholder management", "sustainability or triple bottom line" and finally, "the change the game". Similarly, the other vital dimensions change orientations as they evolve through the five stages.

The companies face different developmental challenges at each stage. Thus, in Stage 1 the challenge is to "gain credibility". As the companies grow toward Stage 5, the challenges are to build capacity, create coherence and deepen commitment. Fig. 1.2 graphically depicts the developmental challenges that trigger the movement of corporate citizenship through the five stages of growth.

Company examples that illustrate the various stages have been identified by Mirvis and Googins. GE in Stage 1 extended its emphasis beyond financial success. Chiquita, Nestle and Shell Oil are represented as companies becoming engaged in Stage 2. In Stage 3, Baxter International and ABB are acknowledged as innovative companies striving to create coherence. In Stage 4, BP is an example of the company which shows commitment to sustainability where the theme is integration. Finally at Stage 5, the experiences of Unilever, widely distinguished for its socio-economic investments in emerging markets and is presented as a company with an emphasis on transformation in its corporate citizenship.

		Stage 1 Elementary	Stage 2 Engaged	Stage 3 Innovative	Stage 4 Integrated	Stage 5 Transforming
Dimensions	**Citizenship concept**	Jobs, Profits and Taxes	Philanthropy, Environmental Protection	Stakeholder Management	Sustainability or Triple Bottom Line	Change the Game
	Strategic Intent	Legal Compliance	License to Operate	Business Case	Value Proposition	Market Creation or Social Change
	Leadership	Lip Service, Out of Touch	Supporter, In the Loop	Steward, On Top of it	Champion, In Front of it	Visionary, Ahead of the Pack
	Structural	Marginal, Staff Driven	Functional Ownership	Cross-Functional Coordination	Organisational Alignment	Mainstream, Business Driven
	Issues Management	Defensive	Reactive Policies	Responsive Programs	Pro-Active Systems	Defining
	Stakeholder Relationships	Unilateral	Interactive	Mutual Influence	Partnership Alliance	Multi-Organisation
	Transparency	Flank Protection	Public Relations	Public Reporting	Assurance	Full Disclosure

Fig. 1.1: Stages of Corporate Citizenship

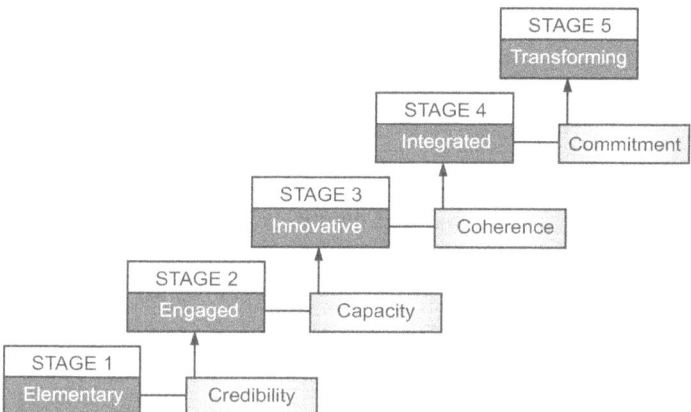

Fig. 1.2: Developmental Challenges Triggering Movement of Corporate Citizenship

Source: Philip Mirvis and Bradley K. Googins, Stages of Corporate Citizenship, A Developmental Framework (Center for Corporate Citizenship and Boston College, Boston 2006), 5. Used with permission

The stages of corporate citizenship model effectively presents the challenges of credibility, capacity, coherence and commitment that firms move through as they come to grips with development of more comprehensive and integrated citizenship agendas. From the researchers work, it is obvious that corporate citizenship is not a stagnant position but is one that steps forward through different themes and challenges as firms get better and better over time.

The terminology and concepts of corporate citizenship are especially attractive because they resonate so well, the business community's attempts to describe its own socially responsive activities and practices. Therefore, it is expected that this concept will be around for some years to come. When reference is made to CSR, social responsiveness, social performance and sustainability, these also embrace activities, programmes and practices that would typically fall under the purview of a firm's corporate citizenship.

1.3 Corporate Social Responsibility and Stakeholders

1.3.1 Meaning of Stakeholder

Stakeholders mean individuals, groups, or organisations that are concerned with the performance of a business. Stakeholders are directly or indirectly affected by performance of the business therefore they are concerned with business activities. Stakeholders can be categorised into two; internal stakeholders and external stakeholders. For decision-making, stakeholders use a variety of information. The information provided to stakeholders depends on whether the stakeholder is an internal or external stakeholder.

A corporate stakeholder is an individual or group who can affect or be affected by the actions of a business. The concept of stakeholder was first used in a 1963 internal memorandum at the Stanford Research Institute. It defined stakeholders as "those groups without whose support the organisation would cease to exist."

In the last decades of the 20th century, the word "stakeholder" has become more commonly used to refer to a person or group that has a legitimate interest in a project or entity. Institutions like large business corporations, government agencies, and non-profit organisations while discussing the decision-making process should include everyone with an interest (or "stake") in what the entity does.

1.3.2 Types of Stakeholder: Internal and External Stakeholders

Various types of stakeholders can be divided into the following two categories:

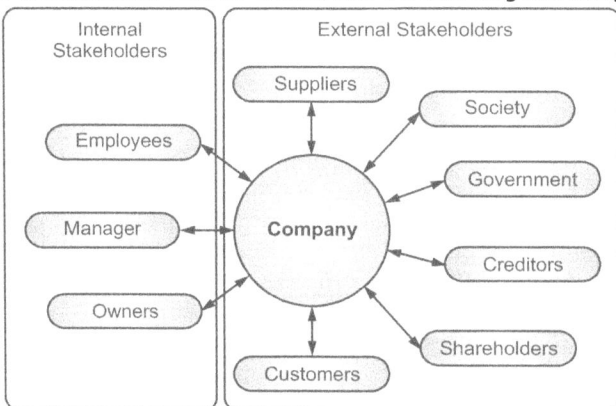

Fig. 1.3: Types of Stakeholders

1. Internal Stakeholders

Internal stakeholders, also known as primary stakeholders, are groups within a business or people who work directly within the business, such as employees, owners, and investors. Employees wish to earn high incomes and maintain their jobs. Owners are concerned with increasing the profit the business makes. Investors are interested in earning income from their investment.

Internal stakeholders are those that are directly affected by the business' performance. Internal stakeholders such as owners, shareholders, creditors, managers, customers, employees, business partners, and suppliers are directly involved with the actions of the business.

Internal stakeholders usually have a great influence on how the company is run. For example, important business decisions will be taken by the company's owners. Customers are also internal stakeholders that are very important to a business as the amount to which their requirements are met will influence the company's sales. Company's managers and workers also influence the company's day to day operations by the various business decisions that they make.

2. **External Stakeholders**

External stakeholders are groups outside a business or people such as customers, suppliers, creditors, community, trade unions, and the government, who are not directly working within the business but are affected from the decisions of the business. The government wants the business to pay taxes, employ more people, follow laws, and truthfully report its financial conditions. Customers want the business to produce quality products at rational prices. Suppliers want the business to continue to buy their products. Creditors want to be repaid on time and in full. The community has a stake in the business as employers of local people.

External stakeholders are individuals, groups, and organisations that are not directly affected by the business' performance. They may or may not be affected by the company's decisions or operations as they are not directly involved in decision-making and other business dealings. External stakeholders consist of government entities, the general public, community businessmen, politicians, analysts, stock brokers, potential investors, etc.

External stakeholders for a number of reasons will use the company's financial information and other publicly available information. Government entities such as Internal Revenue will use this information for assessing tax payments, potential investors will use the information to make investment choices, media will use them for public awareness purposes, and analysts and stock brokers will use them to advise clients or potential investors.

Difference between Internal and External Stakeholders

Stakeholders are the groups, individuals, and organisations that are interested in a business's activities, operations, performance, and success. The motive behind such an interest by these individuals may be that they are affected directly or indirectly by the business' successes or failures. The two types of stakeholders are internal stakeholders and external stakeholders. Internal stakeholders are directly involved in the business operations, and some also have the influence to make important business decisions. External stakeholders may or may not be directly affected by the business' operations but make use of any publicly available information for various purposes.

1.3.3 Responsibilities of Business towards Different Stakeholders

The existence, survival and the growth of any industrial unit largely depends on the social progress in production activity. Social responsibility is a matter of developing the right attitude towards social as well as industrial progress; it is a social discipline for the industrial unit.

It is impossible to promote social progress by imposing legal restrictions on industrial units. Only the positive approach of the top management can meet this obligation. The various responsibilities of business towards the shareholders, workers and public can be stated as below:

(I) Responsibilities towards Customers

The ultimate aim of any production is consumption of goods and satisfactory services to the customers. Hence, responsibilities of the management towards customers are of paramount importance. The consumer's interest and welfare are important considerations. The management must see that customers' requirements are fulfilled. They must get the required goods with perfection in quantity, quality, exactness of place and at reasonable price. This is the basic responsibility of management towards customers. Some of the responsibilities of management towards customers are:

1. **Production According to Requirement:** The management has to produce goods that meet the requirements of the consumers of different classes, tastes, and with varying purchasing powers. It has to ensure continuous supply of goods and services at fair prices.

2. **Prompt and Adequate Service:** The management has to provide prompt, adequate and courteous service to the customers. The management has to ensure cordial relations between the shareholders, employees and managers and have to build up goodwill with customers and prospective customers.

3. **Attention towards Complaints and Objections:** Complaints or objections are based on suspicion or doubts. The management has to handle customer's complaints more carefully. The objections or complaints must be removed by providing satisfactory services to the customer. There should be a prompt redressal of customer's grievances.

4. **Replies to the Enquiries:** The management must give prompt replies to enquiries regarding the company, its products and services, etc. It must be remembered that a mere visitor of today is a definite buyer of tomorrow and to neglect him is to undercut the sales of tomorrow.

5. **Co-operation:** Consumers have their associations and the management must extend its co-operation to them. Their suggestions must be taken into consideration and necessary help should be provided to them by the management.

6. **Consumer and Product Research:** In order to provide satisfactory service to the customers, a detailed study of the needs of customers as well as the product should be made. It certainly increases efficiency of the management in providing satisfactory services. Simplification, specialisation and standardisation are integral parts of product development.

7. **Steps to Correct Imperfection in the Distribution System:** It is necessary to take proper steps to correct imperfections in the distribution system including adulteration, hoarding, black marketing or profiteering, any middlemen or anti-social elements, i.e., avoid unfair and unethical practices.

8. **Improve Efficiency of the Functioning of Business:** An organisation will have to increase productivity and reduce prices, improve quality and smoothen the distribution system so that the goods can be made available easily.

In short, the management must have a firm foundation of sound customer policy.

(II) Responsibilities towards the Shareholders

The shareholders are the owners of an industrial organisation and hence, responsibilities towards shareholders are very important. The responsibilities of management towards the shareholders are:

1. **Safety of Investment/Preservation of Solvency:** The basic responsibility of a business enterprise is to ensure safety of investment, highest long run of return on their investments and a steady capital appreciation. The solvency of the enterprise must be preserved. Capital of the shareholders should be safeguarded. The company should strengthen and consolidate its position.

2. **Payment of Dividend:** In order to provide dividends the company should earn sufficient profits. Adequate reserves should be built up so that it will be in a position to declare reasonable dividends during a lean period as well.

3. **Direct Participation in the Management:** The interests of the shareholders are well protected through either direct participation in management by being elected to its board of directors or through their power to intervene. The shareholders are entitled to seek regular, accurate and full financial information about the company.

4. **Information to the Shareholders:** The management will have to publish news-letters, annual reports, published accounts and outlook on growth potential in future.

5. **Innovation and Growth:** If a company fails to cope up with changes in a changing and dynamic world, its position will be weakened and unstabilised, and the shareholder's interests will be affected. By innovation and through growth the company should consolidate and improve its position and help to strengthen the share prices.

6. **Public Image:** The shareholders are interested not only in the protection of their investment and the returns on it but also in the image of the company. Hence, the company should ensure its public image is such that the shareholders will feel proud of their company.

7. **Shareholders' Obligations:** As a part of an obligation, the shareholders can see with the help of their association and interest that a company is pursuing a dynamic policy and that sufficient profit is ploughed back for innovation and expansion. So they should offer wholehearted co-operation and support, sometimes even foregoing their dividends.

(III) Responsibilities towards Workers/Employees

It must be remembered that the ultimate success of any industrial enterprise depends on the highest productivity of workers.

1. **Fair Wages and Security to the Workers:** It is the responsibility of the management to provide the workers with opportunities for meaningful work. The management must win the co-operation of the workers. The management must provide fair wages and security to the workers. The remuneration of managerial personnel at different levels of the organisation also should be linked up with factors like responsibility, risk-taking, skill and initiative. Incentives, workers' participation in management also help a lot in contented staff.
2. **Opportunities to the Workers:** It is the responsibility of the management to give the workers, the opportunities to develop their capabilities through proper training, education and maintaining a free working atmosphere in the organisation.
3. **Proper Working Conditions and Workers' Welfare:** The management must provide working conditions that meet accepted standards of cleanliness, heat, ventilation, light and safety. The provisions of the Indian Factories Act should be implemented. Certain welfare activities e.g., recreation, sports, hobbies, medical care and help, debates and discussions, pension, education should also be created by the management.
4. **Trade Union Rights:** Trade unions are working efficiently in order to avoid unfair practices. Management should recognise worker's right to membership of trade unions and through them to collective bargaining and their right to strike over correct and just issues. Management must have a positive approach in negotiating with trade unions.
5. **Proper Recognition:** The organisation should make efforts for proper recognition, appreciation and encouragement of special skills and capabilities of workers. Similarly, opportunities to participate in managerial decisions should be provided to them.
6. **Proper Training and Promotion:** The workers should be properly trained and on acquiring additional training they should be promoted to higher positions. Such provision should be made a part of the system and policy.
7. **Grievance Handling System:** The organisation should create an efficient grievance handling system.

8. **A Company Code of Conduct:** A company code of conduct contains a recognised procedure for alleviating grievances and award proper rewards for making useful, valuable suggestions. The code guarantees religious, political and social independence of the worker and makes proper provision for the worker's participation in civil activities which are beneficial for the community. It is the responsibility of the management not to support unfair labour practices. Otherwise disciplinary action must be taken according to the code of conduct.

(IV) Responsibilities towards Community

It is the responsibility of the management to enlighten the community regarding the company's policies, processes, problems, developments of the locality they undertake and the well-being of the community. The responsibilities of the management towards community are:

1. **Spread of Education:** The management must provide its workers opportunities and time off for civil duties and for assisting in technical and other educational programmes. In order to have reliable means of communications, there should be the spread of education, so that education and cultural life of the community will improve.
2. **Meetings:** The management has to organise meetings and discussion groups. Public meetings should be regular, periodic and open to representatives of the customers, employees and community as well as shareholders.
3. **Help to the Local Government:** The management has to help the local government to improve public services and facilities. It has to provide financial and technical help to municipalities and other civic and government organisations. It should contribute to the upliftment of weaker sections of the society.
4. **Other Responsibilities:** The management has to encourage sports, art, music etc. It should provide recreational facilities. There should be a healthy environment free from all types of pollution, tension, worries and anxiety.
5. **Fair Competition:** The management should avoid the tendency to become monopolistic by keeping itself competitive and welcoming competition. It should always engage only in fair competition. It should restrain the community from indulging in anti-social and unethical attitudes and practices.

(V) Responsibilities towards the State / Government

In any country, the Government has to directly or indirectly participate in production, distribution, control and regulation of the business. The following are the responsibilities of management towards the state:

1. **Abide by Laws:** The management must abide by the laws passed by local, state and central governments.

2. **Co-operation:** The management has to co-operate with the formulation, legislation of constructive laws affecting business and also with the executive agencies in administering laws.
3. **Payment of Taxes and Dues:** The business managements should pay taxes and dues regularly, fully and honestly. This particular act should also be treated as co-operation of management with the state.
4. **Other Responsibilities:** Managements should not encourage corruption in public service. It should avoid monopolistic activities and sell commodities without adulterating them.

The general role of management in the economic set-up of any country is rationalised utilisation of available resources for increasing the productive capacity and providing opportunities to the various sections of the society for fruitful activities. In the words of *Peter F. Drucker*, "Management must maintain wealth-producing resources intact by making adequate profits to offset the risk of economic activity. It must besides increasing the wealth-creating and wealth-producing capacity of these resources, also increase the wealth of the society."

Interest in management development is fast increasing in India. Today, Indian management is still on trial. The need for higher standards of good management in business is indeed the challenge of the times. If an organisation is to remain strong, it must be provided opportunities for development and competent replacements for those who die or retire. Management must give the same priority to the development of human assets as it gives to the development of physical assets.

1.3.4 Stakeholder's Interests

The first step is to identify the stakeholders before identifying and addressing stakeholder interests. We have discussed in general terms the categories that stakeholders might fall into, but the list is different for each community and each effort. It's an essential part of one's job to decide who all stakeholders are, and try to engage them in a manner that advances the goals.

After identifying stakeholders, the next job is to understand their interests. Some will have an investment in carrying the effort forward, but others may equally aim on preventing it from happening or making certain it's unsuccessful. Stakeholder analysis (also referred to as stakeholder mapping) will help you choose which stakeholders might have the most influence over the success or failure of the effort, which might be the most important supporters, and which might be the most important rivals. Once you have that information, you can make plans for dealing with stakeholders with different interests and different levels of influence.

1. **Identifying Stakeholders**

    In identifying stakeholders, it's imperative to think beyond the obvious. Beneficiaries, policy makers, etc. are simple to identify, whereas indirect effects—and, as a result, secondary stakeholders—are sometimes harder to see. For example, a push for new regulations on a particular industry might require to a great extent increased paperwork or the purchase of new machinery on the part of that industry's suppliers.

    Given that there are a number of ways to identify stakeholders, often, the use of more than one will yield the best results.

    (a) Brainstorm: Have meetings with people in the organisation, officials, and others already involved in or informed about the effort and start calling out categories and names is referred to as brainstorming. One has to come out with anything that comes to mind, even if it seems impractical. On reflection, the impractical ideas may turn out to be among the best, so be as far-ranging as you can. After 10 or 15 minutes, stop and talk about each idea, possibly identifying each as a primary, secondary, and/or key stakeholder.

    (b) Bring together categories and names from informants in the community (if they're not available to be part of a brainstorming session), particularly members of a population or residents of a geographic area of concern.

    (c) Seek advice from organisations that either are or have been involved in related efforts; or that work with the population or in the area of concern.

    (d) Get more ideas from stakeholders as you identify them.

    (e) If appropriate, advertise. You can use some blend of the media—often free, through various community service arrangements—community meetings, community and organisational newsletters, social media, targeted emails, announcements by leaders at meetings and religious gatherings, and word of mouth to get the word out. You may come across people who think themselves stakeholders, whom you haven't thought about.

2. **Discovering and Understanding Stakeholder Interests**

    Stakeholder interests may differ. Some stakeholders' interests may be best served by carrying the effort forward, others by stopping or weakening it. Even among stakeholders from the same group, there may be contradictory concerns. Some of the many ways that stakeholder interests may manifest themselves:

    (a) Potential beneficiaries may be passionately supportive of an effort, seeing it as a chance or the pathway to an improved life... or they may be unsure or angry toward it. The effort or intervention may be awkward to them (e.g., adult literacy) or may seem troublesome. They may not understand it, or they may not see the benefit that will come from it. They may be scared to attempt something new, on the supposition that they will be unsuccessful, or will end up worse off than they are. They may be skeptical of any people or organisations engaged in such an effort, and experience that they are being looked down upon.

(b) Economic concerns bother some stakeholders. Sometimes these concerns are simply self-centered or greedy—as in the case of a corporation with billions in annual profits reluctant to spend a small part of that money to stop its factories from polluting—but in most cases, they are lawful.

(c) Economic concerns may also work in support of an effort. An initiative to put up one or more community clinics can offer construction jobs, orders for medical equipment, jobs for medical professionals and paraprofessionals, and economic rewards for the community. It might be backed, therefore, by unions, equipment manufacturers, professional associations, and local government, largely for economic reasons.

(d) Business people may have concerns about universal health care or regulation. These may be good for the larger society but they may in fact harm some businesses, especially very small businesses, where a minor alteration in profits may indicate not only a drop in share price, but also the incapability to uphold one's source of revenue. Businesses may have economic concerns in the opposite direction as well. Violence prevention might promise well for businesses in areas that people are uncertain to recurrence because of the threat of violence, and it might also lessen the risk of losses and physical harm to the business owners themselves. Thus, there is optimistic interest in an effective violence prevention effort.

(e) Organisations, agencies, and institutions may have a financial stake in an effort because of funding concerns. Their ability to be funded for conducting activities related to the effort may signify the difference between laying off and keeping staff members, or even between survival and closing the doors.

(f) Efforts that concern issues that are controversial for cultural reasons, such as abortion and gay marriage, may be passionately supported by some segments of the community and severely opposed by others. While such hot-button issues may not be resolvable, it's vital to know the positions of stakeholders on both sides.

(g) Ideological and cultural differences also drive stakeholder interests. Those who think that government shouldn't be seen as the source of anything might oppose government-funded programmes to help the poor, maintain public health, or provide other services that others deem necessary for the well-being of the community. The most fundamental services that people obviously can't provide for themselves such as the military, roads, police, public education are provided by the government.

(h) Legislators and policy makers may be concerned with public perceptions that they are wasting public money by funding a particular effort.

(i) The jobs of organisation staff members engaged in carrying out an effort can be drastically changed by the need to learn new methods, add to paperwork, or any number of other requirements. Depending on the situation, they may be more than willing to take on these responsibilities, and may have ideas about how they can be made less burdensome, or may dislike them.

(j) Family concerns may enter into stakeholder interests as well. Parents cite child abuse when their wards are punished by spankings with a brush or belt. Some people may view this as protecting children and others as interfering with parental rights.

1.3.5 Influence of Various Stakeholder Groups

Stakeholders have increased influence on company business activities in the early 21st century as community citizenship and social responsibility have been consistently integrated into business management. Main stakeholder groups—customers, employees, communities and business partners carry weight in company decisions and activities. Understanding the impact of these stakeholders on business is especially important for small businesses.

1. **Governance and Social Responsibility:** Business governance is the formal organisation of a mission, vision and objectives. In the past, businesses had made maximising profits a prime aim of governance and business operations. Now, social responsibility has encouraged many companies to balance social and environmental responsibilities with profits. Social responsibility in business has existed for some time. Due to pressures from the government and society, some companies have preferred to participate in environment preservation and social responsibility.

2. **Customers and Community:** Customers are the central influence for many companies because they have understood that satisfied customers and long-term relationships are the key to building sustainable success and profiting over time. Many organisations make use of customer relationship management through which companies gather data on customers for more targeted and efficient marketing and sales efforts.

3. **Employees:** Businesses that stick to social responsibility requirements and make community citizenship a main concern have also made employee interests a focal point of their business operations. Companies can be influenced by emphasis on employees as a stakeholder by treating employees as the most valued assets, encouraging a nondiscriminatory work environment and actively involving employees in important decisions.

4. **Business Partners:** The Supply Chain Management (SCM), a popular logistics management system has come into view in the early 21st century. SCM involves close collaboration between suppliers and business buyers that work together to deliver the best value to end customers. This collaboration helps companies to cut costs, have a stronger focus on customer value, improve environmental preservation and build significant relationships with a key group of trusted business partners.

1.4 Bottom of the Pyramid Opportunities: Issues and Opportunities for Business in a Socially and Environmentally Sensitive World

With the end of the Cold War, the former Soviet Union and its allies, as well as China, India, and Latin America, opened their closed markets to foreign investment in a cascading fashion. The new growth opportunities for multinational corporations (MNCs) have been possible due to this significant economic and social transformation; its promise has yet to be realised.

First, the prospect of millions of "middle-class" consumers in developing countries, clamouring for products from MNCs, was wildly oversold. To make matters worse, the Asian and Latin American financial crises have to a great extent reduced the attractiveness of emerging markets. As a result, many MNCs worldwide slowed investments and began to rethink risk–reward structures for these markets. This move back could become even more evident in the rise of the terrorist attacks in the United States on September 11, 2001.

The monotonous nature of most MNCs' emerging market strategies over the past decade does not change the amount of the opportunity, which is in reality much larger than thought beforehand. The real source of market promise are the *aspiring poor* who are joining the market economy for the first time rather than the small number of rich in the developing world, or even the emerging middle-income consumers.

This is a time for MNCs to look at globalisation strategies through a new lens of inclusive capitalism. For companies with the resources and determination to compete at the bottom of the world economic pyramid, the potential rewards include growth, profits, and incalculable contributions to humankind. Countries with less or no modern infrastructure or products to meet basic human needs are an ideal testing ground for developing environmentally sustainable technologies and products for the entire world.

Furthermore, MNC investment at "the bottom of the pyramid" means reducing poverty and desperation, preventing the social decay, political chaos, terrorism, and environmental meltdown that is certain to go on if the space between rich and poor countries continues to broaden.

Doing business with the world's billions of poorest people, two-thirds of the world's population will need major innovations in technology and business models. Therefore, MNCs has to reassess price–performance relationships for products and services. It will demand a new level of capital competence and new methods of measuring financial success. Companies will be forced to transform their understanding of scale, from a "bigger is better" ideal to an ideal of highly distributed small-scale operations married to world-scale capabilities.

1.4.1 Four Consumer Tiers

There are 75 to 100 million affluent Tier 1 consumers from around the world at the very top of the world economic pyramid. (See Fig. 1.4) This is a cosmopolitan group which consists of middle- and upper-income people in developed countries and the few rich elites from the developing world. In the middle of the pyramid, in Tiers 2 and 3, are poor customers in developed nations and the growing middle classes in developing countries, the targets of MNCs' past emerging-market strategies.

Annual Per Capita Income	Tiers	Population in Millions
More than $ 20,000	1	75-100
$1,500-$ 20,000	2 and 3	1,500-1,750
Less than $ 1,500	4	4,000

Fig. 1.4: The World Economic Pyramid

In Tier 4 which is at the bottom of the pyramid their annual per capita income based on purchasing power parity in US dollars is less than $1,500, the minimum considered necessary to sustain a decent life.

The income gap between the rich and poor is increasing. Although the poor represent the majority of the population, they cannot have a say in the global market economy due to this severe inequity of wealth distribution. In fact, given its huge size, Tier 4 represents a multitrillion-dollar market. According to World Bank projections, the population at the bottom of the pyramid could increase to more than 6 billion people over the next 40 years, because the mass of the world's population growth occurs there.

The perception that the bottom of the pyramid is not a viable market also fails to take into account the growing importance of the informal economy among the poorest of the poor, which by some estimates accounts for 40 to 60 percent of all economic activity in developing countries. The majority of Tier 4 people live in rural villages, or urban slums and shantytowns, and they generally do not hold legal title or legal document to their assets (e.g., dwellings, farms, businesses). Mostly, they are illiterate and are hard to reach by means of conventional distribution, credit, and communications. Generally, low quality and quantity of products and services are available in Tier 4. This massive segment of the global population has continued to be unseen to the corporate sector.

Fortunately, the Tier 4 market is wide open for technological innovation. Among the many possibilities for innovation, MNCs can be leaders in leapfrogging to products that don't repeat the environmental mistakes of developed countries over the last 50 years. Today's MNCs evolved in an era of plentiful natural resources and thus tended to make products and services that were resource-intensive and extremely polluting.

1.4.2 The Invisible Opportunity

Perception of market opportunity is a function of the way many managers are socialised to think and the analytical tools they use. Markets are being judged by the MNCs on the basis of income level or selections of products and services appropriate for developed countries, thus most of the MNCs tend to discard the bottom level of the pyramid. To understand the market potential of Tier 4, MNCs must come to conditions with a set of core assumptions and practices that influence their view of developing countries. We have identified the following as widely shared orthodoxies that must be reexamined:

- **Assumption #1:** The poor are not our target consumers because with our current cost structures, we cannot profitably compete for that market.
- **Assumption #2:** The poor cannot afford and have no use for the products and services sold in developed markets.
- **Assumption #3:** Only developed markets appreciate and will pay for new technology. The poor can use the previous generation of technology.
- **Assumption #4:** The bottom of the pyramid is not important to the long-term viability of our business. We can leave Tier 4 to governments and nonprofits.
- **Assumption #5:** Managers are not excited by business challenges that have a humanitarian dimension.
- **Assumption #6:** Intellectual excitement is in developed markets. It is hard to find talented managers who want to work at the bottom of the pyramid.

The challenge for MNCs is to cater to this segment of market by combining features like low cost, good quality, sustainability, and profitability to its products.

Drivers of Innovation	Implications for MNCs
Increased access among the poor to TV and information.	Tier 4 is becoming aware of many products and services and is aspiring to share the benefits.
Deregulation and the diminishing role of governments and the international aid.	A more hospitable investment climate for MNCs entering developing countries and more cooperation from non-governmental organisations.
Global overcapacity combined with intense competition in Tiers 1, 2 and 3.	Tier 4 represents a huge untapped market for profitable growth.
The need to discourage migration of overcrowded urban centers.	MNCs must create products and services for rural populations.

Fig. 1.5: Innovation and MNC Implications in Tier 4

Furthermore, MNCs cannot use these new opportunities without thoroughly rethinking how they go to market. Fig. 1.6 suggests some (but by no means all) areas where an entirely new perspective is required to create profitable markets in Tier 4.

Price Performance	Views of Duality
• Product development • Manufacturing • Distribution	• New delivery formats • Creation of robust products for harsh conditions [heat, dust, etc.]
Sustainability	Profitability
• Reduction in resource intensity • Recyclability • Renewable energy	• Investment intensity • Margins • Volume

Fig. 1.6: New Strategies for the Bottom of the Pyramid

1.4.3 Tier 4 Pioneers

Hindustan Lever Ltd. (HLL) is a subsidiary of Great Britain's Unilever PLC and is broadly considered the best-managed company in India, and has been a pioneer among MNCs surveying markets at the bottom of the pyramid. For more than 50 years, HLL has served people in India having low incomes so that they could afford to buy MNC products. In the 1990s, Nirma Ltd., a local firm began offering detergent products for poor consumers, mostly in rural areas. In fact Nirma adopted a business system that incorporated a new product formulation, low-cost manufacturing process, wide distribution network, special packaging for daily purchasing, and value pricing.

HLL, in typical MNC fashion, initially dismissed Nirma's strategy. First of all HLL did not pay attention to Nirma's strategy. Nirma was taking over the market from its big competitors. However, HLL discarded the traditional business model and looked forward to adopt the new business system followed by Nirma.

HLL's new detergent, called Wheel, was formulated to significantly decrease the percentage of oil to water in the product, responding to the fact that the poor frequently wash their clothes in rivers and other public water systems. HLL decentralised the production, marketing, and distribution of the product to leverage the abundant labour pool in rural India, rapidly creating sales channels through the thousands of small outlets where people at the bottom of the pyramid shop. In order to launch Wheel at a low price, HLL also changed the cost structure of its detergent business.

In the detergent market, Nirma and HLL are close competitors. Unilever's own analysis of Nirma and HLL's competition in the detergent business disclose even more about the profit potential of the marketplace at the bottom of the pyramid.

Table 1.1: Nirma Vs HLL in India's Detergent Market (1999)

	Nirma	HLL (Wheel)	HLL (High-End Products)
Total Sales ($ Million)	150	100	180
Gross Margin (%)	18	18	25
ROCE (%)	121	93	22

Source: Presentation by John Ripley, senior vice president, Unilever at the Academy of Management Meeting, August 10, 1999.

Contrary to popular assumptions, if MNCs modify their business models, the poor can be a very profitable market. Specifically, Tier 4 is not a market that allows for the traditional pursuit of high margins; instead, profits are driven by volume and capital efficiency. Margins are likely to be low (by current norms), but unit sales can be extremely high. Managers who focus on gross margins will miss the opportunity at the bottom of the pyramid; managers who innovate and focus on economic profit will be rewarded.

Nirma has become one of the largest branded detergent makers in the world. As the Unilever example makes clear, the starting assumption must be that serving Tier 4 involves bringing together the best of technology and a global resource base to deal with local market conditions. The potential of Tier 4 cannot be realized without an entrepreneurial orientation.

Serving Tier 4 markets is not the same as serving existing markets better or more efficiently. Managers first must build a commercial infrastructure customised to the wants and challenges of Tier 4. Creating such an infrastructure must be seen as an investment, much like the more familiar investments in plants, processes, products, and R&D.

Further, contrary to more conventional investment strategies, no firm can do this alone. Multiple players must be involved, including local governmental authorities, non-governmental organisations (NGOs), communities, financial institutions, and other companies. Four elements which are the keys to a flourishing Tier 4 market—creating buying power, shaping aspirations, improving access, and tailoring local solutions (See Fig. 1.7).

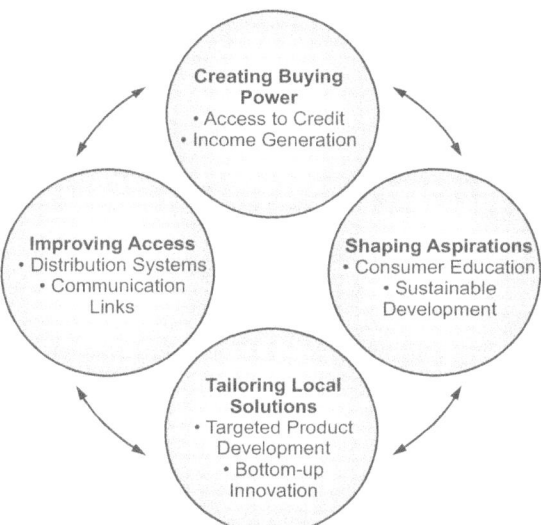

Fig. 1.7: The Commercial Infrastructure at the Bottom of the Pyramid

Each of these four elements demands innovation in technology, business models, and management processes. And business leaders must be willing to experiment, collabourate, empower locals, and create new sources of competitive advantage and wealth.

1.4.4 Creating Buying Power

According to International Labour Organisation report in 2012, more than 197 million people globally or 6% of the world's labour force were without a job. To uplift the poor from the poverty line is an opportunity for the business to do something good for the needy and the nation. By providing access to credit and increasing the earning potential of the poor, business can effectively help the poor. A few perceptive companies have already begun to blaze this path with surprisingly optimistic outcomes.

In the past, commercial credit has been unavailable to the very poor. Even if those living in poverty had access to a bank, without collateral it was hard to get credit from the traditional banking system. Now, people with low incomes are able to build their equity and make major purchases such as houses, cars, and education due to availability of credit.

The vast majority of the poor in developing countries function in the "informal" or extra legal economy, since the time and cost concerned in securing legal title for their assets or incorporation of their microenterprises is prohibitive. Governments of developing countries provide subsidies on products to help the poor so that they can afford things easily. Even if government support is provided to the poor to start small businesses, their dependence on credit from local moneylenders charging usurious rates makes it impossible to do well.

Extending credit to the poor so that they can lift themselves up economically is not a new idea. Computerisation of micro-lending services has made possible to reach many more people and lending money to individuals with no guarantee and no formal address. A number of multinational banks are commencing to provide micro-banking services in developing countries.

1.4.5 Shaping Aspirations

In Tier 4, sustainable product innovations is promoted through consumer education, that may not only completely influence the preferences of people at the bottom of the pyramid, but may eventually reshape the way people in Tier 1 live. In fact, in 20 years, we may look back to see that Tier 4 provided the early market pull for troublemaking technologies that replaced weak technologies in developed countries and advanced the fortunes of MNCs with foresight.

For example, Unilever's HLL subsidiary has dealt with the lack of practical, low-priced, low-energy-consuming refrigeration in India. HLL's laboratories have developed a new refrigeration approach that allows transportation of ice-cream across the country in normal non-refrigerated trucks. The system allows quantum decrease in usage of electricity and makes hazardous and polluting refrigerants unnecessary. As an additional benefit, the new system is cheaper to build and use.

The opportunities in developing countries are electricity, water, refrigeration, and many other essential services. The Solar Electric Light Fund (SELF) which is a US based NGO has creatively adapted technology and applied microcredit financing to bring electrical service to people in remote villages in Africa and Asia who otherwise would spend money to burn hazardous kerosene, candles, wood, or dung for their light and cooking. SELF's rural electrification system is based on small-scale on-site power generation using renewable resources.

The success of SELF and other NGOs paying attention to small-scale distributed energy solutions have begun to draw the attention of Western companies such as the US's Plug Power Inc. (fuel cells) and Honeywell Inc. (micro-turbines). They see the sense in moving into a wide-open market in Tier 4 rather than trying to compel their technology in advance into applications for the developed markets, where incumbents and institutions stand in their way. With several billion potential customers around the world, investments in such innovations should be well worth it.

1.4.6 Improving Access

As Tier 4 communities are often physically and economically cut off, improved distribution systems and communication links are necessary for the growth of the bottom of the pyramid. Few of the large emerging-market countries have distribution systems that reach more than half of the population leading to the continued dependence of the poorest consumers on local products and services and moneylenders. As a result, few MNCs have designed their distribution systems to cater to the requirements of poor rural customers.

MNCs can help bottom-of-the-pyramid enterprises by providing them links to international markets by distributing the products of Tier 4 enterprises in Tier 1 markets. Certainly, it is feasible through partnerships to influence traditional knowledge bases to produce more sustainable, and in some cases, superior products for consumption by Tier 1 customers.

The single major barrier to sustainable development can be shortage of information. It is likely to imagine a single, interconnected market bringing together the world's rich and poor in the pursuit of actual sustainable economic development through telephones and Internet connections. The process could transform the "digital divide" into a "digital dividend."

Bringing such technology to villages in Tier 4 makes possible a number of applications, including tele-education, telemedicine, micro-banking, agricultural extension services, and environmental monitoring, all of which facilitate and encourage microenterprise, economic development, and access to world markets.

1.4.7 Tailoring Local Solutions

As we come into the new century, the combined sales of the world's top 200 MNCs equal nearly 30 percent of the total world gross domestic product. Yet these same corporations employ less than 1 percent of the world's labour force. Of the world's 100 largest economies, 51 are economies internal to corporations. Yet scores of Third World countries have suffered absolute economic stagnation or decline.

To succeed in the 21st century, MNCs must expand their economic base and share it more extensively. They should narrow the gap between the rich and poor. This can be possible only if these companies also produce products for Tier 4 consumers along with the production of global products for Tier 1 consumers. They must look after local markets and cultures, influence local solutions, and make wealth at the lowest levels on the pyramid.

To achieve this, MNCs must merge their superior technology with deep local insights. For example, consider packaging. Consumers in Tier 1 countries have the disposable income and the space to buy in bulk (e.g., 10 kg detergent from superstores like Big Bazaar) and shop less frequently. They use their spending money to "inventory convenience." Tier 4 consumers are short of money and with limited living space, shop every day, but not for much. They look for single-serve packaging. But a consumer with small means is not burdened by large quantities of product and they can change brands every time they buy.

1.4.8 Putting it all Together

The four elements of the commercial infrastructure for the bottom of the pyramid—creating buying power, shaping aspirations, improving access, and tailoring local solutions, are tangled. Innovation in any one element will influence innovation in the others too. Corporations are only one of the actors; MNCs must work together with NGOs, local and state governments, and communities.

However someone must take the go ahead to make this revolution take place. The question is why should it be MNCs?

Even if multinational managers are emotionally convinced, it is not obvious that large corporations have real advantages over small, local organisations. MNCs may never be able to beat the cost or responsiveness of village entrepreneurs. Indeed, empowering local entrepreneurs and enterprises is a way to develop Tier 4 markets. Still, there are several compelling reasons for MNCs to embark on this course:

- **Resources:** Constructing a complex commercial infrastructure for the Tier 4 is a resource—and management-intensive task. Significant research is required in developing environmentally sustainable products and services. Distribution channels and communication networks are costly to build up and maintain. *A small number of local entrepreneurs have the managerial or technological resources to build this infrastructure.*

- **Leverage:** MNCs like Avon, Unilever, Citigroup, and many others can transfer knowledge from one market to another—from China to Brazil or India. Even if practices and products have to be tailored to serve local needs, *MNCs, with their distinctive global knowledge base, have a plus point that is not easily available to local entrepreneurs.*

- **Bridging:** MNCs can be nodes for building the commercial infrastructure, providing access to knowledge, managerial imagination, and financial resources. Without MNCs as catalysts, well-intentioned NGOs, communities, local governments, entrepreneurs, and even multilateral development agencies will carry on to struggle in their efforts to bring growth to the bottom. *MNCs are best placed to connect the range of actors necessary to develop the Tier 4 market.*

- **Transfer:** Not only can MNCs leverage learning from the bottom of the pyramid, but they also have the capacity to transfer innovations up-market all the way to Tier 1. Tier 4 is a testing ground for sustainable living. *Many of the innovations for the bottom can be adapted for use in the resource—and energy-intensive markets of the developed world.*

It is crucial, however, that managers recognise the nature of business leadership required in the Tier 4 arena. Creativity, imagination, tolerance for ambiguity, stamina, passion, understanding, and courage may be as important as analytical skill, intelligence, and knowledge. Leaders must have a deep understanding of the complexity and delicacy of sustainable development in the perspective of Tier 4. Finally, managers must have the interpersonal and intercultural skills to work with a wide array of organisations and people.

There must be a systematic organisational infrastructure build up by MNCs to deal with opportunity at the bottom of the pyramid. This means building a local base of support, reorienting R&D to focus on the needs of the poor, forming new alliances, increasing employment intensity, and reinventing cost structures. These five organisational elements are clearly interconnected and mutually strengthening.

- **Build a Local Base of Support:** The present power structure can be intimidated by empowering the poor. As Cargill Inc. set up its sunflower-seed business in India, the local opposition came forward and Cargill's offices were burned twice. But Cargill continued. Through Cargill's investments in farmer education, training, and supply of farm inputs, farmers have appreciably improved their productivity per acre of land. Today, Cargill is seen as the friend of the farmer. Political opposition has vanished.

- **Conduct R&D Focused on the Poor:** It is essential to carry out R&D and market research focused on the unique necessities of the poor, by region and by country. In India, China, and North Africa, for example, research on matters like to provide safe water for drinking, cooking, washing, and cleaning is a main concern. Research must adapt foreign solutions to local requirements. For example, a daily dosage of vitamins can be added to a wide variety of food and beverage products. For corporations that have distribution and brand presence throughout the developing world, such as Coca-Cola Company, the bottom of the pyramid presents a huge unused market for such products as water and nutritionals.

- **Form New Alliances:** MNCs have conventionally formed alliances only to break into new markets; now they want to expand their alliance strategies. By entering into alliances to expand in Tier 4 markets, MNCs gain insight into developing countries' culture and local knowledge. At the same time, MNCs improve their own reliability. They may also protect preferred or exclusive access to a market or raw material. We foresee three kinds of significant relationships which are alliances with local firms and cooperatives (such as the Khira District Milk Cooperative); alliances with local and international NGOs (like Starbucks's alliance with Conservation International in coffee); and alliances with governments (e.g., Merck & Company's recent alliance in Costa Rica to foster rain forest preservation in exchange for bioprospecting rights).

Given the difficulty and complexity of building business models reliant on relationships with national or central governments (e.g., large infrastructure development), we foresee more alliances at the local and regional level. To achieve something in such alliances, MNC managers must be taught to work with people who may not have the same agenda or the same educational and economic background as they do. The challenge and payoff is how to manage and gain knowledge from diversity—economic, intellectual, racial, and linguistic.

- **Increase Employment Intensity:** MNCs which are adapted to Tier 1 markets think in terms of capital intensity and labour productivity. Exactly the opposite logic applies in Tier 4. The vast number of people at the bottom of the pyramid can be employed because of the production and distribution approach, as in the case of Ruf & Tuf jeans from Arvind Mills. It provided jobs to a mass of local tailors as stockers, promoters, distributors, and service providers, even though the cost of the jeans was 80 percent below that of Levi's. As Arvind demonstrated, MNCs need not employ large numbers of people directly on their payroll, but the organisational model in Tier 4 must enhance employment intensity (and incomes) among the poor and groom them to become new customers.

- **Reinvent Cost Structures:** Managers must radically reduce cost levels relative to those in Tier 1. MNCs must decrease their costs considerably to produce products and services the poor can afford. The complete business process must be rethought with a focus on functionality, not on the product itself. For example, financial services need not be distributed only through branch offices open from 9 a.m. to 5 p.m. but can be at a time—after 8 p.m. and place near their homes. Cash-dispensing machines can be placed in safe areas—police stations and post offices.

Lowering cost structures also forces a debate on ways to decrease investment costs. This will unavoidably lead to greater use of information technology to develop production and distribution systems. As eminent, village-based phones are already transforming the pattern of communications throughout the developing world. Add the Internet, and we have a whole new way of communicating and creating economic development in poor, rural areas. Creative use of IT will come into view in these markets as a means to noticeably lower the costs linked with access to products and services, distribution, and credit management.

1.5 Environmental and Social Issues and How they Shape Market

Environmental and social issues can have noteworthy impacts on the performance and prospects of companies. The possibility and extent of impact of key environmental and social issues will vary by industry and by company. Many of these issues are interrelated and mutually dependent. The landscape of environmental and social issues and risks important to business is depicted in the Global Risks 2011 Sixth Edition report of the World Economic Forum as follows:

1. **Water Scarcity and Quality**

   Some industries depend on a supply of water for their operations (e.g. extractive industries, beverage producers, agriculture growers, bottlers, semi-conductor producers). Likewise, employees and communities require potable water. A price boost would present significant social and business consequences and opportunities for technological innovation.

2. **Climate Change**

   Companies in most industries are affected by the decision regarding reduction of greenhouse gas emissions and adapting to the effects of climate change impacts. Business impacts may include access to affordable insurance, availability and security of energy, and the need for technological innovation and renewable energy solutions. Transportation routes for raw materials and product may also be affected. A number of larger greenhouse gas emitting companies have begun to put a "shadow" price on carbon in their strategic and capital investment planning.

3. **Energy**

   Energy availability, cost, security, production and transportation are all affected by environmental and social considerations that impact all companies and stakeholders. Energy-related environmental and social issues offer opportunities for technological innovation and investment for many companies as the cost of conventional energy sources rises and the search for alternative energy sources expand. There are also opportunities to decrease costs by decreasing energy demand.

4. **Air Pollution**

   The effect of air pollution on human health, agriculture, forests and lakes has led governments to force regulations to control the quantity of pollutants emitted into the environment. These regulations can impact the timing of approvals for new facilities and operations. They also, at times, cause new technological innovations to meet more strict emission standards whether from stationary or mobile sources.

5. **Waste and Waste Management**

   Product design and packaging, production processes and waste disposal practices have direct bottom line impacts. There is an increasing call for "doing more with less"—a growing recognition that natural resources are not infinite and therefore there is a need to consume less without putting at risk product quality.

Reducing material usage, packaging and waste, and improving waste management practices can lead to cost savings and can present opportunities for innovation (e.g., tailings ponds in extractive industries). Recycling of products and components is more and more significant from regulatory and consumer viewpoints and can lead to new business opportunities for some industries and companies.

6. **Biodiversity Loss**

Great attention is paid by the stakeholders in many industries and regions to the extent that industrial practices impact biodiversity (e.g., in extractive industries). The loss of biodiversity affects the productivity and availability of resources in a variety of industries (e.g., fisheries, forestry, agriculture, pharmaceuticals, beverages etc.).

7. **Forest and Soil Degradation**

Deforestation and deterioration of forests impact habitats, biodiversity and air and soil quality, mainly affecting lumber, pulp and paper companies. Agricultural productivity is affected by soil degradation. Sustainability of forest management practices can be an issue for customers and supply chain policies.

8. **Earthquakes and Volcanic Eruptions**

Beyond the site-specific impacts on people, ecosystems and infrastructure, earthquakes and volcanic eruptions can also affect supply chains and travel plans of employees. While earthquakes and volcanic eruptions have always occurred as natural phenomena, with globalisation and the interconnectedness of economies, the reach of their impacts on business is more extensive today.

9. **Population Growth, Urbanization and Demographics**

The export markets, as well as major sources of low-cost labour are available in developing countries due to significant population growth. Urbanisation brings with it growing demands for energy and infrastructure and concerns about air quality; and the demographics of populations, such as ageing, impact workforces, markets, health care and pensions. Urbanisation and population growth also impact the availability of agricultural land and demand for food and call for productivity improvements in agricultural practices. In the short, this may lead to increase in larger or different markets.

10. **Food Production and Safety**

The major concern of many developing nations is to provide sufficient food to sustain increasing populations. New industries have come forward to meet the growing demand for more natural products due to increasing concerns about the safety of food and it's processing. The growing demand for food, coupled with food safety concerns, climate change, water shortage and energy cost issues, contributes to forest and soil degradation as well as an anticipation of increasing food prices. Increased food prices affect disposable income.

11. Poverty

Poverty impacts the demand for and pricing of products (e.g., consumer product companies, telecommunications, pharmaceuticals, automobiles) and can also impact the availability of an educated and healthy work force. Companies operating in poor areas may find that investing in improving community infrastructure decreases risks related to lack of suitable workforce, insufficient transportation and incapability to get or maintain a social license to operate.

12. Human Health and Safety

Healthy communities are needed by most of the companies to have a source of a strong and productive workforce. As per government regulations workplace safety of employees and contractors has long been recognized as a priority in many industries. Companies more progressively recognise the business case for addressing disease prevention, treatment and response, e.g., issues such as obesity, AIDS, healthy lifestyles, pandemics. Some companies are developing new products and services in response to these issues.

13. Human Rights

Companies together with their contractors are held accountable for improper workplace and business practices that impinge on human rights, whether directly or through their supply chains. Consumers, communities, employees and other stakeholders are impacting corporate business practices regarding human rights and affecting a company's social license to operate, particularly given the power of the internet and social media.

14. Corruption

Companies are increasingly held liable for the reliability of their practices in all countries in which they do business. Failure to act with honesty can have major, if not severe, financial consequences. It can also affect corporate reputation and ability to operate.

15. Social Unrest

Besides the several issues mentioned above, other issues such as unemployment, religious conflicts, political instability and terrorism can contribute to social unrest. This, in turn, can produce significant business and operating risks, including threats to facilities, infrastructure, supply chains, markets and workforce.

Points to Remember

- **Social responsibility** is the obligation (of manager) to pursue those policies, to make those decisions, or to follow those lines of action which are desirable in terms of objectives and values of our society.

- Following are the steps of one of the **strategies to implement CSR commitments.**
  1. Develop an integrated CSR decision-making structure.
  2. Plan and execute a CSR business plan.
  3. Set measurable targets and make out performance measures.
  4. Engage employees and others to whom CSR commitments apply.
  5. Design and conduct CSR training.
  6. Create mechanisms for addressing problematic behaviour.
  7. Build internal and external communications plans.
- **Corporate citizenship** refers to the degree to which businesses are socially responsible for meeting legal, ethical and economic responsibilities placed on them by shareholders. The aim of businesses is to provide higher standards of living and quality of life in the communities in which they run while still safeguarding profitability for stakeholders.
- **Stakeholders** mean individuals, groups, or organisations that are concerned with the performance of a business.
- **Various types of stakeholders** can be divided into the following two categories:
  1. Internal Stakeholders
  2. External Stakeholders
- **Investment at "the bottom of the pyramid"** means reducing poverty and desperation, preventing social decay, political chaos, terrorism, and environmental meltdown that is certain to go on if the space between rich and poor countries continues to broaden.

Questions for Discussion

1. Elabourate the concept, nature and relevance of corporate social responsibility.
2. What do you understand by the concept of corporate citizenship?
3. Discuss the types and influence of stakeholders in business.
4. Explain the formulation and implementation of CSR policy.
5. Describe the concept of Bottom of Pyramid in CSR.

Multiple Choice Questions

1. The acronym CSR stands for:
   - (a) Corporate Search and Rescue
   - (b) Corporate Social Responsibility
   - (c) Corporate Sensitive Reliability
   - (d) Corporate Social Reality
2. All those who are affected by or can affect the operations of the organisation are known as:
   - (a) owners
   - (b) interested parties
   - (c) stakeholders
   - (d) stockholders

3. The stakeholder view of social responsibility states that organisations must respond to the needs of
   (a) employees and customers
   (b) shareholders and owners.
   (c) all interested parties.
   (d) all those who might sue the organisation

4. A firm is said to have good corporate social performance when
   (a) stockholders invest in socially responsible causes.
   (b) charitable deductions are automatically deducted from pay without the consent of employees.
   (c) the company has not been convicted of ethical violations for five consecutive years.
   (d) stakeholders are satisfied with its level of social responsibility.

5. A socially responsible mutual fund will only purchase stocks in companies that
   (a) have a no-smoking policy in place.
   (b) have a culturally diverse management team.
   (c) hire some job candidates who are HIV positive.
   (d) have good social performance.

6. A whistle blower is an employee who
   (a) exposes organisational wrongdoing.
   (b) complains a lot to company management.
   (c) engages in unethical behavior.
   (d) referees disputes with other employees.

7. Which one of the following approaches to creating an ethical and socially responsible workplace is likely to be the most powerful?
   (a) Passing out buttons with the statement "Just Say No to Bad Ethics"
   (b) Placing posters about ethics throughout the organisation
   (c) Top management acting as models of the right behaviour
   (d) Including a statement about ethics and social responsibility in the employee handbook

8. A recommended way of minimising unethical behavior is for employees to
   (a) write anonymous notes to ethical violators.
   (b) immediately report all suspicious behaviour to top management.
   (c) spend part of their vacation preparing a personal philosophy of ethics.
   (d) confront fellow employees about ethical deviations.

9. Corporate social responsibility (CSR) consists of which four kinds of responsibilities:
   (a) Economic, ethical, societal, and altruistic
   (b) Economic, legal, ethical, and altruistic
   (c) Fiscal, legal, societal, and philanthropic
   (d) Economic, legal, ethical, and philanthropic
10. Which of the items listed is NOT a product of a "favourable corporate reputation."
    (a) Charge more for its products and services
    (b) Attract, hire and keep higher quality applicants/employees
    (c) Enhance their access to better capital markets
    (d) Ignore the Foreign Corrupt Practices Act
11. Typical Codes of Conduct cover conduct described below. In the aftermath of Bhopal, the chemical industry wishing to demonstrate responsible corporate citizenship has added which additional behaviours set out below.
    (a) Legal compliance
    (b) Continuous improvement, communication with external stakeholders and training of suppliers on the standards
    (c) Pollution prevention
    (d) Safe handling of chemicals from manufacture through disposal
12. Why, according to stakeholder theory, is it in companies' best interests to pay attention to their stakeholders?
    (a) If firms only act in their own self-interest employees may feel exploited.
    (b) If firms only act in their own self-interest government might put more regulation on them.
    (c) If firms only act in their own self-interest customers might not like the image that the company portray.
    (d) If firms only act in their own self-interest and inflict harm on stakeholders then society might withdraw its support.

Answers

1. (b)	2. (c)	3. (c)	4. (d)	5. (d)	6. (a)	7. (c)	8. (d)	9. (d)	10. (d)
11. (b)	12. (d)								

Project Questions

1. To what extent is CSR being practiced in India? Give examples. Do you think Indian corporate adequately give back to society compared to what they have received from it?
2. How is CSR related to corporate citizenship?

■■■

Chapter 2...
Sustainable Development

Contents ...
2.1 Sustainable Development
    2.1.1 Concept and Definitions
    2.1.2 Need and Importance of Sustainable Development
    2.1.3 Education for Sustainable Development
    2.1.4 Philosophical Development of Sustainable Development
    2.1.5 Gandhian Thought on Sustainable Development
    2.1.6 Sustainable Development and Social Framework
        2.1.6.1 Internal
        2.1.6.2 External
    2.1.7 Sustainable Development and Equitable Distribution
    2.1.8 Difference between Sustainable Development and Green Development
    2.1.9 Criticism on Sustainable Development
2.2 Stakeholder
    2.2.1 Meaning of Stakeholder
    2.2.2 Types of Stakeholder
    2.2.3 Role of Stakeholders in Business
    2.2.4 Powers of Stakeholder
2.3 Sustainability Engagement Approaches
    2.3.1 Reducing Socio-environmental Costs and Risks: Managing the Downside
    2.3.2 Driving Revenues and Creating Intangible Value: Managing the Upside
- Points to Remember
- Questions for Discussion
- Multiple Choice Questions
- Project Questions

Learning Objectives ...
- To understand the concept, need and importance of sustainable development
- To study the philosophical development of sustainable development
- To be able to explain the Gandhian thought on sustainable development
- To learn the social framework of sustainability
- To differentiate between sustainable development and green development
- To visualise the powers of stakeholders in a business
- To learn the downside and upside management approaches of Sustainability Engagement

2.1 Sustainable Development

2.1.1 Concept and Definitions

Sustainable development is a road-map, the action plan, for achieving sustainability in any activity that uses resources and where immediate and intergenerational replication is demanded. Sustainable development is development that meets the needs of the present without compromising the ability of future generations to meet their own needs.

It contains two major concepts:

- the concept of needs, in particular the essential needs of the world's poor, to which overriding priority should be given;
- the idea of limitations imposed by the state of technology and social organisation on the environment's ability to meet present and future needs.

Sustainable development implies the implementation of several conditions:

- preserving the overall balance,
- respect for the environment,
- preventing the depletion of natural resources,
- reduced production of waste, and
- the rationalisation of production and energy consumption must be implemented.

Development must combine three main elements in order to be sustainable:

- sociopolitical sustainability,
- environment sustainability, and
- economic sustainability.

Fig. 2.1: The Need for Sustainability Development

If we don't take care of the world we live in now, we won't have anything to leave behind us for the future generations. Sustainability tries to find a way in which human beings live comfortably, but respecting Mother Nature. The world is not something you enjoy today, it was here before you were born and it might be here after you leave. The success of this depends on the consumers accepting certain constraints and citizens observing certain requirements with regard to transparency and participation.

Some important definitions are stated below:

- **Brundtland Commission**

"Sustainable development is the development that meets the needs of the present without comprising the ability of future generations to meet their own needs."

- **Hamilton-Wentworth Regional Council**

"Sustainable development is positive change which does not undermine the environmental or social systems on which we depend. It requires a coordinated approach to planning and policy making that involves public participation. Its success depends on widespread understanding of the critical relationship between people and their environment and the will to make necessary changes."

- **World Business Council on Sustainable Development**

"Sustainable development involves the simultaneous pursuit of economic prosperity, environmental quality and social equity. Companies aiming for sustainability need to perform not against a single, financial bottom line but against the triple bottom line."

"Over time, human and social values change. Concepts that once seemed extraordinary (e.g. emancipating slaves, enfranchising women) are now taken for granted. New concepts (e.g. responsible consumerism, environmental justice, intra- and inter-generational equity) are now coming up the curve."

- **Interfaith Center on Corporate Responsibility (ICCR)**

"Sustainable development is the process of building equitable, productive and participatory structures to increase the economic empowerment of communities and their surrounding regions."

2.1.2 Need and Importance of Sustainable Development

1. **Provide Basic Human Needs:** When population increases, bare essentials such as water, food and shelter are used more. The provision of these essentials is based almost entirely around having an infrastructure that can sustain them for the long-term.

2. **Agricultural Necessity:** Agriculture will have to catch up with that growing population as well, figuring out ways to feed around 3 billion more people. It can become expensive if the same unsustainable tilling, seeding, watering, spraying and harvesting methods are used into the future. Sustainable agriculture practices like crop rotation and effective seeding practices can help to promote high yields while protecting the integrity of the soil as it produces food for larger amounts of people.

3. **Accommodate City Development:** Cities will need to become larger to accommodate the influx of new residents, as the population increases. They will become more and more expensive to build and maintain, since the resources being used to develop the cities will be finite fossil fuels that will only get more expensive as they run out over time. The higher volume of these fuels required to produce energy for this larger population will also negatively impact the air quality of cities. If cities use sustainable development practices, they can conceivably make way for new housing and business developments indefinitely.

4. **Control Climate Change:** Climate change is another issue that can be at least partially remedied through sustainable development. Sustainable development practices would mandate a lower use of fossil fuels, which are not sustainable and which produce greenhouse gases. As the population rises, more people will be requiring more energy and will be putting an even greater strain on the world climate.

5. **Provide Financial Stability:** Financially sustainable economies throughout the world can be produced through sustainable development. Resource-poor economies will gain access to free and accessible energy through renewables while also having the opportunity to train workers for jobs that won't be displaced by the basic reality of finite resources. Jobs built around the "old" model of unsustainable development simply have no place in economies of the future. Industries built around reliance upon a resource that will not be accessible into the future will ultimately fail, leaving sustainable development as the only option moving forward.

6. **Sustain Biodiversity:** Through overconsumption and unsustainable development practices, biodiversity is hit badly. There is the further concern that these species are a part of a food web that humans rely on.

2.1.3 Education for Sustainable Development

"Education is the most powerful weapon you can use to change the world."

- **Nelson Mandela**.

Education is essential to sustainable development. Education for sustainable development allows every human being to acquire the knowledge, skills, attitudes and values necessary to shape a sustainable future. Citizens of the world need to learn their way to sustainability. Education for sustainable development means including key sustainable development issues into teaching and learning; for example, climate change, disaster risk reduction, biodiversity, poverty reduction, and sustainable consumption. It also requires participatory teaching and learning methods that motivate and empower learners to change their behaviour and take action for sustainable development. Education for sustainable development consequently promotes competencies like critical thinking, imagining future scenarios and making decisions in a collaborative way.

Education for Sustainable Development (ESD) is not a particular programme or project, but is rather an umbrella for many forms of education that already exist, and new ones that remain to be created. ESD is the term most used internationally and by the UN. ESD encourages efforts to change systems and educational programmes that support unsustainable societies. All components of education are affected by the ESD:

- legislation,
- policy,
- finance,
- curriculum,
- instruction,
- learning, and
- assessment.

It recognizes the fact that educational needs of people change over their lifetime and hence entitles lifelong learning. Many individuals and organizations around the world already implement ESD. Programmes are developed using the ESD approach which is important for accomplishing sustainability.

Education for sustainable development:
- is based on the principles and values that underlie sustainable development;
- deals with the well-being of all three dimensions of sustainability – environment, society, and economy;
- uses a variety of pedagogical techniques that promote participatory learning and higher-order thinking skills;
- promotes life long learning;
- is locally relevant and culturally appropriate;
- is based on local needs, perceptions and conditions, but acknowledges that fulfilling local needs often has international effects and consequences;
- engages formal, non-formal and informal education;

- accommodates the evolving nature of the concept of sustainability;
- addresses content, taking into account context, global issues and local priorities;
- builds civil capacity for community-based decision-making, social tolerance, environmental stewardship, an adaptable workforce, and a good quality of life;
- is interdisciplinary. No single discipline can claim ESD for itself; all disciplines can contribute to ESD.

To reflect the environmental, social, cultural and economic conditions of each locality, the essential characteristics of ESD can be executed in many ways. It also increases the civil capacity by improving the society by including a formal, non-formal and informal education.

ESD aims at Demonstrating the Following Features:

- **Interdisciplinary and Holistic:** should not be taught as a separate subject but instead should be included in the whole curriculum;
- **Participatory Decision-making:** learners participate in decisions on how they are to learn;
- **Values-driven:** it is important that the shared values and principles underpinning sustainable development should be made clear so that they can be applied, examined and argued on;
- **Locally Relevant:** addressing local as well as global issues, and using the language(s) which learners most commonly use. Concepts of sustainable development must be carefully expressed in other languages - languages and cultures say things differently, and each language has creative ways of expressing new concepts;
- **Critical Thinking and Problem Solving:** leading to confidence in addressing the dilemmas and challenges of sustainable development;
- **Multi-method:** For knowledge to be passed, methods of teaching such as art, debate, experience should be incorporated, so that teachers and learners work together to acquire knowledge and play a role in shaping the environment of their educational institutions;
- **Applicability:** Practical experiences in day to day personal and professional life should be incorporated in the teaching plan.

2.1.4 Philosophical Development of Sustainable Development

Along with the observed circumstances, the way we think about sustainability changes in a constant manner. The most common arguments used in environmental issues may be categorised into three broad groups of conceptions, that is, ***the philosophies of sustainability (Dobson 1998)***. These conceptions attempt to reconstruct the key elements of sustainability so as to make them meaningful, coherent, and rational.

The key questions along which the philosophies of sustainability are:
1. What are we to sustain?
2. Why should it be sustained?
3. How do we sustain it?

The three conceptions described below all give different answers to these questions.

1. **Sustainability Conception A ("Critical Natural Capital")**

   According to conception A, natural resources have only an instrumental role in the world, and the main goal of sustainability is the human (present and future) well-being. What therefore needs to be sustained are those natural resources that are necessary or critical ('critical natural capital') to the production and reproduction of human well-being. It can be a renewable or a non-renewable resource, and this makes a world of a difference in what would be the most sustainable way to use it. In the case of a renewable resource such as forest, the best solution is probably to renew the resource itself, while in the case of a non-renewable resource such as oil, the most sustainable option could be to substitute it by some other energy production resource. Sustainability decisions are made solely in terms of their impacts on human well-being. Whenever substitution of natural resources with some other means would increase human present or future well-being, it is considered to be the most sustainable option.

2. **Sustainability Conception B ("Irreversible Nature")**

   Certain aspects or properties of nature cannot be substituted in conception B. The main focus of sustainability is "irreversible nature", meaning that those aspects of nature which are indispensable, or whose loss would be irreversible, should be sustained whether or not they are regarded as critical to human well-being. As **Andrew Dobson** puts it, *"arguments in favour of downplaying the importance of preserving biodiversity, for instance, are often couched in terms of lists of species that have disappeared from taxonomists' catalogues without making a dent in standards of human welfare. Those who argue for avoiding the irreversible loss of natural objects and features, therefore, might do so in terms of criticality, but they might also do so in terms of arguments relating to the intrinsic value of whatever it is that is irretrievably lost."*

   Options for their sustainable use are either substitution or protection, since irreversible losses cannot be renewed. However, since the irreversible aspects of nature, like endangered species, are valued for their uniqueness rather than their instrumental role for human well-being, the most preferable option in this conception would be mandatory protection.

3. **Sustainability Conception C ("Value of Nature")**

   Conception A gives nature purely instrumental value.

   Conception B considers some irreversible aspects of nature to have intrinsic value as well. Conception C expands this intrinsic value to nature more generally. For instance **Alan Holland** argues for *"the recognition that nature, and its various component events and processes, is a particular historical phenomenon and should be valued as such"*.

2.1.5 Gandhian Thought on Sustainable Development

It is important first to define Gandhiji's understanding of economics as opposed to Adam Smith. Gandhiji was not an economist but his theory is rich in its grasp of the economic processes, thought-provoking and creative in its accent of other alternatives. According to Gandhiji, economics is a part and way of our life and cannot be separated from human life.

He ensured distributive justice by making sure that the production and distribution were not split. Gandhiji's vision of sustainable development challenges the basic assumptions that the capitalist model of development makes about the use of nature and natural resources, the meaning of growth, progress and development, the ways in which society is governed, and the formulation and implementation of public policy.

There are four key concepts in the Gandhian vision of Sustainable Development:

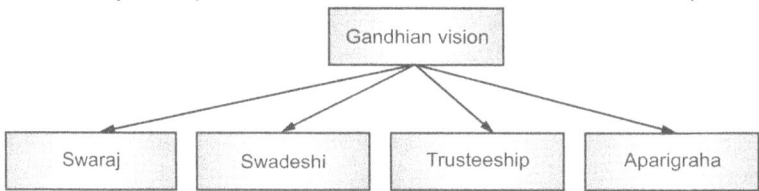

Fig. 2.2: Gandhian Vision

1. Swaraj

Since economics makes the common man helpless in view of the distribution and production of resources, Gandhiji pictured an alternative image through the concept of Swaraj. Swaraj is necessary for the liberation of weaker economies from the commanding position of neoliberal capitalism. Gandhiji visualised each country should stand on its own ability.

Psychology and **ethics** are the two independent variables of Swaraj. Production cannot be increased for an indefinite period as resources are limited. The psychology of wealth is an illogical trend. The main values of economic activity are based on needs and not on wealth as wealth propagates inequality, as it is based on economic distortion.

In the quest to be wealthy, greed springs up and hence this is where psychology plays an important role. Values which condition the mind can change human behaviour and hence the goal of Swaraj limits the human wants.

The main features of Swaraj are:

1. Gandhiji gave adequate importance to the traditional sector. Highest priority is given to agriculture and agro-centric industries. The balance between primary, secondary and tertiary sectors should be skillfully maintained, on the basis of available human resources.

2. Villages must get more importance than cities. Gandhiji observed: *"You cannot build non-violence on a factory civilisation, but it can be built on self-contained villages... You have therefore to be rural-minded, and to be rural-minded, you have to have faith in the spinning wheel."*

2. Swadeshi

Swadeshi is also known as home. We all know that Gandhiji desired to end British colonialism; however, this was only part of his struggles. The major chunk of his work was to renovate India's energy and regenerate its culture. Gandhiji also believed that the soul and spirit of India lay in its village communities. He said: *"The true India is to be found not in its few cities but in its seven hundred thousand villages. If the villages perish, India will perish too."*

The principle of Swadeshi was simple: *"Whatever is made or produced in the village must be used, first and foremost, by the members of the village"*.

The principle spoke about how trading should be limited among villages and between villages and towns and unless the services or goods cannot be generated from the community then it can be bought from outside.

Swadeshi avoids:

- economic dependence on external market forces that could make the village community vulnerable
- unnecessary, unhealthy, wasteful and environmentally destructive transportation.

Members of the village should first give importance to the local goods and services thereby building a strong economic base to satisfy most of the village needs. Mass production forces people to leave their villages, their land, their crafts and their homesteads, and to seek work in the factories. In Swadeshi, the machine would be subordinated to the worker.

Economics should not be separated from the deep spiritual foundations of life. According to Gandhiji, this is achieved when every individual is a part of the community; when homemade handicrafts are given preference; when the economy is local; and when the production of goods is on a small scale.

A society in which workers had to labour at a conveyor belt, in which animals were treated cruelly in factory farms, and in which economic activity necessarily led to ecological devastation, could not be conceived as a civilisation, according to Gandhi. He believed the members would be disturbed, cities would be concrete jungles and the world would be transformed into a desert. In other words, global industrial society, as opposed to a society made up of largely autonomous communities committed to the principle of Swadeshi, is unsustainable.

Gandhiji stated: *"Even Swadeshi, like any other good thing, can be ridden to death, if it is to be made a fetish ... To reject foreign manufacture merely because they are foreign, and to go on wasting national time and money in the promotion of one's country of manufacture for which it is not suited, would be a criminal folly and a negation of the Swadeshi spirit."*

From the above it becomes clear that Gandhiji does not reject trade with other nations, but he is opposed to an international order based solely on considerations of comparative advantage or a system that celebrates global free trade but not fair trade.

3. Trusteeship

Mahatma Gandhiji's efforts towards "spiritualising economics" are reflected in his concept of trusteeship. Based on the first sloka of Isopanisad,

"One is asked to dedicate everything to God, and then use it only to the required extent", Gandhiji conceived the third concept.

In other words, in the first instance, everything must be surrendered to God, and then out of it, one may use only that which is necessary, according to one's strict needs. The spirit behind this concept is service and detachment.

The idea of trusteeship cropped up to Gandhiji from his faith in the law of non-possession and established on Gandhiji's religious belief that everything belonged to God or to Nature. When an individual had more than his respective portion, he became a trustee of that portion. If this principle could be imbibed by people in general, trusteeship would become a legalized institution. Gandhiji wished it to become a gift from India to the world.

Basically, Gandhiji suggested this concept as an answer to the economic inequalities of ownership and income, a kind of non-violent way of resolving all social and economic conflicts in the world. Therefore, man's dignity and not his material prosperity, is the centre of Gandhian economics.

He believed that trusteeship is the only way in which an ideal combination of economics and ethics can be worked out. The basic features of the trusteeship formula are:

1. Trusteeship does not recognise any right of private ownership of property, except so far as it may be permitted by society for its own welfare.
2. It does not exclude legislation of the ownership and use of wealth.
3. Under state-regulated trusteeship, an individual will not be free to hold or use his wealth for selfish satisfaction, in disregard of the interests of society.
4. Just as in the case of a decent minimum living wage, a limit should be fixed for the maximum income that would be allowed to any person in society. The difference between such minimum and maximum incomes should be reasonable and equitable, and variable from time to time, so much so that the tendency should be towards the obliteration of the difference.

5. Under such an economic order, the character of production will be determined by social necessity and not by personal greed.
6. Trusteeship provides a means of transforming the present capitalist order into an egalitarian and sustainable one.

The whole idea of possessing wealth only to guard it from being misused and to distribute it equitably, aims at protecting human dignity. If it is possessed for any other objective, it is objectionable on moral grounds. The concept of trusteeship moves off from the Marxian economic philosophy too. According to Gandhiji a human being, is an ethical being first, and a social being later. Marxian socialism aims at the destruction of the capitalist class, whereas the Gandhian approach is not to destroy the institution but to reform it. Gandhian socialism, being ethical, is different from Marxian socialism. One of the important differences between the two concepts of socialism lies in the way the democratic society is achieved. Gandhiji talks about non-violence and only trust, whereas the Marxian concept promotes violence. The common man trusts his trustee and the latter plays the role of a custodian.

Though this kind of socialism is difficult to achieve, Gandhiji advocated it as he believed in the basic strength of the goodness of man and the value of morals. What must not be forgotten is that at the centre of the concept lies the need to protect human dignity, while promoting egalitarianism and sustainable development.

4. Aparigraha

Since 1987 when the World Commission on Environment and Development (WCED) of the United Nations, chaired by Dr. Gro Harlem Brundtland, submitted its report 'Our Common Future', the idea of sustainable development has become a buzzword in the discourse on international development. According to the **Brundtland Commission Report**, *"Sustainable development is development that meets the needs of the present, without compromising the ability of future generations to meet their own needs."* Over-consumption is the level or quality of consumption that undermines a species' own life-support system and for which individuals and societies have choices in their consumption patterns. The level of consumption of material goods largely determines the size of the ecological footprint, and developed nations like the US and UK has per capita footprints many times the size of developing countries like India and Bangladesh.

The seeds are to be found in the core assumptions of the economics that shapes our societies and our lives. The economics built on this foundation is a wants-based one where the agents are engaged in the quest for material progress. Such consumption cannot but be environmentally destructive.

Gandhiji denounced Britain's industrialized lifestyle as essentially unsustainable and stated:

"God forbid that India should ever take to industrialism after the manner of the west. The economic imperialism of a single tiny island kingdom (England) is today keeping the world in chains. If an entire nation of 300 million took to similar economic exploitation, it would strip the world bare like locusts."

Non-possession or minimisation of wants is a natural consequence of ethical considerations, was Gandhiji's view. He summarises the motivation for aparigraha:

"We notice that the mind is a restless bird; the more it gets, the more it wants, and still remains unsatisfied. The more we indulge our passions, the more unbridled they become."

And again: *"The Moral Law also requires that the strong men of a community or nation should regard it as their paramount duty to protect the weak and the oppressed. If all men realized the obligation of service, they would regard it as a sin to amass wealth; and then there would be no inequalities of wealth, and consequently, no famine or starvation."*

Remember he did not glorify poverty, in fact he labeled it a sin and his system was working towards removing poverty and instead bring along equality. His doctrine is *"not intended as a glorification of austerity but rather as an exercise in the optimisation of overall individual welfare"*.

While pointing out on the interests of the poor, he was at the same time appealing to the upper classes and also to the middle classes to work on a simplicity lifestyle. The Voluntary Simplicity Movement (VSM), with its motto of simple living, restriction of wants and minimisation of the size of our ecological footprint, is slowly gaining ground.

2.1.6 Sustainable Development and Social Framework

Internal as well as external provisions will be needed to support the social well-being as suggested by manufacturers. In terms of job security, benefits and safety, companies address the social concerns, though external measures that go beyond employees working within the company's bounds have become common. The framework also addresses the needs of the stakeholders of the larger manufacturing industry as well as civil society agents (consumers, families of employees, and the community at large, which is represented by nongovernmental organisations (NGOs) and media) and governments.

2.1.6.1 Internal

A company can influence the satisfaction of internal stakeholders through
- rewards,
- pay,
- job safety and
- health.

The appropriate level of provisions for equality, safety, and support for employees remains unclear and has different explanations amongst the stakeholders and the companies.

The most discussed issues regarding social sustainability is the treatment of employees.

The precise definition of what constitutes decent working conditions is highly debatable, even while concerns about the working conditions have grown out of some highly visible problematic cases. Forced labour, child labour and sweatshops should be prohibited. While there are different views of who is ultimately responsible for the well-being of individuals, some researchers have argued that governments should be held responsible, while others are of the opinion that employers have to provide a minimum standard of living for their employees, while there is one more section that views that it is the individual's responsibility to create their own safety net.

Manufacturers are still criticised if any inhumane working conditions are found. While manufacturers only do not have so much control over the working conditions of their suppliers, they do have a choice in where they source their components from and can leverage this power to influence the behaviour of their suppliers. It can be made easier to negotiate adherence to particular specifications when manufacturers have a working relationship with the suppliers.

Baseline standards exist to ensure that manufacturers are at least cognizant of the human rights standards they should maintain. All of these factors leave the most appropriate social standards for the treatment of employees ambiguous. Such standards can be taken from:

- Social Accountability International's SA 8000 standard,
- The UN's International Labour Organisation (ILO) Conventions,
- Universal Declaration of Human Rights, and
- Convention on the Rights of the Child.

These standards hold some importance to consumers, as evidenced by their willingness to pay for products that are created under good working conditions. Consumers have become increasingly critical of the working conditions under which products arc created; while the public may not be aware of the exact conditions under which employees work, past incidents, of poor working conditions have brought bad publicity to some of the world's largest producers.

Verification of compliance for working conditions is especially problematic, whatever standards are chosen.

2.1.6.2 External

Stakeholders outside of the company are also part of the social framework of sustainability.

Logan defines **corporate citizenship** *"as the activities that make the organisation accountable to its stakeholders, including employees, shareholders, consumers, suppliers, and the communities in which they are located"*. Others define social accountability as the total contribution that a company will make to the society.

Azapagic defines social accountability as *"related to wider responsibilities that business has to communities in which it operates and to society in general, including both present and future generations."*

Meanwhile **Business for Social Responsibility** considers corporate social responsibility *"as a way of conducting business that meets or exceeds societies' ethical, legal, commercial, and public expectations"*.

With so many different views on the social scope of manufacturing impacts, let us look at the role the external factors play, such as larger industry, consumers, NGOs, media and the community.

Consumer interests in issues of sustainability, such as human health, depletion of resources, pollution, waste creation, and climate change, have grown over the years.

Meulenberg defines **sustainable consumption** as *"a process by which social responsibility and impacts on future generations are incorporated with the needs and desires of consumers"*.

The ethical consumer will see a connection between the purchases made and the social issues, through the product choice. **Cohen** points out that *"these consumers, a demographic known as LOHAS (Lifestyles of Health and Sustainability), spends upwards of $300 billion each year in the USA."* Thus, finding ways to clearly communicate aspects of sustainability with this segment can have substantial financial incentives for producers.

The health and safety aspects of a product are the most direct social impacts manufacturers have on consumers. In terms of sustainability, the question that arises is whether producers should take the initiative to improve the health impacts of their products, like for example, Unilever, who have improved the nutritional value of their food items.

Various research efforts have been dedicated to calculating the sustainability impacts that entities have on communities. These relate to the equity of relationships between businesses and communities, the standards of living in communities where businesses exist and the investments businesses make to improve such standards. Information about their philanthropic efforts is added by the companies in their annual report. In addition some methodologies exist at the product level to identify goods for the impacts they have on workers and communities. The methodology for assessing community impacts at the process level remains unclear.

The most subjective and hardest to determine of all social impacts are the community-based social impacts. Assessing what these conditions are is more complex than how an organization contributes to the social conditions. Many efforts to measure social conditions have been at the geographic level (e.g., national and city). Many of these assessments attempt to adjust to replace the measure of GDP to include some social measures on issues like the population's health and education.

Manufacturers often participate in industry level coalitions or voluntary agreements in order to build support to either drive an industry forward or to maintain the status quo. The way that one company treats its various stakeholders can influence others within the industry. Members can more easily influence acceptable standards for others within the industry. Some industries are associated with specific social problems or generously thought of for creating social benefits. By becoming more sustainable, industries have the potential to improve or maintain their impacts long-term. These assessments not only calculate the economic, social, and environmental impacts of a given industry, but also help decision makers guide national development in a more sustainable way, through policies and subsidies.

2.1.7 Sustainable Development and Equitable Distribution

Sustainable development requires an equitable distribution of the world's resources among today's societies, bearing in mind the requirements of future generations. Industrialised and developing countries have a common but differentiated role to play in addressing environmental degradation. Rich countries should take the lead by engaging in vigorous environmental action at home and making the necessary financial and technical resources available for sustainable development worldwide. At the same time, developing countries should critically examine domestic spending priorities to ensure that they are sustainable.

Sustainability is presently not really either understood by theorists or addressed by corporations, despite the many claims that are being made. Sustainability cannot exist without equity in the distributional process. Central to the argument therefore is that an understanding of sustainability must include not just what raw materials are used by the organisation, or even how they are used. It must also take into consideration an evaluation of how the effects – both positive and negative – are distributed to the various stakeholders concerned. This requires some rethinking of organisational activity and a revision of processes and effects.

2.1.8 Difference between Sustainable Development and Green Development

Though the words sustainable and green are used interchangeably, the two words are not the same thing.

Green is defined *as products and services that reduce health and environmental impacts compared to similar products and services used for the same purpose*, whereas **Sustainability**, on the other hand, *can be represented with a three-legged stool having a leg for environmental, social and financial responsibility*, according to Jim Newman, owner of Newman Consulting Group.

The consideration about people and staff is limited to direct exposures from products or services in green. Sustainability talks about the implications of products and services used over a much longer period of time, and considers social and financial impacts as well.

Sustainable Development is a product being capable of being continued with minimum effect on the environment.

Any product or process that can be reused or re-grown over and over is said to be sustainable. A community can be sustainable, which basically means that sustainable communities are places where people reside or work presently or in the future. They meet the diverse needs of existing and future residents, are sensitive to their environment, and contribute to a high quality of life. They are safe and inclusive, well planned, built and run, and offer equality of opportunity and good services for all. A great example of sustainable product is bamboo as it can grow to be harvested in 5 years and then it is cut and it re-grows on its own again.

Green Development: Green is also associated with regeneration, fertility and rebirth for its connections to nature. Many political groups use green in their symbol, symbolising environmental protection and social justice and in this sense they feel like they are part of the green revolution and are environment friendly.

Green is the word often used to talk about being environmentally friendly or saving the environment – for example – Go Green. Green is more of a catch phrase for protecting our environment. Some are more extreme than others, but still usually fall in the earth-friendly group.

2.1.9 Criticism on Sustainable Development

1. **Growth:** Growth is said to be the primary cause of nature being overused. Hence it is said that the problem cannot be the solution. Dingler argues that unlimited growth is not possible and states that intra-economical limits to growth could exist.

    If we want to build two houses we will need more resources than to build one house and hence growth is not separable from removing the resources from nature. The fact that ecological systems have limits in providing resources and take-up capacities, leads to the fundamental insight that nature has limits for human emissions. Hence a sustained growth cannot exist, and a conception of sustainable development claiming sustained growth is inconsistent with its goals.

2. **Efficiency, De-coupling and Dematerialisation:** Any company, that cannot increase its efficiency, cannot continue to exist, and hence increase in efficiency is essential for capitalist firms. Increasing efficiency decreases the production costs of the company. When there is an increase in efficiency it is more of an economic mechanism that of an ecological mechanism. When efficiency is increased it is said to be a part of the economical rationality, and leads to over-using natural resources. Hence efficiency makes the ecological crisis escalate and does not fix it also and since efficiency has to

be present always, this strategy cannot succeed. However, an increase in efficiency can change the urge to change, since the same amount of resources can be used for a longer time. This holds true only if the total amount of consumption stays.

The marginal gain of an increase in efficiency would meet the marginal costs of itself, sooner or later.

3. **Environmental Management:** It will not be possible to collect all data and information about a specific ecosystem. Therefore, only incomplete management of nature is possible. Non-linear systems are characterised by unpredictability and thus cannot be managed based on informed decisions. Even if management tries to take place, predictions can always be counteracted by the instability/inadequacy of the known system.

4. **Poverty and Population Growth:** When poverty strikes, nature is over-used though often it is the industrialised countries that over-use nature. Instead of the poverty of people in developing countries, it is the lifestyle of the people in developed countries which is responsible for the environmental crisis. An increase in population can increase over-using of nature. Yet, it is not the lifestyle of the poor that affects the environmental crisis but the lifestyle of the people of industrialised countries. If the poor people of developing countries also lead their lives in the same way as the people from industrialised countries, then there will surely be an increase in the crisis.

5. **The Concept "Needs":** Since the future generation does not exist it is difficult to know their needs and hence in order to evaluate them, we have to assume certain values whereby we can judge their needs for the future. The idea is deconstructed by Dingler who concludes that needs are historically, socially, and culturally shaped; they are constructed in discourses, which take place in the context of power-relations.

The definition of sustainable development's "future needs" is useless. If future generations should have the same options as we have today, we would need to stop any interventions in nature. Future generations might want to use the resources in a totally different manner. Thus, sustainable development should not be defined based on the idea of "needs" or "options", but discuss in how far it is acceptable in a certain historically, socially, and culturally shaped context to cut options for future generations normatively.

6. **Divergence between Ecological and Economical Developments:** The economic subsystem struggles to be independent of the ecological sub-system. Economically resources are transported and processed very fast; ecologically these resources are changed slowly. Economy tries to a great extent to unify singularities, to make them tradable, whereas ecology depends on diversity. Distances are economically bridged easily, but ecologically it is more difficult to transport. Dingler concludes that the orders of both subsystems cannot go together and therefore would produce instabilities.

7. **Participation** recognises the need to strengthen major groups: *"Moving towards real social partnership in support of common efforts for sustainable development"*. However, companies are more equal in participation than most other groups. This can be explained based on **Abels and Bora's** *"participation is a political means of inclusion.* Some people or stakeholders are included, and others not. Usually participation is supposed to increase the legitimacy of a decision-making process. Only then solutions to problems *"have some chance of success"*.

8. **Scientification and Technocentrism:** Scientification and technology have been named as causes of the environmental and developmental crisis. Even Gore hints that it would be a myth that technology is "good" all the time. Local and traditional knowledge of the peripheral countries is often non-recognised and accepted by the dominating mainstream philosophy of science. However, within the hegemonic discourse it is claimed, that this mainstream science shall provide the solutions to the crisis. It has been shown that total control of nature is not possible; environmental management cannot prevent over-using of nature.

Science cannot carry out all the relevant valuations neutrally and isolated, but values have to be discussed with all affected humans or even other beings.

2.2 STAKEHOLDER

2.2.1 Meaning of Stakeholder

Stakeholders can be defined in many ways and different kinds of entities can be stakeholders, such as persons, groups inside as well as outside an organisation. Stakeholders are also defined as any person or organisation that has legitimate interest in project, who can affect or be affected by organisations with their managerial behaviours and by the product throughout the product's life cycle; those who share a particular set of understandings and meanings concerning the development of a given technology, having a moral and non-negotiable rights to influence its outcome and; having material, political affiliation; informational, symbolic or spiritual interests in a company and that are able to advocate these interests through formal economic or political power. The stakeholders act according to their interest and use their power to influence the product in the direction they desire. The definition of stakeholder by **Freeman** as *"any group or individual who can affect or is affected by the achievement of the organisation's objectives"* has been agreed by many scholars.

However, **Glicken** argues that all definitions of stakeholders or interested parties are that they identify and define groups relative to a specific issue. While some of these groups may exist over time as formal organisations, they become stakeholders only in reference to a particular issue. Thus stakeholder is therefore a relative term.

2.2.2 Types of Stakeholders

A stakeholder is anyone with an interest in a business. Stakeholders are individuals, groups or organisations that are affected by the activity of the business. They include:
1. Owners who are interested in how much profit the business makes.
2. Managers who are concerned about their salary.
3. Workers who want to earn high wages and keep their jobs.
4. Customers who want the business to produce quality products at reasonable prices.
5. Suppliers who want the business to continue to buy their products.
6. Lenders who want to be repaid on time and in full.
7. The community which has a stake in the business as employers of local people. Business activity also affects the local environment.

Internal stakeholders are groups within a business - e.g. owners and workers.

External stakeholders are groups outside a business - e.g. the community.

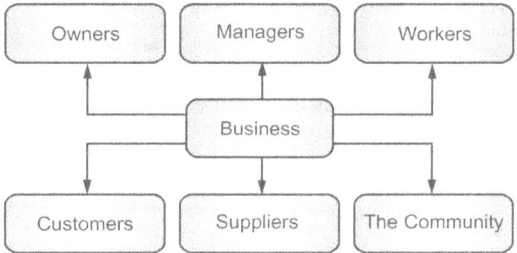

Fig. 2.3: Types of Stakeholders

2.2.3 Role of Stakeholders in Business

A stakeholder is usually an investor in your company whose actions determine the outcome of your business decisions. They do not have to be equity shareholders. Employees can also have a stake in your company's success and an incentive for your products to succeed. They can be business partners, who depend on the success to keep the supply chain going on. The roles of stakeholders differ between businesses, dependent on the rules and responsibilities laid out at the founding of your company or as your business evolved over the years. The most common definition of a stakeholder, however, is a large investor that has the clout to hold a viable "stake" in your company.

1. **Decision-making:** The most common gathering of stakeholders in a publicly traded company is the board of directors, comprised of high-ranking executives and occasional outsiders who hold large amounts of equity in the company. These stakeholders have the power to disturb the proceedings or by introducing new ideas to the company. The board of directors has the power to appoint the senior managers which include the CEO and also to remove them if necessary. Members of the board dictate the future of the company and are involved in all major business decisions.
2. **Direct Management:** Some stakeholders prefer to directly assume management positions. They can take some departments such as HR or R&D to insure the success. In privately owned and publicly traded companies, large investors often directly participate in business decisions on the management level.
3. **Investors:** Stakeholders are regarded as large investors, who will either increase or decrease their stakes in your company according to your financial performance. They act as angels as they pressure the management to change tactics if necessary and some stakeholders, often known as activist investors, will make unpredicted investments to attract media attention and thereby increase the share price,
4. **Corporate Conscience:** Large stakeholders are generally high profile investors, and would like to push companies that tread on human rights and environmental laws. They may vote against your business decisions if they are deemed harmful to the company's long-term goals and also monitor your company's outsourcing activities.
5. **Other Responsibilities:** Stakeholders mostly care about these four issues, but some short-term profits take precedence over long-term sustainability. While stakeholders may own your company, it's easier to control your investors when your company is privately held than publicly traded. Often times, the large influx of cash from a successful IPO turns out to be a deal with the devil when your company is suddenly taken over by a board of directors that ousts you. Stakeholders can keep your company grounded and focused on its most profitable products and sustain your company's earnings growth.

2.2.4 Powers of Stakeholder

All individuals and groups in society who are affected by a business and its practices hold a stake in that business, in the stakeholder concept of business ethics. Shareholders, customers and company officers are the most directly affected and the most directly powerful; other stakeholders can influence a business' practices as well in a variety of ways. Basically there are four distinct categories for stakeholder power:

1. **Voting Power:** Company shareholders have the most direct power over companies through voting. Prior to or during annual meetings, shareholders may cast votes proportionate to the amount of stock they hold to influence or direct a business' future actions. This power is unique to shareholders unless contractually awarded to other parties; for example, a few companies have given labour unions a voting voice.
2. **Economic Power:** Customers and shareholders commonly hold great economic power over a business, but the banks that lend to the company; creditors who extend credit and even governments (through tax levies) also wield economic power. Suppliers and retailers also hold economic power in that they may refuse to supply to or sell products from a company.
3. **Political Power:** Most often expressed through how those companies are taxed, regulated and permitted to exist. Governments hold direct political power over companies. Voters and activist organisations may use voting and political pressure to influence political power in democratically organised countries. In countries with other types of governance, political power may be wielded for or against companies in different ways, as when a country decides to nationalise a privately held business.
4. **Legal Power:** Stakeholders directly and indirectly impacted by a company may bring legal power to bear against a corporation. Employees who feel they have been treated unfairly may bring lawsuits. Labour unions, environmentalists, customers and even governments are also able to file lawsuits against companies.
5. **Other Types of Stakeholder Power:** Stakeholders may exercise power to influence business practices in other ways. Technology, cultural norms, the environment and direct persuasion of groups have also been cited as areas of stakeholder power.

2.3 Sustainability Engagement Approaches

Harvard Business School's **Michael Porter** describes two basic categories of competitive advantages:

1. Lower its costs compared with the competitor.
2. Differentiate its product on quality, features or service.

Some costs are obvious and relatively short-term: inputs used, energy consumed, time and money spent on meeting regulatory requirements. The resource productivity of a business - the amount of material or energy needed per unit of output - goes straight to the bottom line and needs to be improved. By avoiding products, chemicals or processes that require special care and documentation, lower overhead, regulatory burdens can be eliminated.

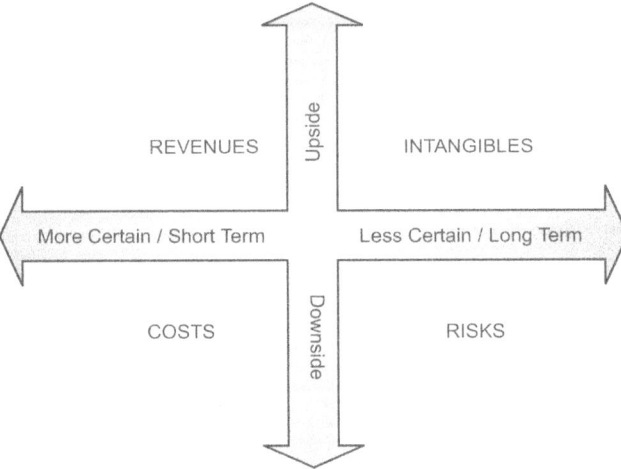

Fig. 2.4: Strategy Framework

Companies that successfully manage environmental risk:

- lower operating costs
- reduce the cost of capital
- drive up stock market valuation
- keep insurance premiums reasonable
- avoid the indirect costs of business interruption and lost goodwill

The benefits of differentiation through good environmental stewardship are sometimes concrete - like commanding a price premium or just selling more - but are largely intangible strengthened relationships with customers, employees and other stakeholders, on the revenue side. Some say that these intangibles are too vague to be measured, but they are wrong.

- How much does it cost to acquire a new customer to replace a lost one? That's the rough value of increasing loyalty.
- How about employee churn?
- If improving morale and employee engaged in the company's mission lowers turnover, how much would that save?
- And what about community support?

Table 2.1: Sustainability Objectives, Strategies and Tactics

Objective	Strategy	Tactic
I. Controls Managing the Downside	**(A) Costs** Reducing operational costs and environmental expenses	1. **Efficiency:** Improving resource productivity and usage by enhancing efficiency, e.g. waste elimination or utilisation, pollution prevention and energy conservation. 2. **Regulations:** Decreasing disposal costs, regulatory fines, compliance expenses, etc., e.g. eliminating costs associated with waste disposal and pollution control, including time and money spent. 3. **Value-chain engagement:** Capturing the value of reduced environmental burdens through primary, secondary, internal and external functions to include supply-chain management (when not referring to disk management specifically) e.g. more efficiency packaging, supply-chain efficiency, maximising usage of space, sourcing and distribution.
	(B) Risks Identifying and reducing risk exposure	4. **Risk management:** Anticipating and addressing issues, regulations and mandates; ensuring compliance and minimizing exposure to financial, strategic, operational and hazard risk e.g. liability, competitive, consumer, supply-chain regulatory, natural and employment risks.
II. Opportunities Building the Upside	**(C) Revenue** Driving revenues by providing products that meet demand	5. **Product design:** Making environmentally friendly products i.e. designing, redesigning, modifying or improving current products to meet the demands of green-conscientious consumers. 6. **Sales and marketing:** Building competitive positions for current products or generating consumer loyalty based on sustainability and green attributes.

contd. ...

		7. **Growth:** Driving growth by promoting innovation i.e. development of new products or new markets that are completely different from current products' purpose or geographic markets.
	(D) Intangible Creating value with overall corporate sustainability	8. **Value:** Building corporate reputation and brand value - e.g. share-price performance, customer loyalty, brand image, access to capital.

2.3.1 Reducing Socio-environmental Costs and Risks: Managing the Downside

By changing one process of the production of adipic acid, DuPont has cut its contribution to global warming by 72 percent, over the last 15 years. Modifying this little change, eliminated emissions of nitrous oxide, a potent greenhouse gas that causes far more warming than carbon dioxide. Over the past decade, this strategy has saved DuPont $2 billion.

The company also vowed to smoothen its energy use at

- the primary source of its greenhouse gas emissions and
- no matter how fast the company's top line grew, it found 100 ways to meet its energy targets.

Green-to-Gold Play 1:

Eco-Efficiency – Improve Resource Productivity

- WaveRiders get the same output with lower inputs. In improving resource productivity, their actions stand out as the classic win-win environmental strategy.

Green-to-Gold Play 2:

Eco-Expense Reduction – Cut Environmental Costs and Regulatory Burden

- This Green-to-Gold Play centres on the time and money consumed by pollution control and environmental management. In addition to millions of dollars or euros spent on waste disposal and pollution-control equipment, this includes the managerial time and money spent filling out forms, the sometimes crippling cost of fines for mismanaging environmental issues and the general business slowdown caused by jumping regulatory hurdles.

Green-to-Gold Play 3:

Value Chain Eco-Efficiency – Lower Costs Upstream and Downstream

- Many companies have found ways to lower value chain costs by cutting the environmental and financial expenses of product distribution. IKEA is proud of its "flat packaging."
- Efforts to squeeze millimeters out of every box have allowed the company to pack its trucks and trains tighter. That saves up to 15 percent on fuel per item.

Green-to-Gold Play 4:

Eco-Risk Control – Manage Environmentally Driven Business Risk

- WaveRiders find issues before problems find them. They examine not only the supply chain, but the entire value chain. Identifying enterprise risk means understanding exactly how a company affects the environment and how the constraints of nature affect the company.

2.3.2 Driving Revenues and Creating Intangible Value: Managing the Upside

Environmental strategy has been there for around 40 years, focusing on compliance and on cost and efficiency, and now to a more strategic view centered on growth opportunities.

The following Green-to-Gold Plays are about the growth of

- sales,
- brand value, and
- stakeholders' trust.

Green-to-Gold Play 5:

Eco-Design – Meet Customer Environmental Needs

- Identifying customer needs or desires and designing a product to meet them is never easy. With growing environmental consciousness, the opportunities to seize Eco-Advantage through green marketing are expanding. Companies can avoid the worst stumbles by following a few simple lessons.
- Meet a need that exists; don't ignore other needs of the customer; and pay attention to your own costs.

Green-to-Gold Play 6:

Eco-Sales and Marketing – Build Product Position and Customer Loyalty on Green Attributes

- Every day more consumers are including environmental factors in their buying equation. In parallel, companies are finding that there is money to be made from meeting the growing demands for green products.

Green-to-Gold Play 7:

Eco-Defined New Market Space – Promote Value Innovation and Develop Breakthrough Products

- Toyota saw the Green Wave coming and responded with the energy-efficient "hybrid" Prius. The company promoted value innovation and ended up with a breakthrough product that enhanced profits and sustained shareholder value.

Green-to-Gold Play 8:

Intangible Value — Build Corporate Reputation and Trusted Brands

- Positioning a brand as environmentally friendly only works if it's true. The 1980s and 1990s saw a flurry of bogus green claims. Some were just plain laughable. Hefty's highly touted biodegradable garbage bags broke down in sunlight, but not in the landfills where they would actually end up.

Points to Remember

- **Sustainable development** is a road-map, the action plan, for achieving sustainability in any activity that uses resources and where immediate and intergenerational replication is demanded.
- Development must combine three main elements in order to be sustainable. In order to be sustainable, development must combine three main elements:
  1. fairness, sociopolitical sustainability,
  2. protection of the environment sustainability, and
  3. economic sustainability efficiency.
- **Hamilton-Wentworth Regional Council** defines sustainable development as a *"positive* change *which does not undermine the environmental or social systems on which we depend." It requires a coordinated approach to planning and policy making that involves public participation. Its success depends on widespread understanding of the critical relationship between people and their environment and the will to make the necessary changes."*
- **Need and Importance of Sustainable Development:**
  1. Provide basic human needs
  2. Agricultural necessity
  3. Accommodate city development
  4. Control climate change
  5. Provide financial stability
  6. Sustain biodiversity
- Education for Sustainable Development allows every human being to acquire the knowledge, skills, attitudes and values necessary to shape a sustainable future.

- The three conceptions described below all give different answers to these questions.
    1. Sustainability Conception A ("Critical Natural Capital")
    2. Sustainability Conception B ("Irreversible Nature")
    3. Sustainability Conception C ("Value of Nature")
- There are four **key concepts in the Gandhian vision** of Sustainable Development which are
    1. Swaraj
    2. Swadeshi
    3. Trusteeship
    4. Aparigraha
- A company can influence the satisfaction of internal stakeholders, through
    1. rewards,
    2. pay,
    3. job safety, and
    4. health.
- **Green** is defined as products and services that reduce health and environmental impacts compared to similar products and services used for the same purpose, whereas **sustainability**, on the other hand, can be represented with a three-legged stool having a leg for environmental, social and financial responsibility, according to Jim Newman, owner of Newman Consulting Group.
- Sustainability talks about the implications of products and services used over a long period of time and also consider social and financial impacts.
- The definition of stakeholder by Freeman as "any group or individual who can affect or is affected by the achievement of the organisation's objectives" has been agreed by many scholars.
- **Types of Stakeholder**
    1. Owners who are interested in how much profit the business makes.
    2. Managers who are concerned about their salary.
    3. Workers who want to earn high wages and keep their jobs.
    4. Customers who want the business to produce quality products at reasonable prices.
    5. Suppliers who want the business to continue to buy their products.
    6. Lenders who want to be repaid on time and in full.
    7. The community which has a stake in the business as employers of local people.
- **Powers of Stakeholders**
    1. Voting power
    2. Economic power
    3. Political power
    4. Legal power

Questions for Discussion

1. Define sustainable development and discuss its need and importance.
2. Discuss the philosophical development of sustainable development.
3. Explain the Gandhian thought on sustainable development.
4. Describe the social framework of sustainability.
5. Differentiate between sustainable development and green development.
6. What are the types and powers of stakeholders in a business?
7. Elaborate the managing downside and upside approaches of sustainability engagement.

Multiple Choice Questions

1. Sustainable development will not aim at:
   (a) Social economic development which optimise the economic and societal benefits available in the present, without spoiling the likely potential for similar benefits in the future.
   (b) Reasonable and equitably distributed level of economic well-being that can be perpetuated continually.
   (c) Development that meets the need of the present without compromising the ability of future generations to meet their own needs.
   (d) Maximising the present day benefits through increased resource consumption.
2. Which of the following statements in relation to sustainable development is not true?
   (a) Sustainable development is defined as the development that meets the needs of present without compromising the ability of our future generations to meet their own needs.
   (b) Sustainability has the main objective of purely focussing on the natural environment.
   (c) Sustainable development of various countries and the entire world is the only solution left with mankind to survive for a longer period on Earth.
   (d) Sustainable development not only considers the protection of the environment but also the maintenance of economic viability as well as the social and ethical considerations.
3. The term sustainability refers to _____.
   (a) Maintaining resource use at current or higher levels
   (b) Keeping the natural environment and human society in a happy, healthy and functional state
   (c) Holding or increasing the current quality of human life
   (d) Always focusing on fulfilling short-term needs
   (e) Opposing change from current policies

4. Social sustainability refers to what?
   (a) The concept of the enterprise supporting jobs and delivering income to communities in the long term
   (b) Stewardship of resources and managing and conserving the environment
   (c) The concept of the enterprise supporting jobs and delivering income to communities in the short term
   (d) Sharing benefits fairly and equitably and respecting the quality of life of communities and of human rights
5. The Brundtland definition comprises of which three parts?
   (a) Development, Needs and Future Responsibility
   (b) Development, Issues and Future Generations
   (c) Development, Needs and Future Generations
   (d) Growth, Needs and Future Generations
6. What is the most commonly cited definition for, and accepted thinking about, sustainable development?
   (a) Brundtland World on Committee Environment and Sustainable Development
   (b) Bruntland World Committee on Environment and Development
   (c) Brundtland World Commission on Environment and Sustainable Development
   (d) Brundtland World Commission on Environment and Development
7. Which one of the following characteristics is widely regarded as being an important aspect of sustainable development?
   (a) Inter-generational equity
   (b) Increasing consumption expenditure
   (c) Intra-generational inequity
   (d) Increased levels of saving
8. A "green transport plan" is:
   (a) An environmentally acceptable travel plan devised by a local authority for its area
   (b) An internationally agreed strategy for reducing the impact of international transport activity on the global environment
   (c) A plan devised by a company or organisation to reduce the environmental impact of the transport demands generated by itself and its employees
   (d) The UK government's plan for a sustainable transport sector
9. Food, space, disease, natural disasters, climate, competition and predation are example of what?
   (a) Capacity Factors
   (b) Limiting Factors
   (c) Predation Factors
   (d) Sustainable Factors

10. Sustainable Development focuses on more use of:
    (a) Renewable resources
    (b) Abiotic resources
    (c) Agricultural resources
    (d) Natural resources

Answers

| 1. (d) | 2. (b) | 3. (a) | 4. (d) | 5. (c) | 6. (d) | 7. (a) | 8. (c) | 9. (d) | 10. (a) |

Project Questions

1. What are, in your opinion, the main paradoxes of sustainable development?
2. What do you think the role of business in the process of sustainable development?

Chapter 3...

Business Case for Sustainable Development

Contents ...

3.1 Three Dimensions of Sustainable Development
3.2 Environmental Dimension
    3.2.1 Environmental Management
    3.2.2 Management of Human Consumption
3.3 Economic Dimension
    3.3.1 Decoupling Environmental Degradation and Economic Growth
    3.3.2 Nature as an Economic Externality
    3.3.3 Economic Opportunity
3.4 Social Dimension
    3.4.1 Peace, Security, Social Justice
    3.4.2 Sustainability and Poverty
    3.4.3 Human Relationship to Nature
    3.4.4 Human Settlements
3.5 Ecological Footprint
3.6 Eco-Tracking
3.7 Carbon Marketing
3.8 Carbon Credit
3.9 Design for Environment
    3.9.1 Origins and Definition of Design for Environment
    3.9.2 Approach to Improve the Environmental Performance
    3.9.3 Implementation of Design for Environment
3.10 Greening the Supply Chain
    3.10.1 Business Value of GSC Initiatives
3.11 Regulation
    3.11.1 Key Indian Legislations Relevant to Sustainable Development
3.12 Business Models for Sustainable Development
3.13 Sustainability Reporting
    3.13.1 The Triple Bottom Line Defined
    3.13.2 Content of Sustainability Reports
    3.13.3 Corporate Social Responsibility (CSR) Reporting
    3.13.4 Social Accounting
    3.13.5 Environmental Accounting

3.14 Social Responsibility Standard: ISO 26000
    3.14.1 Definition of Social Responsibility
    3.14.2 Seven Principles
    3.14.3 Seven Core Subjects
    3.14.4 ISO 26000 - Guidance on Social Responsibility
3.15 Global Compact Principles
3.16 Environmental Impact Assessment
3.17 Life Cycle Analysis or Life Cycle Assessment (LCA)
3.18 Social Impact Assessment (SIA)
- Points to Remember
- Questions for Discussion
- Multiple Choice Questions
- Project Questions

Learning Objectives ...

- To discuss in detail the three dimensions of sustainable development i.e. Environmental, Economic and Social
- To study terms like ecological footprint, eco-tracking, carbon marketing, carbon credits etc.
- To understand the business models for sustainable development in Indian and global perspectives
- To learn the concepts related to sustainability reporting
- To be able to explain the concepts related to social accountability standards

3.1 Three Dimensions of Sustainable Development

The definition of sustainable development was expressed during the World Commission on Environment and Development in 1987, chaired by **Gro Harlem Brundtland** which states that "mankind has the ability to ensure a sustainable development, meaning that the present necessities are met without compromising the ability of future generations to meet their own needs".

The central concept of this definition is the need for intergenerational equity; future generations have the same rights as the present ones. Intergenerational equity refers to the same generation persons have the same rights belonging to different political, economical, social and geographical groups. The success of this concept, mostly of ecological source, has stimulated international debate and led to many in-depth studies and more elaborations, so that over time it has come to include all dimensions that add to development.

From this viewpoint, development is seen as a continuing process that implies the integration of the three vital and inseparable features of development- the Environmental, Economic and Social dimensions.

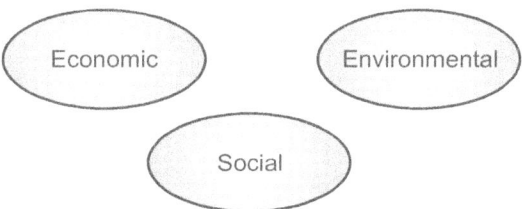

Fig. 3.1: Three Dimensions of Sustainable Development

- **Environmental Sustainability:** Environmental Sustainability can be defined as the ability to protect over time the three fundamental functions of the environment which are the resource supply function, the waste receiver function and that of direct utility. In other words, within a territory (area/region), environmental sustainability means the capacity to augment and introduce the importance of the environment and its peculiarities, while promising the safety and the renewal of natural resources and the environment.

- **Economic Sustainability:** Economic Sustainability is referred as the capacity of an economic system to create a stable and improving development of its economical indicators. Especially, the ability to make incomes and employment in order to uphold the populations. Within a territorial system, economic sustainability means the capability to create and maintain the highest added value through the most efficient mix of resources in order to improve the specificity of territorial products and services.

- **Social Sustainability:** Social Sustainability can be defined as the ability to assure welfare (security, health, education), equitably distributed among social classes and genders. Within a territory, social sustainability means the ability of the different social actors (stakeholders), to interact efficiently, to aim towards the same goals, encouraged by the close interaction of the institutions, at all levels.

3.2 Environmental Dimension

Healthy ecosystems offer vital goods and services to humans and other organisms. There are two main methods of minimising harmful human impact and improving ecosystem services which are environmental management and management of human consumption of resources. Environmental management is a direct approach which is based mainly on information gained from earth science, environmental science and conservation biology. However, this is management at the end of a long series of indirect causal factors that are initiated by human consumption, so a second approach is through demand management of human resource use.

Management of human consumption of resources is an indirect approach based largely on information gained from economics. The three broad criteria for ecological sustainability suggested by Herman Daly are:

(a) Renewable resources should provide a sustainable yield (the rate of harvest should not exceed the rate of regeneration);

(b) For non-renewable resources there should be equivalent development of renewable substitutes;

(c) Waste generation should not exceed the assimilative capacity of the environment.

3.2.1 Environmental Management

In the broadest sense, at the global scale sustainability and environmental management involves managing the oceans, freshwater systems, land and atmosphere, as indicated by sustainability principles.

Land use alteration is very significant to the operations of the biosphere because alterations in the relative segment of land dedicated to urbanisation, agriculture, forest, woodland, grassland and pasture have a noticeable outcome on the global water, carbon and nitrogen biogeochemical cycles. Management of the Earth's atmosphere involves evaluation of all aspects of the carbon cycle to recognize opportunities to deal with human-induced climate change and this has turn out to be a center of attention of scientific research because of the potential disastrous effects on biodiversity and human communities. Ocean circulation patterns have a strong impact on climate and weather and, in turn, the food supply of both humans and other organisms.

(A) Atmosphere

In March 2009 meeting of the Copenhagen Climate Council, 2,500 climate experts from 80 countries issued a crucial statement that there is now "no excuse" for failing to take action on global warming and that with no strong carbon reduction "abrupt or irreversible" shifts in climate may occur that "will be very difficult for contemporary societies to cope with". Management of the global atmosphere now involves assessment of all aspects of the carbon cycle to recognise opportunities to address human-induced climate change and this has become a center of attention of scientific research because of the potential disastrous effects on biodiversity and human communities.

Other human impacts on the atmosphere include the air pollution in cities, the pollutants including toxic chemicals like nitrogen oxides, sulphur oxides, volatile organic compounds and airborne particulate matter that generate photochemical smog and acid rain, and the chlorofluorocarbons that degrade the ozone layer. Anthropogenic particulates such as sulphate aerosols in the atmosphere decrease the direct irradiance and reflectance (albedo) of the Earth's surface. Known as global dimming, the decrease is estimated to have been about 4% between 1960 and 1990 while the trend has then reversed. Global dimming may have disturbed the global water cycle by decreasing evaporation and rainfall in some areas. It also creates a cooling effect and this may have to some extent covered the effect of greenhouse gases on global warming.

(B) Freshwater and Oceans

Water covers 71% of the Earth's surface. Of this, 97.5% is the salty water of the oceans and only 2.5% freshwater, most of which is locked up in the Antarctic ice sheet. The remaining other freshwater sources are glaciers, lakes, rivers, wetlands, the soil, aquifers and atmosphere. Due to the water cycle, fresh water supply is repeatedly replenished by precipitation, though there is still inadequate demanding management of this resource. During the 20th century, awareness of the global importance of preserving water for ecosystem services has emerged as more than half the world's wetlands have been lost along with their valuable environmental services. Growing urbanisation contaminates clean water supplies and much of the world still does not have access to clean, safe water. Greater stress is now being positioned on the better management of blue (harvestable) and green (soil water available for plant use) water, and this applies at all scales of water management.

The climate and weather are strongly influenced by ocean circulation patterns and, in turn, the food supply of both humans and other organisms. Scientists have cautioned about the possibility of an unexpected change in circulation patterns of ocean currents that could severely change the climate in some regions of the globe. Ten per cent of the world's population – about 600 million people – live in low-lying areas susceptible to sea level rise.

(C) Land use

Loss of biodiversity is mainly due to the habitat loss and fragmentation produced by the human appropriation of land for development, forestry and agriculture as natural capital is gradually converted to man-made capital. Land use change is fundamental to the operations of the biosphere because alterations in the relative proportions of land dedicated to urbanisation, agriculture, forest, woodland, grassland and pasture have a marked effect on the global water, carbon and nitrogen biogeochemical cycles and this can impact negatively on both natural and human systems. At the local human scale, major sustainability benefits grow from sustainable parks and gardens and green cities.

Since the Neolithic Revolution about 47% of the world's forests have been vanished to human use. Existing forests inhabit about a quarter of the world's ice-free land with about half of these occurring in the tropics. In temperate and boreal regions forest area is progressively increasing (with the exception of Siberia), but deforestation in the tropics is of major concern.

Food is essential to life. Feeding more than seven billion people takes a heavy duty on the Earth's resources. This commence with the appropriation of about 38% of the Earth's land surface and about 20% of its net primary productivity. Further, the resource-hungry activities of industrial agribusiness require everything from need for irrigation water, synthetic fertilisers and pesticides to the resource costs of food packaging, transport (now a major part of global trade) and retail. The environmental problems related with industrial agriculture and agribusinesses are now being resolved through such movements as sustainable agriculture, organic farming and more sustainable business practices.

3.2.2 Management of Human Consumption

The human consumption is most important of direct human impacts on the environment. This impact is minimised by not only consuming less but by also making the full cycle of production, use and disposal more sustainable. Consumption of goods and services can be analysed and managed at all scales through the chain of consumption, starting with the effects of individual lifestyle alternatives and spending patterns, through to the resource demands of specific goods and services, the impacts of economic sectors, through national economies to the global economy. The study of consumption patterns relates to utilising resource to the environmental, social and economic impacts at the scale or context under research. The ideas of embodied resource use (the total resources needed to produce a product or service), resource intensity, and resource productivity are important tools for understanding the impacts of consumption. The key resource categories concerning to human needs are food, energy, materials and water.

In 2010, the International Resource Panel, hosted by the United Nations Environment Programme (UNEP), published the first global scientific assessment on the impacts of consumption and production and identified priority actions for developed and developing countries. According to this study, ecosystem health, human health and resource depletion are the most serious impacts. From a production perspective, it was found that fossil-fuel combusting processes, agriculture and fisheries have the most significant impacts. In the meantime, from a final consumption perspective, it found that household consumption associated to mobility, shelter, food and energy-using products leads to the greater part of life-cycle impacts of consumption.

(A) Energy

Through the process of photosynthesis the Sun's energy is stored by plants (primary producers) and passed through the food chain to other organisms to finally power all living processes. Since the industrial revolution as fossil fuels which are the result of the concentrated energy of the Sun stored in fossilised plants has been a major driver of technology which, in turn, has been the source of both economic and political power. In 2007 climate scientists of the IPCC concluded that there was at least a 90% probability that increase of CO_2 gas in atmosphere was human-induced, mostly as a consequence of fossil fuel emissions but, to a lesser amount from changes in land use. Stabilising the world's climate will necessitate high-income countries to lessen their emissions by 60–90% over 2006 levels by 2050 which should hold CO_2 levels at 450–650 ppm from current levels of about 380 ppm. Above this level, temperatures could rise by more than 2 °C to produce "catastrophic" climate change. Decrease in current CO_2 levels must be achieved against a background of global population increase and developing countries aspiring to energy-intensive high consumption Western lifestyles.

Reduction of greenhouse emissions is being undertaken at all scales, ranging from tracking the passage of carbon through the carbon cycle to the commercialisation of renewable energy, developing less carbon-hungry technology and transport systems and efforts by individuals to lead carbon neutral lifestyles by monitoring the fossil fuel use embodied in all the goods and services they use. Engineering of emerging technologies such as carbon-neutral fuel and energy storage systems such as power to gas, compressed air energy storage, and pumped-storage hydroelectricity are necessary to store power from transient renewable energy sources including emerging renewables such as airborne wind turbines.

(B) Water

Water security and food security are inextricably linked. In the decade 1951–60 human water withdrawals were four times greater than the previous decade. This rapid increase in water withdrawals resulted from scientific and technological developments impacting through the economy – especially the increase in irrigated land, growth in industrial and power sectors, and intensive dam construction on all continents. This changed the water cycle of rivers and lakes, affected their water quality and had a significant impact on the global water cycle. Currently towards 35% of human water use is unsustainable, drawing on diminishing aquifers and reducing the flows of major rivers. This percentage is likely to boost if climate change impacts become more severe, populations increase, aquifers become gradually used up and supplies become polluted and unhygienic. From 1961 to 2001 demand of water became double- agricultural use increased by 75%, industrial use by more than 200%, and domestic use more than 400%. In the 1990s it was estimated that humans were using 40–50% of the globally available freshwater in the approximate proportion of 70% for agriculture, 22% for industry, and 8% for domestic purposes with total use gradually increasing.

Water efficiency is being improved on a global scale by increased demand management, improved infrastructure, improved water productivity of agriculture, water recycle, minimising the water intensity (embodied water) of goods and services, addressing shortages in the non-industrialised world, concentrating food production in areas of high productivity, and planning for climate change. People have become more independent at the local level by harvesting rainwater and reducing use of mains water.

(C) Food

The American Public Health Association (APHA) defines a "sustainable food system" as "one that provides healthy food to meet current food needs while maintaining healthy ecosystems that can also provide food for generations to come with minimal negative impact to the environment. A sustainable food system also supports local production and distribution infrastructures and makes nutritious food available, accessible, and affordable to all. Further, protecting farmers and other workers, consumers, and communities is a kind and just effort". Concerns about the environmental impacts of agribusiness and the severe difference between the obesity problems of the Western world and the poverty and food insecurity of the developing world have caused a strong movement towards healthy, sustainable eating as a main element of overall ethical consumerism. The environmental effects of different dietary patterns depend on many factors, including the proportion of animal and plant foods consumed and the method of food production.

The World Health Organisation has published a Global Strategy on Diet, Physical Activity and Health report which was endorsed by the May 2004 World Health Assembly. Mediterranean diet is advised which is related with health and long life. This diet should be low in meat, rich in fruits and vegetables, low in added sugar and limited salt, and low in saturated fatty acids. The conventional source of fat in the Mediterranean is olive oil, rich in monounsaturated fat. The Japanese diet which is healthy rice-based is also high in carbohydrates and low in fat. Both diets are low in meat and saturated fats and high in legumes and other vegetables. They are associated with a low occurrence of illness and low environmental impact.

Through sustainable agriculture and organic farming environmental impact of agribusiness is being addressed at the global level. At the local level there are various movements working towards local food production, more productive use of urban wastelands and domestic gardens including permaculture, urban horticulture, local food, slow food, sustainable gardening and organic gardening.

Sustainable seafood is seafood from either fished or farmed sources that can maintain or enhance production in the future without endangering the ecosystems from which it was acquired. The sustainable seafood movement has gained thrust as more people become conscious about both overfishing and environmentally destructive fishing methods.

(D) Materials, Toxic Substances, Waste Management

The use of variety of materials increased in volume, diversity and distance transported as global population and prosperity has augmented. Included here are raw materials, minerals, synthetic chemicals (including hazardous substances), manufactured products, food, living organisms and waste. By 2050, humanity could consume a predicted 140 billion tonnes of minerals, ores, fossil fuels and biomass per year (three times its current amount) unless the economic growth rate is decoupled from the rate of natural resource consumption. Developed countries' citizens consume an average of 16 tonnes of those four key resources per capita (ranging up to 40 or more tonnes per person) in some developed countries with resource consumption levels far ahead of what is probably sustainable.

Sustainable use of materials has targeted the idea of dematerialisation, converting the linear path of materials (extraction, use, disposal in landfill) to a circular material flow that reuses materials as much as possible, much like the cycling and reuse of waste in nature. Especially, at individual countries and the global economy, this approach is supported by product stewardship and the increasing use of material flow analysis at all levels. The renewable sources should be used that can be recycled is preferred over non-renewables sources.

Synthetic chemical production has escalated following the stimulus it received during the Second World War. Chemical production includes everything from herbicides, pesticides and fertilisers to domestic chemicals and hazardous substances. Apart from greenhouse gas emissions, chemicals of particular concern include heavy metals, nuclear waste, chlorofluorocarbons, persistent organic pollutants and all harmful chemicals proficient of bioaccumulation. All the synthetic chemicals are not harmful therefore rigorous testing of new chemicals is required. International legislation has been established to manage the global distribution and management of hazardous goods. The effects of some chemical agents require long-term measurements and a lot of legal battles to realise their danger to human health. The classification of the toxic carcinogenic agents is managed by the International Agency for Research on Cancer.

Every economic activity produces material that can be classified as waste. To decrease waste industry, business and government are now imitating nature by turning the waste produced by industrial metabolism into resource. Dematerialisation is being encouraged through the ideas of industrial ecology, ecodesign and ecolabelling. In addition to the well-established "reduce, reuse and recycle," shoppers are using their purchasing power for ethical consumerism.

3.3 Economic Dimension

On one account, sustainability "relates to the specification of a set of actions to be taken by present persons that will not reduce the prospects of future persons to benefit from levels of consumption, wealth, utility, or welfare comparable to those enjoyed by present persons." Sustainability interfaces with economics through the social and ecological consequences of economic activity. Sustainability economics corresponds to a broad interpretation of ecological economics where environmental and ecological variables and issues are fundamental but part of a multidimensional viewpoint. Social, cultural, health-related and monetary/financial aspects should be included into the analysis. Nevertheless, the concept of sustainability is much broader than the concepts of sustained yield of welfare, resources, or profit margins.

Presently, the average per capita consumption of people in the developing world is sustainable but population numbers are increasing and individuals are aspiring to high-consumption Western lifestyles. The developed world population is only increasing slightly but consumption levels are unsustainable. The challenge for sustainability is to control and manage Western consumption while increasing the standard of living of the developing world without increasing its resource use and environmental impact. This must be done by using strategies and technology that break the link between, on the one hand, economic growth and on the other, environmental damage and resource depletion.

A latest UNEP report recommends a green economy defined as one that improves human well-being and social equity, while considerably minimising environmental hazards and ecological shortages. Instead of favouring political perspective, it works to decrease excessive depletion of natural capital. The report finds three key factors that:

1. Greening not only cause increase in wealth, particularly a gain in ecological commons or natural capital, but also (over a period of six years) makes a higher rate of GDP growth;
2. There is an inextricable link between poverty eradication and better maintenance and conservation of the ecological commons, arising from the benefit flows from natural capital that are received directly by the poor;
3. In the transition to a green economy, new jobs are produced, which in time exceed the losses in "brown economy" jobs. However, there is a period of job losses in transition, which requires investment in re-skilling and re-educating the workforce.

For economic analysis and reforms, a number of key areas have been targeted such as the environmental effects of unconstrained economic growth, the consequences of nature being treated as an economic externality, and the prospect of an economics that takes greater account of the social and environmental consequences of market behaviour.

3.3.1 Decoupling Environmental Degradation and Economic Growth

In times gone by there has been a close connection between economic growth and environmental degradation. As communities grow, so the environment declines. This trend is clearly demonstrated on graphs of human population numbers, economic growth, and environmental indicators. Unsustainable economic growth has been severely compared to the malignant growth of cancer because it eats away the Earth's ecosystem services which are its life-support system. There is concern that, unless resource use is checked, modern global civilisation will follow the path of ancient civilisations that collapsed through overexploitation of their resource base. While conventional economics is concerned largely with economic growth and the efficient allocation of resources, ecological economics has the explicit goal of sustainable scale (rather than continual growth), fair distribution and efficient allocation, in that order. The World Business Council for Sustainable Development states that "business cannot succeed in societies that fail".

In economic and environmental fields, the term decoupling is becoming increasingly used in the context of economic production and environmental quality. When used in this way, it refers to the ability of an economy to grow without incurring corresponding increases in environmental pressure. Ecological economics includes the study of societal metabolism, the throughput (output relative to input) of resources that enter and exit the economic system in relation to environmental quality. An economy that is able to sustain GDP growth without having a negative impact on the environment is said to be decoupled. Exactly how, if, or to what extent this can be achieved is a subject of much debate. In 2011 the International Resource Panel, hosted by the United Nations Environment Programme (UNEP), warned that by 2050 the human race could be devouring 140 billion tonnes of minerals, ores, fossil fuels and biomass per year – three times its current rate of consumption – unless nations can make serious attempts at decoupling. The report noted that citizens of developed countries consume an average of 16 tonnes of those four key resources per capita per annum (ranging up to 40 or more tonnes per person in some developed countries). By comparison, the average person in India today consumes four tonnes per year. Sustainability studies analyse methods to decrease resource intensity (the amount of resource e.g. water, energy, or material needed for the production, consumption and disposal of a unit of good or service) whether this be attained from enhanced economic management, product design, or new technology.

There are contradictory views whether developments in technological efficiency and innovation will allow full decoupling of economic growth from environmental degradation. On the one hand, it has been claimed frequently by efficiency experts that resource use intensity (i.e., energy and materials use per unit GDP) could in principle be decreased by at least four or five-fold, thereby allowing for continued economic growth without rising resource depletion and related pollution. Alternatively, a wide historical analysis of technological efficiency improvements has conclusively revealed that improvements in the efficiency of the use of energy and materials were almost forever outpaced by economic growth, in large part because of the rebound effect (conservation) or "Jevons Paradox" resulting in a net increase in resource use and related pollution. In addition, there are inbuilt thermodynamic and practical limits to all efficiency improvements.

For example, there are definite minimum inevitable material requirements for growing food, and there are limits to making automobiles, houses, furniture, and other products lighter and thinner without the threat of losing their essential functions. Since it is both theoretically and practically unfeasible to increase resource use efficiencies indefinitely, it is equally impossible to have continued and infinite economic growth without a related increase in resource depletion and environmental pollution, i.e., economic growth and resource depletion can be decoupled to some degree over the short run but not the long run. Consequently, long-term sustainability requires the transition to a steady state economy in which total GDP remains more or less constant, as has been advocated for decades by Herman Daly and others in the ecological economics community.

3.3.2 Nature as an Economic Externality

The economic significance of environment is indicated by the use of the term 'ecosystem services' to emphasize the market relevance of an increasingly limited natural world that can no longer be regarded as both unlimited and free. In general, as a commodity or service becomes inadequate, the price increases and this acts as a restraint that encourages frugality, technical innovation and alternative products. Though, this only applies when the product or service falls within the market system. As ecosystem services are usually treated as economic externalities they are not priced and as a result overused and degraded. This situation is referred the "Tragedy of the Commons".

One approach to this problem has been the effort to "internalise" these "externalities" by using market strategies like ecotaxes and incentives, tradable permits for carbon, and the encouragement of payment for ecosystem services. Community currencies associated with Local Exchange Trading Systems (LETS), a gift economy and Time Banking has also been encouraged as a way of supporting local economies and the environment. Green economics is another market-based attempt to address issues of equity and the environment. The global recession and a range of associated government policies are likely to bring the biggest annual fall in the world's carbon dioxide emissions in 40 years.

3.3.3 Economic Opportunity

Treating the environment as an externality may generate short-term profit at the cost of sustainability. On the other hand, sustainable business practices integrate ecological concerns with social and economic ones (i.e., the triple bottom line). Growth that depletes ecosystem services is referred as "uneconomic growth" as it leads to a decline in quality of life. Local businesses can take opportunities by minimising such growth. For example, industrial waste can be treated as an "economic resource in the wrong place". The benefits of waste reduction include savings from disposal costs, fewer environmental penalties, and reduced liability insurance. This may lead to improved market share due to an improved public image. Energy efficiency can also increase profits by reducing costs.

The organisations such as the Sustainability Consortium of the Society for Organisational Learning, the Sustainable Business Institute, and the World Council for Sustainable Development have been formed on the idea of sustainability as a business opportunity. Research focusing on progressive corporate leaders who have rooted sustainability into commercial strategy has given way to a leadership competency model for sustainability. The expansion of sustainable business opportunities can contribute to job creation through the introduction of green-collar workers.

3.4 Social Dimension

Sustainability issues are generally expressed in scientific and environmental terms, as well as in ethical terms of stewardship, but implementing change is a social challenge that entails, among other things, international and national law, urban planning and transport, local and individual lifestyles and ethical consumerism. "The relationship between human rights and human development, corporate power and environmental justice, global poverty and citizen action, suggest that responsible global citizenship is an inescapable element of what may at first glance seem to be simply matters of personal consumer and moral choice."

3.4.1 Peace, Security, Social Justice

Social disruptions like war, crime and corruption divert resources from areas of greatest human need, damage the capacity of societies to plan for the future, and generally threaten human well-being and the environment. Broad-based strategies for more sustainable social systems include: improved education and the political empowerment of women, especially in developing countries; greater regard for social justice, notably equity between rich and poor both within and between countries; and intergenerational equity. Depletion of natural resources including fresh water increases the likelihood of "resource wars". This aspect of sustainability has been referred to as environmental security and creates a clear need for global environmental agreements to manage resources such as aquifers and rivers which span political boundaries, and to protect shared global systems including oceans and the atmosphere.

3.4.2 Sustainability and Poverty

The main obstacle to achieve sustainability is the alleviation of poverty. It has been broadly accepted that poverty is one major source of environmental degradation. Such acknowledgment has been made by the Brundtland Commission report "Our Common Future and the Millennium Development Goals". There is a increasing realisation in national governments and multilateral institutions that it is not possible to separate economic development issues from environment issues. According to the Brundtland report, "poverty is a major cause and effect of global environmental problems. It is therefore futile to attempt to deal with environmental problems without a broader perspective that encompasses the factors underlying world poverty and international inequality." People below poverty line tend to depend greatly on their local ecosystem as a source for basic needs (such as nutrition and medicine) and general well-being. As population growth continues to increase, increasing pressure is being placed on the local ecosystem to provide these basic essentials. According to the UN Population Fund, high fertility and poverty have been strongly interrelated, and the world's poorest countries also have the highest fertility and population growth rates.

The word sustainability is also used extensively by western country development agencies and international charities to focus their poverty lessening efforts in ways that can be sustained by the local populous and its environment. For example, teaching water treatment to the poor by boiling their water with charcoal would not generally be considered a sustainable strategy, whereas using PET solar water disinfection would be. Also, sustainable best practices can involve the recycling of materials, such as the use of recycled plastics for lumber where deforestation has devastated a country's timber base.

3.4.3 Human Relationship to Nature

According to Murray Bookchin, the idea that humans must dominate nature is common in hierarchical societies. Bookchin contends that capitalism and market relationships, if unchecked, have the capacity to reduce the planet to a mere resource to be exploited. Nature is thus treated as a commodity. "The plundering of the human spirit by the market place is paralleled by the plundering of the earth by capital." Social ecology, founded by Bookchin, is based on the conviction that nearly all of humanity's present ecological problems originate in dysfunctional social arrangements. Whereas most authors carry on as if our ecological problems can be fixed by applying recommendations which stem from physical, biological, and economic studies, Bookchin's claim is that these problems can only be resolved by understanding the fundamental social processes and superseding in those processes by applying the concepts and methods of the social sciences.

Deep ecology establishes principles for the well-being of all life on Earth and the richness and diversity of life forms. This requires a substantial decrease in human population and consumption along with the reduction of human interference with the nonhuman world. This can be achieved if ecologists support policies for basic economic, technological, and ideological structures that will improve the quality of life rather than the standard of living. Those who subscribe to these principles are appreciative to make the necessary change happen. The concept of a billion-year "sustainocene" has been developed to initiate policy consideration of an earth where human structures power and fuel the needs of that species (for example through artificial photosynthesis) allowing the Rights of Nature.

3.4.4 Human Settlements

One approach to sustainable living, illustrated by small-scale urban transition towns and rural ecovillages, seeks to build self-reliant communities based on principles of simple living, which make best use of self-sufficiency particularly in food production. These principles, on a broader scale, strengthen the concept of a bioregional economy. These approaches often utilise common based knowledge sharing of open source suitable technology.

Other approaches like loosely based around New Urbanism, are successfully reducing environmental impacts by changing the built environment to build and preserve sustainable cities which support sustainable transport. Residents in compact urban neighbourhoods drive fewer miles, and have significantly lower environmental impacts across a range of measures, compared with those living in sprawling suburbs. In sustainable architecture the recent movement of New Classical Architecture promotes a sustainable approach towards construction that appreciates and develops smart growth, architectural tradition and classical design. This is in contrast to modernist and globally uniform architecture, as well as opposing solitary housing estates and suburban sprawl. Both trends started in the 1980s. The concept of circular flow land use management has also been introduced in Europe to promote sustainable land use patterns that strive for compact cities and a reduction of greenfield land take by urban sprawl.

The community choices and the built environment are influenced by large scale social movements such as Eco-municipalities. Eco-municipalities follow a systems approach, based on sustainability principles. The eco-municipality movement is participatory, involving community members in a bottom-up approach.

There is a wealth of advice accessible to individuals wishing to decrease their personal and social impact on the environment through small, low-cost and easily achievable steps. But the transition necessary to reduce global human consumption within sustainable limits involves much larger changes, at all levels and contexts of society. The United Nations has recognised the central role of education, and has stated a decade of education for sustainable development, 2005–2014, which intends to "challenge us all to adopt new behaviours and practices to secure our future". The Worldwide Fund for Nature proposes a strategy for sustainability that goes ahead of education to undertake basic individualistic and materialistic societal values head-on and strengthen people's connections with the natural world.

3.5 Ecological Footprint

The ecological footprint is an accounting tool for ecological resources. Categories of human consumption are translated into areas of productive land necessary to provide resources and incorporate waste products. The ecological footprint is expressed in "global hectares." Each unit corresponds to one acre of biologically productive space with "world average" productivity. Ecological footprint can be summarise as a measure of the sustainability of our lifestyles.

The ecological footprint offers a broad comparison of natural resources demand and supply availability. The ecological footprint investigation compares the actual geographic area or footprint of a region (e.g., city, country, etc.) with the practical footprint that would be essential for that region to be sustainable. Rees & Wackernackel, the originators of the concept, estimate that the residents of the Earth are currently consuming resources at a rate that would require four times the Earth's resources in order to be sustainable. The analysis is mainly based on data published by United Nations agencies and the Intergovernmental Panel on Climate Change. In summary, ecological footprint can be used as a measure, or indicator, of progress towards sustainability, rather than a tool to develop the environmental performance of an organisation. The data resulting from such measurement can be used for communication purposes both internally and external to an organisation.

Users of Ecological Footprint

1. **Industry:** Ecological footprint calculations are typically applied to communities and are used in industrial operations. However, the quantifiable nature of the concept is relevant to private industry and could be used as an evaluative tool. Industry would benefit from an understanding of the implications of corporate decisions significant to the ecological footprint. Such a measurement may arouse the emphasis on environmental initiatives to decrease an individual company's ecological footprint.

2. **Government:** The United Nations computes the ecological footprint for nations. National consumption is calculated as domestic production plus imports minus exports. This balance is calculated for 72 categories such as cereals, timber, fishmeal, coal and cotton.

3. **Organisations:** Local interest groups, NGOs and environmental organisations make use of the calculated ecological footprint to describe issues of concern and strengthen the need for environmental and sustainability initiatives in developed

countries. Several web sites and resources let basic personal ecological footprint calculations to emphasise the environmental consequences of the modern Western lifestyle.
4. **Individuals:** A person's ecological footprint can be calculated using a "top-down approach," by dividing the regional or national total consumption by its population size. The footprint can also be determined using a "bottom-up approach," by estimating the footprint of individuals, households or communities from the results of a lifestyle questionnaire. The bottom-up approach is an example of direct measurement.

3.6 Eco-Tracking

The Eco-Advantage Mindset is an influential motivator and the central part of the environmental lens that aids companies step up to challenges and get opportunities for grabbing benefit. But it's just the beginning. Companies require tool to get going. We start here with the elements of the toolkit that help companies understand where they are.

Getting the lay of the land requires thinking and analysis that might not come naturally. Eco-Tracking helps to answer fundamental but sometimes unfamiliar questions:

1. What are the company's big environmental impacts?
2. When and where do those impacts arise? During manufacturing? During shipping and distribution? Upstream in the supply chain? Or downstream in the hands of customers?
3. How do others view the company's environmental performance?

These questions can be difficult to answer. However, top companies make use of core set of Eco-Tracking tools to build up an environmental self-portrait and facilitate the companies to manage for Eco-Advantage.

Following their lead, we suggest that you:

1. Trace your environmental footprint.
2. Capture data and create metrics.
3. Set-up environmental management systems.
4. Partner for advantage.

You require a systematic approach to capture and then utilize that valuable information to set off your internal focus on environmental issues. This tacking needs to be made using consistent metrics which are applied globally. The optimum approach applied by a lot of corporations is to set up one data warehouse where the company's environmental from all around the world is measured and analysed using consistent metrics and assessment methodologies. In this way, progress can be monitored.

Eco-tracking tools need to be available which:
1. **Allow you to trace your environmental footprint** - taking into account all the activities in your value chain. If you exploit more resources else the pollution you create, the bigger your footprint will be.
2. **Capture data and create metrics** - so you can observe where problems subsist and what progress is being made in addressing those issues.
3. **Set-up an environmental management system** - which will assist managers to squeeze out waste and run everything more efficiently.
4. **Help your partner for advantage** - with non-government organisations, environmental experts, government agencies, community leaders and others. Many companies set up in environmental impact advisory board that assess their environmental efforts and recommend new directions.

In business, what gets managed gets managed. If you want to have any trustworthiness as an environmentally sound company, you have to be putting plans into action to make a sustainable competitive advantage. Eco-tracking tools allow you to do precisely that.

3.7 Carbon Marketing

Carbon marketing is a method that encourages developed countries to help less developed countries to invest in and use clean energy technologies (that is, those which produce less greenhouse gases).

It is a bid to reduce the emission of carbon and other greenhouse gases which experts claim are changing the global climate drastically. The developed countries can then use the emission-reduction credits to meet their own nation's emission reduction goals.

Strengthening the concept of Law Carbon Marketing

It is an enterprise production and management concept to around the centre of reducing carbon emission and protecting environment, be guided by the sustainable development of enterprises and society. Enterprise managers require to be trained and be aware of to carry out new marketing model under the low carbon economy era, from low carbon marketing consciousness. Enterprises need to form the traditional management pattern, redesign and optimise enterprise business processes, establish scientific corporate governance structure, strengthen the internal control system, completely understand the necessity and urgency of grabbing network information market, grasp the positive opportunity to carry out the network marketing.

3.8 Carbon Credit

Carbon credits and carbon markets are elements of national and international efforts to reduce the increase in concentrations of greenhouse gases (GHGs). One carbon credit is equal to one metric tonne of carbon dioxide, or in some markets, carbon dioxide equivalent gases. Carbon trading is an application of an emissions trading approach. Greenhouse gas emissions are capped and then markets are used to allocate the emissions among the group of regulated sources.

The aim is to permit market mechanisms to drive industrial and commercial processes in the path of low emissions or less carbon intensive approaches than those used when there is no cost to emitting carbon dioxide and other GHGs into the atmosphere. Since GHG reduction projects produce credits, this approach can be used to finance carbon reduction schemes between trading partners around the world.

There are as well numerous companies that trade carbon credits to commercial and individual customers who are involved in lessening their carbon footprint on a voluntary basis. These carbon off-setters purchase the credits from an investment fund or a carbon development company that has collected the credits from individual projects. The Carbon Trade Exchange is like a stock exchange for carbon credits which the buyers and sellers can also use as an exchange platform to trade. The quality of the credits is based in part on the validation process and sophistication of the fund or development company that acted as the sponsor to the carbon project. This is reflected in their price; voluntary units typically have less value than the units sold through the strictly validated Clean Development Mechanism.

3.9 Design for Environment

In a period of mass production, when all activities inclined to be planned in detail, design becomes a powerful instrument by which mankind counterfeit the world we live in. The reach of this instrument undoubtedly also extends to the management of environmental problems.

Design basically consists of moulding material and energy flows for the reason of fulfilling the wants of people, eventually becomes a process of transformation when the needs generating it are contextualised in the patterns and flows of natural systems, incorporating the organising principles of the ecosphere.

The study of the main factors influencing the environmental efficiency of industrial systems, allows the identification of the contexts most appropriate for a design intervention directed at environmental protection. Especially, it highlights the significance of product and process design on the efficiency of working, re-collecting, recycling materials, and preventing pollution. As a result of its great potential, design becomes one of the most powerful factors in the development of sustainable production systems and products.

3.9.1 Origins and Definition of Design for Environment

A full understanding of the potential and responsibility that the vast typology of design interventions has toward the environmental question has been slow to arrive. Although attention was first drawn to the necessary influence of socio-ecological systems on technical design in the early 1960s, the transition from a "design for needs" to a "design for environment" first began in the early 1970s. Actually, this period saw the first ideas which determinedly raised the environmental question and emphasized its revolutionary effects on the structure of conventional design, initially from different points of view. In the perspective of the culture of design, by now an explicit reference to the potential of using biological systems as worthy models for systems developed by mankind and resulting in opportunities of reusing, remanufacturing and recycling artifacts (see figure). Starting out from different viewpoints, economic and social in character, different authors highlighted related aspects, with a obvious emphasis on the design phase:

- The significance of moving in the direction of the optimisation of production systems, supporting the standard of attaining the utmost well-being with the least possible consumption of resources.
- The need to extend a right perception of the environmental question among consumers, essential to encouraging an industrial production directed at limiting the obsolescence of products and at encouraging their recycling.

These first incentives to revising conventional design paradigms were consolidated over the following decade. Taking up some concepts already discussed about the non-sustainability of a development completely oriented toward economic expansion, the new paradigms of design must take motivation from alternative models of development. Against specialised industrial products with limited functionality and of short duration, a new "post-industrial design" phase contrasts multifunctional products, repairable and durable, taking the form of a design which is socially responsive and eco-sustainable. Conventional product requirements regarding functionality and cost are integrated with new requisites: energy efficiency, duration, and recyclability appeal to consumers sensitive to environmental issues. Simultaneously, it is highlighted that this extension in product requirements must not be seen as a drawback by the manufacturer. The environmentally compatible products should be economically competitive, as well as innovative and particularly attractive for the consumer.

At the beginning of the 1990s it was thus possible to have an overall vision of the effects of environmental issues on the design activity, extending to the most diverse areas, and clarified by the results of the first experiences. These experiences were followed by a phase of greater understanding of new needs to safeguard resources, which consolidated in a wide diffusion of new ideas developed with the clear objective of integrating environmental demands in traditional design procedures. Thus, a new approach was formed to design intervention, known as Design for Environment (DFE), Green Design (GD), Environmentally Conscious Design (ECD), and Ecodesign and was characterised by the priority purpose of reducing the impact of products on the environment already in the design phase.

The definition of Design for Environment, which at least initially was not clearly univocal, has developed over the last decade. First presented in a reductive manner as a design approach directed at the decrease of industrial waste and the optimisation of the use of materials, it then gained a more apt dimension. Maintaining the needed attention on the management of waste and resources, and integrating it in a system's vision was clearly inspired by the principles of industrial ecology. It can be understood more completely as "a design process that must be considered for conserving and using again the earth's limited resources. If energy and material consumption is optimised, minimal waste is produced and output waste flows from any process can be used as the raw materials (inputs) of another".

Design for Environment can be defined as a methodology directed at the systematic reduction or elimination of the environmental impacts implicated in the whole life cycle of a product, from the extraction of raw materials to disposal. This methodology is based on assessing the possible impacts during the complete course of the design process. In addition to its specific primary objective and its orientation toward the life cycle, DFE is characterised by two other aspects (see figure):

- the dual level of intervention, concerning both products and processes
- the proactive action of intervention, based on the assumption of the greater effectiveness of intervening early in the product development process preferably in the early design phases

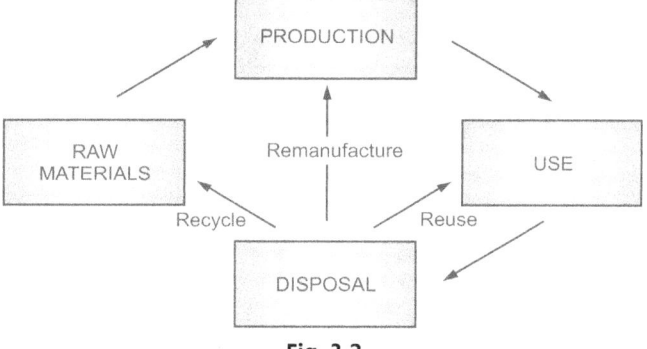

Fig. 3.2

3.9.2 Approach to Improve the Environmental Performance

The central theme unifying the a variety of experiences of Design for Environment can be recognized in the common purpose of dropping the environmental impact of a product over its whole life cycle, from design to disposal. The concept of "reduction of the environmental impact" is not, however, limited to the simple quantification and minimisation of direct impacts on the ecosystem. Rather, in this context it has to be understood in wider terms, as the improvement of the environmental performance, which includes a more distinct range of aspects:

- decrease of scrap and waste, allocating a more efficient use of resources and a reduction in the quantity of refuse, and more usually a decrease in the impact related with the management of waste materials.
- Optimal management of materials, consisting of the accurate use of materials on the basis of the performance required, in their recovery at the end of the product's life and in the reduction of toxic or polluting materials.
- Optimisation of production processes, consisting of the planning of processes which are energetically efficient and result in limited emissions.
- Upgradation of the product, with particular regard to its behaviour during the phase of use, to lessen the consumption of resources or the need for further additional resources during its operation.

It is clear that with these premises Design for Environment acts as a bridge connecting two traditionally separate functions – production development and environmental management. The aim of design for environment is to bring these two functions into close contact and giving importance to those problems of a product life cycle which are frequently overlooked.

3.9.3 Implementation of Design for Environment

Whether the subject of environmental improvement is a product, a process or each single flow of resources, DFE is implemented in design practice through three successive phases:

- **Scoping:** Scoping consists of defining the target of the intervention (product, process, resource flow), identifying possible alternatives, and determining the depth of analysis.
- **Data Gathering:** It consists of obtaining and assessing the more important environmental data.
- **Data Translation:** It involves transforming the outcomes from the preliminary analysis data into tools (from simple guidelines and design procedures to more sophisticated software systems assisting the design team to apply environmental data in the design process).

In fact, the second and third phases are executed by means of two instrument typologies:

- Tools aiding the analysis of the life cycle (Life Cycle Assessment, Life Cycle Cost Analysis), allowing the acquisition, elaboration and interpretation of environmental data.
- Tools aiding the design or redesign (Product and Process Design, Design for Use, Design for End-of-Life, or more generally Design for X).

These tools and issues like assessment of the environmental impact of products and processes, selection of materials and processes, disassembly of the product or subsystems, extension and optimisation of the useful life, recovery at end-of-life through reuse of components and the recycling of materials are the specific subject of our research activity. However, it should be noted here that these tools are based on a wide-ranging series of suggestions and guidelines for the designer which can be summarised as follows:

- Reducing the use of materials, using recycled and recyclable materials, reducing toxic or polluting materials.
- Making best use of the number of replaceable or recyclable components.
- Minimising emissions and waste in production processes.
- Growing energy efficiency in phases of production and use.
- Increasing reliability and maintainability of the system.
- Assisting the use of materials and recovery of resources by planning the disassembly of components.
- Expanding the product's useful life.
- Planning strategies for the recovery of resources at end-of-life, facilitating reuse, remanufacturing and recycling, and reducing waste.
- Controlling and limiting the economic costs incurred by design interventions aimed at improving the environmental performance of the product.
- Respecting current legal constraints and evaluating future regulations in preparation.

Applying these guidelines in relation to the main phases of the product's life cycle, as a general rule it is possible to obtain useful information and to explore the whole set of environmental opportunities for an eco-efficient intervention in the product design and development process.

3.10 Greening the Supply Chain

The term "Greening the Supply Chain" has come out to explain a broad array of actions that a number of companies (chiefly western companies) are presently performing to establish greater performance strictness and operational control over their extended supply chains. Greening the Supply Chain initiatives are part of a process for implementing a sustainable development plan aimed at achieving improved environmental, health and safety performance; increasing efficiencies in the use of energy, water or other natural resources or raw materials; reducing the environmental and societal impact of business operations upon local communities and the global biosphere; and expanding economic and quality of life enhancing opportunities that result from the company's business activities.

The term "Greening the Supply Chain" refers to the following elements of a company's interactions with its suppliers:

- Applying common environmental and related standards and programs across the parent company and its suppliers, taking into consideration local legal frameworks and cultural characteristics.
- Extending management system implementation to ensure greater accountability of supplier performance on health, environment, safety, resource consumption and social factors.
- Examining opportunities for business process redesign or innovation, materials substitution or product design.
- Adopting specific performance goals and metrics to evaluate the performance of specific suppliers over time.
- Practicing greater transparency in reporting performance results.
- Developing partnerships with government agencies, non-government organisations and other institutions to improve specific aspects of performance beyond a company's specific capabilities or to leverage access to technical, managerial or financial resources.

3.10.1 Business Value of GSC Initiatives

- **Mitigating Risks to the Business:** The incentive to put into practice GSC initiatives takes place at a time of growing awareness and concern among developing country policy makers and citizens to decrease environmental pollution; stakeholder, business, peer and marketplace pressures to adopt formal sustainable development policies; developing legal requirements; and a rising expectation for enhanced corporate governance of supplier performance. Reducing threats to the business from current environmental, health and safety factors, or responding to expectations of future controls on carbon emissions or other substances can both advance company-supplier learning and increase the operational reliability of business processes across the supply chain to form business value.
- **Reducing Costs:** At a time of rising costs from energy consumption and other resource and raw material inputs, global companies have more direct incentives to improve the efficiencies of a variety of operating processes. These range from research and development priorities; building design and maintenance; manufacturing process design and operations; heating, ventilation and air conditioning systems; refrigeration; storage facilities; vehicle fleet maintenance and purchasing; procurement; materials and product distribution; and materials re-cycling and re-use.

High cost structures are often rooted in each of these functions many of which result from continuing reliance upon preceding generation technologies or operating standards and practices that result in higher than required consumption of energy, water and other inputs.

- **Motivating Better Performing Suppliers:** The characteristic of supply chain management processes in global companies generates both rising economies of scale in the marketplace and increased interdependencies and complexity in product development and distribution. Such features can also produce higher levels of susceptibility to the corporate customer if suppliers do not reach projected levels of performance. Given the increasingly complex and extended supply chains of global companies—and the well documented performance shortcomings of suppliers in a variety of business sectors—the implementation of sustainability initiatives creates an opportunity to further focus and rationalise supply chains by removing low performers and focusing on a fewer number of suppliers that can meet more accurate sustainability performance criteria while meeting the needs of the marketplace. On the other hand, GSC projects generate the opportunity for customers to further become stable and proceed business relationships with their suppliers through a sustained, mutually advantageous partnership.

- **Preserving Business Continuity:** Business operations in emerging markets often experience trouble from the disruption of electricity supplies or other energy or natural resource inputs required for production. Green supply chain initiatives focus on energy efficiency and other aspects of sustainability can shield business processes from such interruption while contributing to emission reductions.

- **Enhancing Market Access and Strategic Degrees of Freedom:** Whether in emerging or developed markets, global companies seek to maximise the degree of freedom they possess to produce products in a market-based system. In some sectors, however, the need for business access to a natural resource competes with society's growing need for the same resource. Nowhere is this competition more direct than in the growing demand for water resources or for food supply ingredients that are also valuable for producing transportation fuels.

Companies looking to manage their demand for such resources while integrating the requirements of civil society will achieve superior long-term control over their business strategy by combining business process innovation with answers to societal problems. For example, The Coca-Cola Company has formed a corporate objective of becoming "water neutral" by replenishing the amount of water used in generating a variety of its beverage products, thus minimising the competition for access to a inadequate resource and avoiding the achievement of its business goals in competition with those of consumers. Companies that do not bring together their business strategy with societal objectives raise the risk of becoming the center of attention of growing societal conflict and political action. This result will decrease the ultimate control of their business strategy and result in the important diversion of management time and other resources.

3.11 Regulation

India has many laws which take care of the three pillars of sustainable development which are environment, social and economic (including trade and IPR legislation). Most of these demonstrate a high degree of integration or interrelationship between the different pillars of sustainable development, an important feature of sustainable development law. To cite an example, the Biological Diversity Act seeks to conserve bio-resources in addition to offer legal entitlements to the communities who have maintained them over centuries as well as enables them to benefit economically from the resource.

In a similar way, the Forest Rights Act identifies social and economic rights of forest inhabitants and forest dependent communities and brings together it with the need of creating protected areas for wildlife. Similarly, NREGA sets out to attain sustainable development in a comprehensive manner given a legal right to livelihood to rural people. It also seeks to protect the environment with employment being suggested to manage environmental issues like drought, deforestation and soil erosion apart from eradicating rural poverty and ensuring food security. For example, the Wildlife Protection Act in its original form did not recognise the rights of forest dependent communities, but an attempt to have a more participatory and inclusive approach is seen in the later amendments.

Although there has been significant growth in Indian legal provisioning on sustainable development, a few challenges still persist mainly with respect to implementation. It is well recognised that key to enhanced implementation is the capacity building and improved financial and technical resourcing of executing agencies.

3.11.1 Key Indian Legislations Relevant to Sustainable Development

1. **Environment**
    (a) The Forest Act, 1927.
    (b) The Wildlife (Protection) Act, 1972.
    (c) Water (Prevention and Control of Pollution) Act, 1974.
    (d) The Forest (Conservation) Act, 1980.
    (e) Air (Prevention and Control of Pollution) Act, 1981.
    (f) Environmental (Protection) Act, 1986.
    (g) Motor Vehicles Act, 1988.

2. **Social**
   (a) Protection of Human Rights Act, 1993.
   (b) National Trust Act, 1999.
   (c) Commissions for the Protection of Child Rights Act, 2005.
   (d) Right to Information Act, 2005.
   (e) Gram Nyayalayas Act, 2008.
   (f) Right of Children to Free and Compulsory Education Act, 2009.

3. **Economic**
   (a) Foreign Trade (Development and Regulation) Act, 1992 .
   (b) Competition Act, 2002.
   (c) Fiscal Responsibility and Budget Management Act, 2003.
   (d) Micro, Small and Medium Enterprises Development Act, 2006.

4. **Socio-ecological (Environment and Social)**
   (a) Public Liability Insurance Act, 1991.
   (b) National Environment Tribunal Act, 1995 (Repealed).
   (c) The National Environment Appellate Authority Act, 1997 (Repealed).
   (d) National Green Tribunal Act, 2010.

5. **Social Equity (Economic and Social)**
   (a) Person with Disabilities Act, 1995(right to employment of the disabled).
   (b) The Geographical Indications of Goods (Registration and Protection) Act, 1999.
   (c) Protection of Plant Varieties and Farmer's Right Act, 2001.
   (d) The Patents (Amendment) Act, 2005.
   (e) Maintenance and Welfare of Parents and Senior Citizens Act, 2007.

6. **Green Economy (Economic and Environment)**
   (a) Energy Conservation Act, 2001.
   (b) The Electricity Act, 2003.

7. **Sustainable Development (Social, Environment and Economic)**
   (a) The (Wildlife Protection Act), 1972 and its amendments in 1991, 2002.
   (b) Panchayat Extension to Scheduled Areas Act, 1996.
   (c) Biological Diversity Act, 2002 and the Biological Diversity Rules, 2004.
   (d) National Rural Employment Guarantee Act, 2005.
   (e) Forests Rights Act, 2006.

3.12 Business Models for Sustainable Development

'Value proposition' is the focal point of any company's business model is defined as the products and services that yield tangible results for the company's target customers. A company's value proposition distinguishes it from its competitors.

The production and marketing are the two broad areas for possible adaptation and innovation of a business model. The production side consists of the set of activities, mechanisms and relationships for providing a good or service—in other words, 'creating value'. The marketing side comprises the activities, mechanisms and relationships for selling that good or service—in other words, 'capturing value'.

The aim of business models for sustainable development is to bring economic, social and environmental benefits which are the three pillars of sustainable development through core business activities. In these models, the value proposition comprises of social, environmental and economic values, while value distribution within the whole market chain is a key feature.

Key Factors of Success

A number of factors have been identified that add to the success of business models for sustainable development:

- Businesses require constructing their own capacities and strategic alliances with other enterprises, government agencies and development practitioners.
- Involving local communities as partners and co-designers of new models that enhance local buy-in and ownership.
- Self-sustaining business models for sustainable development are required in the long term. Though, significant investment of time and resources at the beginning is the key for successful innovation and scale-up.
- Trade-offs among different sustainable development goals are economic, social, environmental which need to be recognised and addressed.
- Ongoing monitoring and evaluation need to be built into the business model.

3.13 Sustainability Reporting

A sustainability report is a report published by a company or organisation about the economic, environmental and social impacts caused by its daily activities.

A sustainability report also shows the organisation's values and governance model, and exhibit the link between its strategy and its commitment to a sustainable global economy.

Companies would like to make their operations sustainable and contribute to sustainable development. Organisations can measure, understand and communicate their economic, environmental, and social and governance performance with the help of sustainability reporting.

Systematic sustainability reporting facilitates organisations to measure the impacts they cause or experience, set goals, and manage change. A sustainability report is the key platform for communicating sustainability performance and impacts whether positive or negative.

To make a regular sustainability report, organisations set up a reporting cycle which is a program of data collection, communication, and responses. Sustainability performance of the organisation is monitored on an ongoing basis. To bring changes to the organisation's strategy and policies, and improve performance data can be provided on a regular basis to senior decision makers.

Sustainability reporting is as a result a fundamental source for managing change towards a sustainable global economy, one that merge long term profitability with ethical behaviour, social justice and environmental care.

In the past decade, the main goal of businesses, nonprofits and governments has been sustainability, so far measuring the degree to which an organisation is being sustainable or pursuing sustainable growth can be difficult.

3.13.1 The Triple Bottom Line Defined

John Elkington strove to measure sustainability during the mid-1990s by encompassing a new framework to measure performance in corporate America. This accounting framework, called the triple bottom line (TBL), went ahead of the traditional measures of profits, return on investment, and shareholder value to comprise environmental and social dimensions. Triple bottom line reporting can be a significant tool to sustain sustainability goals by focusing on comprehensive investment results, that is, with respect to performance along the interrelated dimensions of profits, people and the planet.

The TBL is an accounting framework that incorporates three dimensions of performance which are social, environmental and financial. This differs from traditional reporting frameworks as it includes ecological (or environmental) and social measures that can be difficult to assign appropriate means of measurement. The TBL dimensions are also commonly called the three Ps: people, planet and profits. We will refer to these as the 3Ps.

Calculating the TBL

The 3Ps do not have a common unit of measure. Profits are measured in dollars. What is social capital measured in? What about environmental or ecological health? Finding a common unit of measurement is one challenge.

Some advocate monetising all the dimensions of the TBL, including social welfare or environmental damage. While that would have the benefit of having a common unit—dollars—many object to putting a dollar value on wetlands or endangered species on strictly philosophical grounds. Others question the method of finding the right price for lost wetlands or endangered species.

An additional solution would be to compute the TBL in terms of an index. Like this, one removes the unsuited units issue and, as long as there is a universally accepted accounting method, allows for comparisons between entities, e.g., comparing performance between companies, cities, development projects or some other benchmark.

For example, the Indiana Business Research Centre's Innovation Index compares a county versus the nation's performance for a variety of components. However, there remains some subjectivity even when using an index. For example, how is the index components weighted? Would each "P" get equal weighting? What about the sub-components within each "P"? Do they each get equal weighting? Is the people category more important than the planet? Who decides?

Another alternative would do away with measuring sustainability using dollars or using an index. If the users of the TBL had the stomach for it, each sustainability measure would stand alone. "Acres of wetlands" would be a measure, for example, and progress would be gauged based on wetland creation, destruction or status quo over time. The downside to this approach is the increase of metrics that may be relevant to measuring sustainability. The TBL user may get metric fatigue.

Having discussed the difficulties with calculating the TBL, we turn our attention to potential metrics for inclusion in a TBL calculation. Following that, we will discuss how businesses and other entities have applied the TBL framework.

What Measures go into the Index?

For calculating the TBL, no universal standard method is followed. Neither is there a universally accepted standard for the measures that comprise each of the three TBL categories. This can be viewed as a strong point because it allows a user to adapt the general framework to the needs of different entities (businesses or nonprofits), different projects or policies (infrastructure investment or educational programs), or different geographic boundaries (a city, region or country).

Both a business and local government agency may measure environmental sustainability in the same terms, say decreasing the amount of solid waste that goes into landfills, but a local mass transit might calculate success in terms of passenger miles, while a for-profit bus company would calculate success in terms of earnings per share. The TBL can accommodate these differences.

Additionally, the TBL is able to be case (or project) specific or allow a broad scope measuring impacts across large geographic boundaries or a narrow geographic scope like a small town. A case (or project) specific TBL would gauge the effects of a particular project in a specific location, such as a community building a park. The TBL can also be valid to infrastructure projects at the state level or energy policy at the national level.

The level of the entity, type of project and the geographic scope will drive many of the decisions about what measures to include. The set of measures will finally be determined by stakeholders and subject matter experts and the ability to gather the necessary data. While there is significant literature on the appropriate measures to use for sustainability at the state or national levels, in the end, data availability will drive the TBL calculations. Many of the traditional sustainability measures, measures vetted through academic discourse, are presented below.

1. **Economic Measures**

    Economic variables ought to be variables that deal with the bottom line and the flow of money. It could look at income or expenditures, taxes, business climate factors, employment, and business diversity factors. Specific examples include:
    - Personal income
    - Cost of underemployment
    - Establishment churn
    - Establishment sizes
    - Job growth
    - Employment distribution by sector
    - Percentage of firms in each sector
    - Revenue by sector contributing to gross state product.

2. **Environmental Measures**

    Environmental variables should signify measurements of natural resources and reflect potential influences to its viability. It could include air and water quality, energy consumption, natural resources, solid and toxic waste, and land use/land cover. Preferably, having long-range trends available for each of the environmental variables would aid organisations recognize the impacts a project or policy would have on the area. Specific examples include:
    - Sulphur dioxide concentration
    - Concentration of nitrogen oxides
    - Selected priority pollutants
    - Excessive nutrients
    - Electricity consumption
    - Fossil fuel consumption
    - Solid waste management
    - Hazardous waste management
    - Change in land use/land cover.

3. **Social Measures**

Social variables refer to social dimensions of a community or region and could include measurements of education, equity and access to social resources, health and well-being, quality of life, and social capital. The examples listed below are a small snippet of potential variables:

- Unemployment rate
- Female labour force participation rate
- Median household income
- Relative poverty
- Percentage of population with a post-secondary degree or certificate
- Average commute time
- Violent crimes per capita
- Health-adjusted life expectancy.

Data for many of these methods are collected at the state and national levels, but are also accessible at the local or community level. Many are apt for a community to utilize when constructing a TBL. However, as the geographic scope and the nature of the project narrow, the set of appropriate measures can change. For local or community-based projects, the TBL measures of success are best determined locally.

There are several similar approaches to protect stakeholder participation and input in designing the TBL framework such as developing a decision matrix to incorporate public preferences into project planning and decision-making, using a "narrative format" to solicit shareholder participation and comprehensive project evaluation, and having stakeholders rank and weigh components of a sustainability framework according to community priorities. For example, a community may consider a significant measure of success for an entrepreneurial development program to be the number of woman-owned companies formed over a five-year time period. Ultimately, it will be the organisation's responsibility to produce a final set of measures applicable to the task at hand.

Variations of the Triple Bottom Line Measurement

The use of the TBL by businesses, nonprofits and governments are motivated by the principles of economic, environmental and social sustainability, but vary with a view to the way they measure the three categories of outcomes. Proponents who have developed and applied sustainability evaluation frameworks like the TBL encountered many challenges, chief among them, how to make an index that is both comprehensive and meaningful and how to identify suitable data for the variables that compose the index.

The Genuine Progress Indicator (GPI), for example, consists of 25 variables that encompass economic, social and environmental factors. Those variables are converted into monetary units and summed into a single, dollar-denominated measure. Minnesota developed its own progress indicator comprised of 42 variables that focused on the goals of a healthy economy and gauged progress in achieving these goals.

There is a large body of literature on integrated assessment and sustainability measures that grew out of the disciplines that measure environmental impact. These are not controlled by stringent economic theory for determining changes in social welfare. Researchers in environmental policy argue that the three categories economic, social and environmental must be incorporated in order to make out the complete picture of the consequences that a regulation, policy or economic development project may have and to measure policy options and tradeoffs.

Who uses the Triple Bottom Line?

Businesses, nonprofits and government entities alike can all use the TBL.

1. **Businesses**

The TBL and its core value of sustainability have become convincing in the business world due to accumulating subjective evidence of greater long-term profitability. For example, minimising waste from packaging can also decrease costs. Examples of the firms that have been following these approaches are General Electric, Unilever, Proctor and Gamble, 3M and Cascade Engineering. Although these companies do not have an index-based TBL through which one can see how they measure sustainability using the TBL concept. Cascade Engineering, for example, a private firm that does not need to file the detailed financial paperwork of public companies, has identified the following variables for their TBL scorecard:

- **Economic**
    - Amount of taxes paid.
- **Social**
    - Average hours of training/employee
    - From welfare to career retention
    - Charitable contributions.
- **Environmental/Safety**
    - Safety incident rate
    - Lost/restricted workday rate
    - Sales dollars per kilowatt hours
    - Greenhouse gas emissions
    - Use of post-consumer and industrial recycled material
    - Water consumption
    - Amount of waste to landfill.

2. **Non-profits**

   TBL have been implemented by many non-profit organisations and some organisations have partnered with private firms to address broad sustainability issues that have an effect on mutual stakeholders. Companies recognise that aligning with non-profit organisations makes good business sense, mainly those non-profits with objectives of economic prosperity, social well-being and environmental protection.

   The Ford Foundation has funded studies that used variations of the TBL to determine the effects of programs to enhance wealth in dozens of rural regions across the United States. Another example is RSF Social Finance, a non-profit organisation that exceptionally focuses on how their investments develop all three categories of the TBL. While RSF takes an original approach to the TBL concept, one can see how the TBL can be adapted to nearly any organisation. Their approach includes the following:

   - **Food and Agriculture** (economic): Investigate new economic models that support sustainable food and agriculture while raising public awareness of the value of organic and biodynamic farming.
   - **Ecological Stewardship** (environmental): Give financial support to organisations and projects dedicated to sustaining, regenerating and preserving the earth's ecosystems, particularly integrated, systems-based and culturally relevant approaches.
   - **Education and the Arts** (social): Fund education and arts projects that are holistic and therapeutic.

3. **Government**

   TBL and analogous sustainability assessment frameworks are increasingly adopted by the State, regional and local governments and as decision-making and performance-monitoring tools.

   Policy-makers apply these sustainability assessment frameworks to make a decision which actions they should or should not take to make society more sustainable. Policy-makers would like to make out the cause and effect relationship between actions—projects or policies—and whether the results move society toward or away from sustainability.

   Internationally, the European Union apply integrated assessment to make out the "likely positive and negative impacts of proposed policy actions, enabling informed political judgments to be made about the proposal and recognize trade-offs in achieving competing objectives." The EU guidelines have themselves been the subject of analysis and have undergone several rounds of improvement. The process of refining the guidelines shows both the transparency of the process and the EU commitment to integrated assessment.

3.13.2 Content of Sustainability Reports

(i) **Welcome Letter from the Board Chair and/or President/CEO**
(ii) **Table of Contents**
(iii) **Corporate sustainability Vision/Mission/Values**
- Vision Statement
- Mission Statement
- Statement of Values

(iv) **Key Sustainability Results Overview**
- Economic (KPIs)
- Environmental (KPIs)
- Social (KPIs)

(v) **Annual Initiatives and Achievements**
- Economic Sustainability Initiatives and Achievements.
- Environmental Sustainability Initiatives and Achievements.
- Social Sustainability Initiatives and Achievements.

(vi) **Organisational Profile**
- Corporate Facts At-a-Glance (e.g. when founded, headquarters/satellite locations, products/services provided, revenue, number of employees and key customers/suppliers).
- Sustainable Technologies (e.g. use of technology to minimise environmental impact, reduce process cycle-time, improve overall questions and improve customer service).
- Financial information (e.g. total revenue, net income, operating expenses, income taxes, total assets, long-term debt and shareowners equity).
- Governance and Management Structures (e.g. listing of specific governance/management structures, controls and processes to ensure the interests of stakeholders/shareowners are protected).
- Key Business Processes (e.g. business Plan review, Formal Process Documentation System, Standard Operating Procedures Flowcharting Process, ISO 14001 Certification, Six Sigma Projects, Global Product Development System, Order-To-Delivery System and Just-in-Time Inventory System.
- Ethics (e.g. listing of the organisations code of ethics statement, ethics questionnaires, vendor ethics and ethics resulting among the workforce).
- Corporate Compliance (e.g., Listing of all industry regulatory requirements and results obtained).

(vii) **Corporate Awards and Recognition**
- Workforce
- Diversity
- Community
- Environmental
- Financial
- Brand Excellence
- Industry
- Global.

(viii) **History of the Organisations Corporate Sustainability Report**
- Reasons for Issuing the Report.
- Corporate Progress in Sustainable Practice addressed in the Report.
- Performance Indicators used to measure overall Corporate Sustainability listed in the Report.
- Reporting Guidelines (e.g., based on Global Reporting Initiative (GRI) guidelines known as GRI-G3. The GRI is an independent institution that provides a framework for corporate sustainability reporting. See website www.globalreporting.org
- Highlights of the Report focus on Economic, Environmental and Social Sustainability.

(ix) **Economic Sustainability Highlights**
- Economic Value Generated and Distributed (e.g., revenues, operating costs, employee compensation, donations, community investments, retained earnings and payments to capital providers and governments).
- Coverage of the organisations defined benefit plan obligations.
- Significant financial assistance received from Government Programs/Grants.
- Policy, practices and proportion of spending on locally based suppliers.
- Development and impact of infrastructure investments and services.
- Procedures for local wring and proportion of senior management hired from the local community where business is conducted.
- Development and impact of infra-structure investments and services provided for public benefit.

(x) Environmental Sustainability Highlights

- Greening the supply chain.
- Development of an environmental statement.
- Addressing greenhouse gas emissions and climate charge issues that are impacted by corporate initiatives.
- Investments in fuel-saving technologies.
- Conservation of energy via facility design, operational practices, renewal energy and retrofitting.
- Optimisation of the corporate transportation network to minimise miles driven/flown.
- Employee engagement programs.
- Fuel and energy conservation programs.
- Construction projects that are LEED certified.
- Recycling and waste management programs.
- Disposal of hazardous and non-hazardous wastes.
- Environment Management Systems patterned after the ISO14001 Standard

(xi) Social Sustainability Highlights (Examples Listed)

- Global workforce development initiatives.
- Workforce diversity and equal opportunity.
- Supplier diversity program.
- Employee health and safety programs.
- Primary corporate-wide safety initiatives.
- Employee feedback and opinion surveys.
- Community engagement projects.
- Human rights practices/policies required of corporate vendors.
- Training and education of the workforce.
- Percentage and total number of business units analysed for risks.
- Actions taken in response to incidents of corruption.
- Monetary value of significant fines and total number of non-monetary sanctions for non-compliance with laws and regulations.
- Life cycles states in which health and safety impacts of products/services are assessed for improvement.

(xii) Future Corporate Sustainability Plans
- Looking ahead for the future (e.g. detail a set of new and/expanded targets and goals as they relate to economic, environmental and social performance).
- Future economic initiatives (e.g. address issues such as rewarding shareholders, providing jobs and creating a positive economic impact on communities were business is conducted).
- Future environmental initiatives (e.g. address issues such as improving environmental strategies and results, deploying technologies to reduce the organisations carbon footprint, further reduction of carbon emissions and saving millions of gallons of fuel on the organisations transportation fleet).
- Future social initiatives (e.g. address issues such as increasing the organisations commitment to communities were business is conducted, better leverage of the organisations intellectual and physical assets, increase funds and workforce expertise to help non-profit organisations).
- Future Key Performance Indicators (e.g. address future Key Performance Indicators KPIs for Economic, Environmental and Social initiatives).

Appendix Sustainability Results

Global Reporting Initiative – GRI (GRI-G3) can be positioned in the Appendix and serve as the foundation for displaying key performance indicators applicable to the Organisations business and it offers a reliable framework for sustainability reporting. Information on the GRI can be downloaded on the www.globalreporting.org website. The GRI has become the global de-facto standard in sustainability reporting since its inception in 1997) The GRI Index appears in Appendix G of this Manual and can be downloaded from this CD-ROM.

3.13.3 Corporate Social Responsibility (CSR) Reporting

Nowadays, Stakeholders are holding companies liable for non-financial performance on issues such as product quality, employee equity, community engagement, and environmental stewardship. Many stakeholders are trying that companies 'prove themselves' by openly sharing information on social and environmental policies, programs, and performance.

Effective CSR reporting and communication programs can build trust by sharing successes, challenges, risks, opportunities and strategic vision with consumers, employees, communities and investors. Reporting can also act as a management framework to systematically track, evaluate and improve a company's CSR performance over time.

Companies progress along a reporting continuum. Reporting difficulty and transparency increases as companies move along the CSR continuum, from focusing mainly on maintaining regulatory observance through to being a transformational leader.

Disclosure	Internal Accountability	External Accountability	Transparency
Ensuring that the level of disclosure meets regulatory requirements so that the company is able to maintain its license to operate. Reporting criteria are draw exclusively from permit conditions and/or regulatory requirements.	Conducting an internal review of CSR activities, to ensure that they are addressing key operational needs including meeting permit conditions and/or regulatory requirements, respecting international voluntary standards and consistent with commonly used reporting methodologies such as Global Reporting Initiative (GRI). There is an internal check and balance on the quality of information included in the report.	Using a materiality analysis to prioritize what is reported, ensuring that the most relevant issues are included in the report. Validating the accuracy of the data through third party assurance and/or engagement with impacted stakeholders to increase the level of transparency and acceptance of report conclusions.	Involving stakeholders in the development of strategic priorities, including the review of key policies, programs and performance. External outreach is done to ensure that perceptions and expectations of key stakeholders are understood and addressed, so that reporting focuses on significant issues. This external focus is an important step to developing a robust reporting strategy.

Corporate CSR reports differ to a great extent in format, length and detail. There are, though, certain elements and disclosures that consistently come into view in such reports. Those elements and disclosures include (1) an opening letter from the company's CEO and/or chief CSR executive (noting the company's commitment to CSR issues and its willingness to discuss challenges and promote successes relating thereto), (2) the company's CSR policy or mission statement, (3) a "forward-looking statements" disclaimer and (4) most significant, disclosures addressing issues most important to each of the company's key stakeholders, for example:

- **Shareholders:** Addressing the company's business model and corporate governance, including disclosing the role of the board in risk management, in sustainability reporting and in evaluating CSR performance.
- **Employees:** Addressing diversity, health and safety, training and mentoring, employee relations, and wages and benefits.
- **Customers:** Addressing customer service and privacy.

- **Suppliers:** Addressing labour standards and whether suppliers are required to implement their own CSR programmes.
- **Communities:** Addressing corporate philanthropy and charitable contributions, community investment and partnerships, volunteerism and the environmental impact of operations.
- **Governments and Regulators:** Addressing lobbying, public policy and the effects of and compliance with environmental regulations.

3.13.4 Social Accounting

Social accounting (also known as social accounting and auditing, social and environmental accounting, corporate social reporting, corporate social responsibility reporting, non-financial reporting or accounting) is defined as the process of communicating the social and environmental effects of organisations' economic actions to specific interest groups within society and to society at large.

Social accounting is usually applied in the perspective of business, or corporate social responsibility (CSR). Although any organisation such as, NGOs, charities, and government agencies may take help of social accounting. Social accounting can also be used in combination with Community-Based Monitoring (CBM). For a toolkit on Community-Based Monitoring methodology, see www.communitymonitoring.org.

Social accounting highlights the idea of corporate accountability. D. Crowther defines social accounting in this sense as "an approach to reporting a firm's activities which stresses the need for the identification of socially relevant behaviour, the determination of those to whom the company is responsible for its social performance and the growth of appropriate measures and reporting techniques."

Social accounting is often used as an umbrella term to describe a broad field of research and practice. The application of more narrow terms to express a specific interest is thus not uncommon. Environmental accounting may specifically refer to the research or practice of accounting for an organisation's impact on the natural environment. Sustainability accounting is often used to express the measuring and the quantitative analysis of social and economic sustainability.

Purpose

Social accounting challenges financial accounting for giving a narrow image of the interaction between society and organisations, and as a result, artificially confining the subject of accounting.

Social accounting seems to expand the scope of accounting in the sense that it should:
- Concern itself with more than only economic events
- Not be exclusively expressed in financial terms
- Be accountable to a broader group of stakeholders
- Broaden its purpose beyond reporting financial success

It points to the fact that companies through their actions influence their external environment (sometimes positively and many a times negatively) and should as a result account for these effects as part of their standard accounting practices. Social accounting is in this sense closely associated to the economic concept of externality.

Social accounting recommends an alternative account of important economic entities. It has the "potential to expose the tension between pursuing economic profit and the pursuit of social and environmental objectives".

The principle of social accounting can be approached from two different perspectives, namely for management control purposes or accountability purposes.

Accountability vs. Authority enjoyed

Social accounting for accountability reasons is intended to support and assist the search of society's objectives. These objectives can be multiple but can characteristically be expressed in terms of social and environmental desirability and sustainability. So as to create informed choices on these objectives, the flow of information in society in general, and in accounting specially, needs to provide for democratic decision-making. In democratic systems, Gray argues, there must then be flows of information in which those controlling the resources offer accounts to society of their use of those resources: a system of corporate accountability.

Society is seen to benefit from executing a social and environmental approach to accounting in a number of ways like:

- Honouring stakeholders' rights of information
- Balancing corporate power with corporate responsibility
- Increasing transparency of corporate activity
- Identifying social and environmental costs of economic success

Management Control

Social accounting for the function of management control is considered to support and help the achievement of an organisation's own objectives.

Because social accounting is concerned with considerable self-reporting on a systemic level, individual reports are often referred to as social audits. The first complete internal model for social accounting and audit, 1981, was designed for social enterprises to assist plan and calculate their social, environmental and financial progress towards attaining their planned objectives.

Organisations are seen to benefit from implementing social accounting practices in a number of ways like:

- Increased information for decision-making
- More accurate product or service costing

- Enhanced image management and public relations
- Identification of social responsibilities
- Identification of market development opportunities
- Maintaining legitimacy

According to BITC the "process of reporting on responsible businesses performance to stakeholders" (social accounting) facilitates combining such practices into business practices, as well as recognizing future risks and opportunities.

The management control view thus focuses on the individual organisation.

Critics of this approach indicate that the kind nature of companies is assumed. Here, responsibility, and accountability, is mainly left in the hands of the organisation concerned.

Scope

1. **Formal accountability**

    In social accounting larger organisations are the center of attention such as multinational corporations (MNCs), and their visible, external accounts rather than informally produced accounts or accounts for internal use. The need for making MNCs liable is specified by the financial and cultural distance of these organisations to those who are affecting and affected by it.

    Social accounting also questions the decrease of all significant information to financial form. Financial data is seen as only one element of the accounting language.

2. **Self-reporting and third party audits**

    In most countries, existing legislation only controls a fraction of accounting for socially related corporate activity. As a result, most accessible social, environmental and sustainability reports are created willingly by organisations and in that sense often look like financial statements. While companies' efforts in this regard are typically admired, there seems to be a tension between voluntary reporting and accountability, for companies are likely to generate reports supporting their interests.

    The re-arrangement of social and environmental data companies already produce as part of their normal reporting practice into an independent social audit is called a silent or shadow account.

    An alternative phenomenon is the formation of external social audits by groups or individuals independent of the respected organisation and typically without its support. External social audits thus also attempt to blur the boundaries between organisations and society and to establish social accounting as a fluid two-way communication process. Companies are sought to be held accountable in spite of their approval. It is in this sense that external audits part with attempts to establish social accounting as an intrinsic feature of organisational behaviour. The reports of Social Audit Ltd. in the 1970s on Tube Investments, Avon Rubber and Coalite and Chemical Products Ltd. laid the foundations for much of the later work on social audits.

3. **Reporting areas**

Unlike in financial accounting, the substance of concern is by definition less specific in social accounting; this is due to an aspired all-encompassing approach to corporate activity. It is usually decided that social accounting will cover an organisation's relationship with the natural environment, its employees, and ethical concerns focussing on consumers and products, and local and international communities. Other issues comprise corporate action on matter of ethnicity and gender.

4. **Audience**

Social accounting take the place of the traditional audit audience, which is mainly consist of a company's shareholders and the financial community, by providing information to all of the organisation's stakeholders. A stakeholder of an organisation is anyone who can influence or is influenced by the organisation. This often includes, but is not limited to, suppliers of inputs, employees and trade unions, consumers, members of local communities, society at large and governments. Different stakeholders have different rights of information. These rights can be stipulated by law, but also by non-legal codes, corporate values, mission statements and moral rights. The rights of information are thus determined by "society, the organisation and its stakeholders".

3.13.5 Environmental Accounting

Environmental accounting which is a division of social accounting emphasises on the cost structure and environmental performance of a company. It chiefly explains the preparation, presentation, and communication of information related to an organisation's interaction with the natural environment. Although environmental accounting is most commonly undertaken as voluntary self-reporting by companies, third-party reports by government agencies, NGOs and other bodies positioned to pressure for environmental accountability.

Accounting for impacts on the environment may occur within a company's financial statements, concerning to liabilities, commitments and contingencies for the remediation of contaminated lands or other financial concerns arising from pollution. Such reporting basically expresses financial issues arising from environmental legislation. More typically, environmental accounting describes the reporting of quantitative and detailed environmental data within the non-financial sections of the annual report or in separate (including online) environmental reports. Such reports may account for pollution emissions, resources used, or wildlife habitat damaged or re-established.

Large companies usually in their reports put prime highlighting on eco-efficiency, referring to the decline of resource and energy use and waste production per unit of product or service. A complete picture which accounts for all inputs, outputs and wastes of the organisation, might not necessarily emerge. Whilst companies can often exhibit immense success in eco-efficiency, their ecological footprint, that is an estimate of total environmental impact, may move independently following changes in output.

Legislation for compulsory environmental reporting exists in some form in Denmark, Netherlands, Australia, the UK and Korea. The United Nations has been greatly concerned with the implementation of environmental accounting practices, remarkably in the United Nations Division for Sustainable Development publication Environmental Management Accounting Procedures and Principles (2002).

3.14 Social Responsibility Standard: ISO 26000

ISO 26000 presents practical assistance on socially responsible behaviour and possible actions. It intends at assisting organisations to become aware of, analyse and address issues concerning social responsibility. It is built as an overarching document that can be used for a wide variety of countries, organisations, operations, roles in the supply chain context and type of activity.

ISO 26000 contains the following elements:

3.14.1 Definition of Social Responsibility

ISO 26000 defines the social responsibility of an organisation as "the responsibility for the impacts of its decisions and activities on society and the environment, through transparent and ethical behaviour that:
- adds to sustainable development, health and the welfare of society.
- takes into account the expectations of stakeholders.
- is in compliance with applicable law and consistent with international norms of behaviour and
- is integrated throughout the organisation and practiced in its relationships.

This definition is based on international standards of corporate behaviour identified in reference instruments such as the ILO (International Labour Organisation) standards, the Universal Declaration of Human Rights, the OECD guidelines and the UN Global Compact.

3.14.2 Seven Principles

Organisations using ISO 26000 should respect the following seven principles:
- Accountability for the organisation's impacts on society and the environment.
- Transparency in the organisation's decisions and activities that have impact on society and the environment.

- Ethical behaviour at all times.
- Respect, consider and respond to the interests of the organisation's stakeholders (employees).
- Accept that respect for the rule of law is mandatory.
- Respect international norms of behaviour, while adhering to the principle of respect for the rule of law and
- Respect human rights and recognise both their importance and their universality.

3.14.3 Seven Core Subjects

After recognising the seven principles, an organisation should concentrate on the subsequent core subjects in order to recognize the issues and priorities that are applicable for the organisation:

- Organisational governance.
- Human rights.
- Labour practices.
- Environment.
- Fair operating practices.
- Consumer issues and
- Community involvement and development.

3.14.4 ISO 26000 - Guidance on Social Responsibility

The International Standards Organisation (ISO) recognised the need for guidance in this area with the development of a new standard, ISO 26000 – Guidance on Social Responsibility. For the duration of the six- year development of this standard, ISO recognized and sought input from key stakeholder groups including representatives from industry, labour, government, consumers and NGOs.

The standard offers guidance on the following core SR subjects which are organisational governance, human rights, labour practices, the environment, fair operating practices, consumer issues, community involvement and development. To provide further guidance on the topics enclosed by the clauses of ISO 26000, Annex A of the standard provides an informative list of current cross-sector initiatives and tools such as:

- The Global Reporting Initiative (GRI)
- CSR 360 – Global Partner Network (Business in the Community [BITC] UK)
- EFQM Framework for CSR & Excellence Model
- Social Accountability International (SAI – SA8000 standard)

The final draft was recently approved by ISO members (September 2010) for publication in November 2010 and adoption as an Irish Standard. It should be noted that **ISO 26000 is not intended for certification purposes** and is a guidance standard.

3.15 Global Compact Principles

The UN Global Compact's ten principles in the areas of human rights, labour, the environment and anti-corruption enjoy universal consensus and are derived from:
- The Universal Declaration of Human Rights
- The International Labour Organisation's Declaration on Fundamental Principles and Rights at Work
- The Rio Declaration on Environment and Development
- The United Nations Convention Against Corruption

The UN Global Compact asks companies to embrace, support and enact, within their sphere of influence, a set of core values in the areas of human rights, labour standards, the environment and anti-corruption:

1. **Human Rights**

   Principle 1: Businesses should support and respect the protection of internationally proclaimed human rights.

   Principle 2: Make sure that they are not complicit in human rights abuses.

2. **Labour**

   Principle 3: Businesses should uphold the freedom of association and the effective recognition of the right to collective bargaining.

   Principle 4: The elimination of all forms of forced and compulsory labour.

   Principle 5: The effective abolition of child labour.

   Principle 6: The elimination of discrimination in respect of employment and occupation.

3. **Environment**

   Principle 7: Businesses should support a precautionary approach to environmental challenges.

   Principle 8: Undertake initiatives to promote greater environmental responsibility.

   Principle 9: Encourage the development and diffusion of environmentally friendly technologies.

4. **Anti-Corruption**

   Principle 10: Businesses should work against corruption in all its forms, including extortion and bribery.

3.16 Environmental Impact Assessment

Environmental Impact Assessment (EIA) is a key aspect of many large scale planning applications. It is a technique which is devised to help organisations know the potential environmental impacts of key development proposals. Both the process and the result of EIA can be complex and confusing leaving local communities uncertain as to how a development might influence them. This guide is planned as a wide introduction to the Environmental Impact Assessment (EIA). The material is drawn from regulations, circulars and guidance and is designed to help individuals understand what EIA is and in what situations it should be applied. The guide is not planned to provide guidance on how to prepare an EIA. For example it does not clarify how to prepare an archaeological survey or landscape evaluation. The overall theme of this guide is to encourage local communities to engage in the EIA process. Experts don't always know best and by ignoring local knowledge their decision may have a disastrous consequence for local people living near development sites.

In a nutshell EIA is an information gathering exercise carried out by the developer and other bodies which facilitates a local planning authority to recognize the environmental effects of a development before making a decision whether or not it should go ahead. Infact, significant thing about environmental assessments is the emphasis on using the best available sources of objective information and in carrying out a systematic and holistic process which should be bias free and allow the local authority and the whole community to properly appreciate the impact of the proposed development. Environmental assessment should lead to improved standards of development and in some cases development not happening at all. Where developments do go ahead environmental assessments should help to recommend proper mitigation measures. Environmental impact assessment is meant to be a systematic process which leads to a final product, the Environmental Statement (ES).

Steps in EIA

Although legislation and practice differ around the world, the basic components of an EIA would essentially comprise of the following stages:

1. Screening to find out which projects or developments need a full or incomplete impact assessment study.
2. Scoping to recognize which potential impacts are applicable to assess (based on legislative requirements, international conventions, expert knowledge and public involvement), to recognize alternative solutions that avoid, lessen or compensate unfavorable impacts on biodiversity (including the option of not proceeding with the development, finding alternative designs or sites which avoid the impacts, including safeguards in the design of the project, or providing compensation for adverse impacts), and to conclude to derive terms of reference for the impact assessment.
3. Assessment and evaluation of impacts and development of alternatives, to forecast and identify the likely environmental impacts of a projected project or development, including the detailed elaboration of alternatives.

4. Reporting the Environmental Impact Statement (EIS) or EIA report, including an environmental management plan (EMP), and a non-technical summary for the general audience.
5. Review of the Environmental Impact Statement (EIS), based on the terms of reference (scoping) and public (including authority) participation.
6. Decision-making on whether to approve the project or not, and under what conditions and
7. Monitoring, compliance, enforcement and environmental auditing. Monitor whether the predicted impacts and proposed mitigation measures occur as defined in the EMP. Verify the compliance of proponent with the EMP, to ensure that unpredicted impacts or failed mitigation measures are identified and addressed in a timely fashion.

3.17 Life Cycle Analysis or Life Cycle Assessment (LCA)

Life cycle assessment (LCA) is a technique of examining the environmental impacts of a process, product or activity along its life cycle, for example from 'the cradle to the grave'.

The objective of most LCA studies is to assist food producers, manufacturers, mining companies and product producers inspect inputs (such as resources, materials and electricity) and outputs (such as waste) and the impacts of these to develop efficiencies and make out where better environmental performance can be achieved.

The LCA approach forms the basis for a range of well-known 'footprint' assessments including 'carbon footprinting'.

Carbon Footprints

Carbon footprints give a means of quantifying the amount of global warming potential or greenhouse gas equivalents (as units of carbon dioxide) emitted through the whole life cycle of a product or consumer or business activities.

It is used to determine the amount of offsets necessary by a business to sell their product as 'carbon neutral' but is not used to determine carbon liability (for tax or emissions trading scheme). It is also valuable for determining where in the operations changes can be made to become more carbon neutral and in many cases save money.

Carbon footprinting has gained wide-scale public awareness through programs like the Planet Ark and the Carbon Trust UK's Carbon Reduction Label and a publicly available specification (PAS 2050 2008) sets the benchmark for assessing product life cycle GHG emissions using an LCA approach.

Strengths and Weaknesses of LCA

One of the strong points of LCA is that scientists can comprise the consumption or production of resources such as energy or carbon emissions, though the products are moved to another geographic location or if changed from one form to another.

For example, inputs can be followed along the lifespan of producing tinned vegetables covering things like energy used to produce fertiliser, transport seeds to the farm, run refrigerators, process the vegetable, package the product and then process the waste at the end of the product's life.

Some of the disadvantages of LCA include:

- Results obtained can be definite and it can be hard to extrapolate out to all industries or all farms
- Insufficient inventory data may be accessible and best estimates are required
- Gathering this data is time-consuming and costly

Sharing of information can help to overcome some of these challenges and CSIRO is establishing various databases to facilitate more efficient and economical LCA studies in the future.

Steps in LCA

Life Cycle Assessment evolved from the 1960s and is now defined with an International Standard, meaning that there are strict rules about how it is to be applied and relied upon.

Step 1: Defining the goals and boundaries

The three most common goals for using LCA are to:

- Quantify product impacts
- Identify main areas for improvements
- Compare alternative life cycle scenarios

After deciding the goals, scientists must decide on what features of the product are to be examined. Some examples may be the cause of production on the environment, the impact of consuming the product on nutrition or the impacts from production or decisions on economic factors.

A consistent unit must be decided like impact per kilogram of product, depending on what is being examined. This will facilitate comparisons between alternative life cycle scenarios. In the case of beef production a 'per kilo' assessment is done.

It is significant to have clearly defined system boundaries for any LCA project with clear objectives about how much information is required for each step and how strong or specific the conclusions can be at the end.

It is also necessary to balance the nature of the information available and what is required to help make the best decisions. In some cases LCAs are done with 'best available' information meaning that the results often need to be considered with certain restrictions.

Step 2: Building the Life Cycle Inventory

LCAs need a lot of data on the product, production processes and impacts, often meaning significant research to collect the data. Through 'Life Cycle Inventory' (LCI), all this information is gathered together.

To carry out LCI, it is important to examine and split up the processes involved in producing the product. If we take the example of an LCI for a food product, the main stages may be examining the agricultural crops and products such as meat, vegetable, grains, herbs, spices; the food additives such as salt, flavours, additives; the packaging process; and the transport processes.

LCI for each individual component must be attained by gathering information for each life cycle stage for completing the study. In many cases, data may be available from crop growers or product suppliers but sometimes data may need to be collected.

When this is not possible, generic information from commercial databases such as Ecoinvent, LCA Food DK Database and Australasian LCA Database, may be used. On the other hand, using generic information will have an impact on the LCA result as environmental impact may differ depending on the location of the supply.

Step 3: Assessing Impact and determining Improvements

When the LCI is done the information needs to be transformed to suitable impact factors such as water or carbon footprints. It is significant to note that studies focusing on a single issue, for example freshwater use, do not provide indicators of overall environmental sustainability, and there may in fact be other impacts that have not been considered.

The decision to focus on certain environmental impacts must be made with the explicit awareness of the potential implications of leaving other factors out. For example, in manufacturing processes, minimising the amount of water being flushed down drains may raise levels of toxicity due to a lower dilution factor.

To correctly interpret LCA results, it is important to explore these relationships to define the information. In many cases, using LCA results should be done only after considering all of the relevant environmental impacts as well as other social and economic concerns.

3.18 Social Impact Assessment (SIA)

Social Impact Assessment (SIA) is predicated on the idea that development interventions have social ramifications and it is imperative that decision-makers understand the consequences of their decisions before they act and people affected get the opportunity to participate in designing their future. Social assessment facilitates to create the project responsive to social development concerns. Developmental initiatives informed by social assessment alleviate poverty, enhance inclusion and build ownership while minimising and compensating for adverse social impacts on the vulnerable and the poor.

Social Impact Assessment can be defined in terms of attempts to assess or estimate, in advance, the social consequences that are likely to follow definite policy actions (including programs and the adoption of new policies), and specific government actions. It is a process that offers a structure for prioritising, gathering, analysing, and including social information and participation into the design and delivery of developmental interventions. It ensures that development interventions: (i) are informed and take into account the key relevant social issues; and (ii) incorporate a participation strategy for involving a wide range of stakeholders.

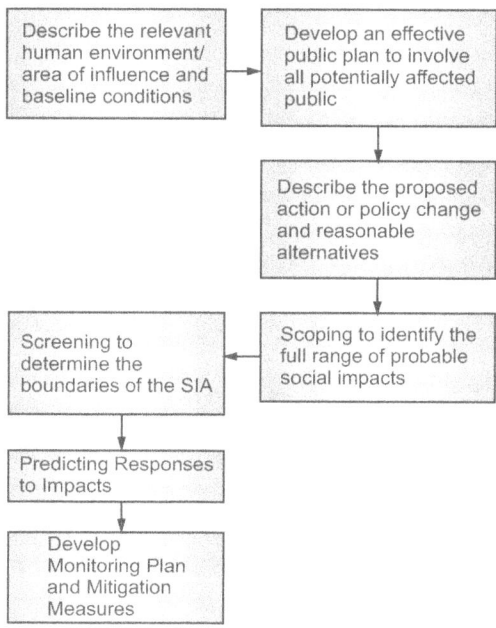

Fig. 3.3: Stages in Social Impact

Step 1: Baseline Conditions

The baseline conditions are the existing conditions and past trends related with the human environment in which the projected activity is to occur. This differs with the kind of project being taken up. For example, in the case of construction projects, the baseline unit may be a cluster of population identified along with the distribution of special populations at risk. The appropriate human environment may be a more discrete set of concerned and affected public, interest groups, organisations and institutions. The generic set of factors for analysis should include (a) population characteristics (b) community and institutional structures (c) political and social resources (d) individual and family changes and (e) community resources.

Step 2: Public Involvement

In this step identifying and working with all potentially affected groups starting at the very beginning of planning for the proposed action(s). Groups affected by proposed actions comprise of those who live nearby; those who will be affected by the development intervention; those who are forced to relocate because of a project; and those who have interest in a new project or policy change but may not live in proximity. Others affected include those who might normally use the land on which the project is located (such as farmers who have to plough along a transmission line). Still others include those affected by the influx of seasonal residents who may have to pay higher prices for food or rent, or pay higher taxes to cover the cost of expanded community services.

Once identified, representatives from each group should be systematically interviewed to establish potential areas of concern/impact, and ways each representative might be involved in the planning decision process. Public meetings by themselves are insufficient for collecting information about public perceptions. Survey data can be used to define the potentially affected population. In this first step, the pieces are put in place for a public involvement programme which will last throughout the environmental and social impact assessment process.

Step 3: Project Description and Identification of Alternatives

In the next step, the proposed action is described in sufficient detail to enable identification of the data requirements to frame the SIA. This should include:

1. Location
2. Land requirements
3. Needs for ancillary facilities (roads, transmission lines, sewer and water lines)
4. Construction schedule
5. Size of the workforce (construction and operation, by year or month)
6. Facility size and shape
7. Need for a local workforce
8. Institutional resources

It is equally important to recognize feasible alternatives for proposed actions within the ambit of the project.

Step 4: Screening

Screening is done to determine the boundaries of SIA. It is concerned with selecting 'developments' that necessitate assessment and avoiding 'developments' that do not require one. Conduct of screening thus involves making a proposal on the 'developments' in terms of its impact on people and of its relative importance. A certain level of basic information about the proposal and its location is necessary for this purpose. Screening procedures employed can be based on the already existing legal frameworks.

Step 5: Scoping

After initial screening, the SIA variables require to be selected for further assessment. Consideration needs to be given both to the impacts perceived by the acting agency and to those perceived by affected groups and communities. The principal methods to be used by experts are reviews of the existing social science literature, public scoping, public surveys and public participation techniques. It is significant for the views of affected people to be taken into consideration. Ideally, all affected people or groups contribute to the selection of the variables assessed through either a participatory process or by review made by responsible officials.

Relevant criteria for selecting significant impacts include the

1. Probability of the event occurring
2. Number of people including indigenous populations that will be affected
3. Duration of impacts (long-term vs. short-term)
4. Value of benefits and costs to impacted groups (intensity of impacts)
5. Extent to which the impact is reversible or can be mitigated
6. Likelihood of causing subsequent impacts
7. Relevance to present and future policy decision
8. Uncertainty over possible effects
9. Presence or absence of controversy over the issue

Step 6: Predicting Responses to Impacts

"Social impacts" refer to the consequences to human populations of any public or private actions that modify the ways in which people live, work, play, relate to one another, organise to meet their needs and generally cope as members of society. The term also includes cultural impacts involving changes to the norms, values, and beliefs that guide and reduce their cognition of themselves and their society.

Adverse social impacts could be in the form of:

1. Loss of land
2. Loss of structures

3. Loss of livelihood
4. Loss of crops/trees
5. Loss of access to community infrastructure/public utility lines

After the direct impacts have been estimated, how the affected people will react in terms of attitudes and actions must be taken into account. Their attitudes before implementation predict their attitudes afterwards, though there are growing data that show fears are often exaggerated and that expected benefits fail to meet expectations. The actions of affected groups can be estimated using comparable cases and consultations and interviews. A lot depends on the nature of local leadership (and the objectives and strategies of these leaders) – this makes such assessments highly uncertain. However, such an exercise enables policy makers to be attentive of potential problems and unexpected results. This step is also important because adoption and response of affected parties can have consequences of their own – whether for the agency that proposes an action (as when political protests stalls a proposal) or for the affected communities, whether in the short-term or in the long-term.

Patterns in previous assessments guide this analysis, and expert judgment and field investigations are used to see whether the study case follows the typical patterns or is it developing uniquely. Being able to demonstrate potentially affected people that significant impacts are being incorporated into the assessment is critical to the achievement of this step.

Step 7: Management and Monitoring

Use of social impact assessment is not just to predict impacts – it should identify means to lessen adverse impacts. This includes the possibility of avoiding the impact by not considering the project at all, if the felt impact is likely to be too severe. Alternately if the forecasted impact is minimal and can be managed, mitigation measures must be put in place. This could be in the form of:

1. Modification of the specific event in the project
2. Operation and redesign of the project or policy
3. Compensation for the impact by providing substitute facilities, resources and opportunities.

Ideally, mitigation measures should be built into the selected alternative, but it is appropriate to identify improvement measures even if they are not immediately adopted or if they would be the responsibility of another person or government unit. Ideally effort should be to avoid all unfavorable impacts.

A Social Management Plan must be set. The components of the SMP must include the following:

1. Enumeration of the Project Affected Persons/Families
2. Measures to Minimise Resettlement

3. Consultation and involvement of PAPs
4. Entitlement Framework
5. Institutional Arrangements

A monitoring programme should be developed that is capable of identifying deviations from the proposed action and any main unanticipated impacts. This should track project and program development and compare real impacts with projected ones. It should spell out (to the degree possible) the nature and extent of additional steps that should take place when unexpected impacts or those larger than the projections occur.

Points to Remember

- The development is seen as a continuing process that implies the integration of the three vital and inseparable features of development- the Environmental, Economic and Social dimensions.
- **Environmental Sustainability** can be defined as the ability to protect over time the three fundamental functions of the environment which are the resource supply function, the waste receiver function and that of direct utility.
- **Economic Sustainability** is referred as the capacity of an economic system to create a stable and improving development of its economical indicators.
- **Social Sustainability** can be defined as the ability to assure welfare (security, health, education), equitably distributed among social classes and genders.
- **Green economy** is defined as one that improves human well-being and social equity, while considerably minimising environmental hazards and ecological shortages.
- As ecosystem services are usually treated as economic externalities they are not priced and as a result overused and degraded. This situation is referred the "Tragedy of the Commons".
- Social ecology, founded by Bookchin, is based on the conviction that nearly all of humanity's present ecological problems originate in dysfunctional social arrangements.
- Ecological footprint can be summarise as a measure of the sustainability of our lifestyles expressed in "global hectares.
- **Carbon marketing** is a method that encourages developed countries to help less developed countries to invest in and use clean energy technologies (that is, those which produce less greenhouse gases)
- **Value proposition** is the focal point of any company's business model is defined as the products and services that yield tangible results for the company's target customers.

- **A sustainability report** is a report published by a company or organisation about the economic, environmental and social impacts caused by its daily activities.
- **Triple bottom line** reporting can be a significant tool to sustain sustainability goals by focusing on comprehensive investment results, that is, with respect to performance along the interrelated dimensions of profits, people and the planet.
- **Social accounting** is defined as the process of communicating the social and environmental effects of organisations' economic actions to specific interest groups within society and to society at large.
- **Environmental Impact Assessment (EIA)** is a key aspect of many large scale planning applications. It is a technique which is devised to help organisations know the potential environmental impacts of key development proposals.
- **Life Cycle Assessment (LCA)** is a technique of examining the environmental impacts of a process, product or activity along its life cycle, for example from 'the cradle to the grave'.
- **Carbon footprints** give a means of quantifying the amount of global warming potential or greenhouse gas equivalents (as units of carbon dioxide) emitted through the whole life cycle of a product or consumer or business activities.

Questions for Discussion

1. Discuss in detail the three dimensions of sustainable development.
2. Describe the components of environmental dimension of sustainable development.
3. Explain the economic dimension of sustainable development.
4. Elaborate the social dimension of sustainable development.
5. Describe the terms ecological footprint, eco-tracking, carbon marketing, carbon credits etc.
6. Explain the business models for sustainable development in Indian and global perspectives.
7. Define sustainable reporting and describe the Triple Bottom Line reports.
8. What do you understand by social accountability standards?

Multiple Choice Questions

1. The definition of sustainable development was expressed during the World Commission on Environment and Development in 1987, chaired by.
   - (a) Gro Harlem Brundtland
   - (b) Murray Bookchin
   - (c) Rees & Wackernackel
   - (d) John Elkington

2. Which of the following statement is correct?
   (a) Renewable resources should provide a sustainable yield (the rate of harvest should not exceed the rate of regeneration).
   (b) For non-renewable resources there should be equivalent development of renewable substitutes.
   (c) Waste generation should exceed the assimilative capacity of the environment.

   (a) a & c   (b) b & c
   (c) a & b   (d) none

3. Dematerialisation is being encouraged through the ideas of industrial ecology, _____ and _____ .
   (a) Ecodesign   (b) Ecolabelling
   (c) Both 1 and 2   (d) None of the above

4. The ecological footprint is an _____ tool for ecological resources.
   (a) Accounting   (b) Management
   (c) Decision making   (d) Financial

5. Eco-tracking tools need to be available which
   (a) Do not allow you to trace environmental footprint
   (b) Avoids data collection
   (c) Set-up an environmental management system
   (d) Help in decision making

6. A sustainability report is the key platform for communicating _____ and impacts whether positive or negative.
   (a) Sustainability performance   (b) Management decisions
   (c) Financial analysis   (d) Information

7. Adverse social impacts could be in the form of _____.
   (a) Loss of land   (b) Loss of structures
   (c) Loss of livelihood   (d) All of the above

8. Who uses the Triple Bottom Line?
   (a) Businesses   (b) Non-profit organisations
   (c) Government entities   (d) All of the above

9. Under which ISO Standard the Guidance on Social Responsibility was recognized?
   (a) ISO 26000   (b) ISO 27000
   (c) ISO 22000   (d) ISO 14000

10. Carbon footprints is used to determine the amount of offsets necessary by a business to sell their product as '_____' but is not used to determine carbon liability.
    (a) Carbon neutral
    (b) Carbon dating
    (c) Carbon cutting
    (d) Carbon rating

Answers

| 1. (a) | 2. (c) | 3. (c) | 4. (a) | 5. (c) | 6. (a) | 7. (d) | 8. (d) | 9. (a) | 10. (a) |

Project Questions

1. How do investors in organisations view the value of sustainability reporting and the various frameworks in particular? What do they want from sustainability reporting? What are the barriers to delivery?

2. Name one company that is making strides toward more sustainable water practices. What are the strengths of the plan and what are its weaknesses?

Chapter 4...

Corporate Governance

Contents ...

4.1 Corporate Governance
    4.1.1 Introduction
    4.1.2 Meaning and Definitions of Corporate Governance
    4.1.3 Constituents of Good Corporate Governance
    4.1.4 OECD Principles of Corporate Governance
    4.1.5 Difference between Governance and Management
    4.1.6 Purpose of Good Corporate Governance
    4.1.7 Potential Consequences of Poor Corporate Governance
    4.1.8 Business Failure and the Contribution of Poor Governance

4.2 Relevant Theories of Corporate Governance
    4.2.1 Agency Theory
    4.2.2 Transaction Cost Theory
    4.2.3 Stakeholder Theory
    4.2.4 Friedman's Theory of CSR

4.3 The Stakeholder Value Approach
    4.3.1 Enlightened Stakeholder Theory
    4.3.2 Balancing of Conflicting Objectives

4.4 Key Issues in Corporate Governance

4.5 Applying Best Practice in Governance
    4.5.1 Voluntary vs. Mandatory
    4.5.2 Rules and Principles-based Approaches
    4.5.3 Concept of 'Comply or Explain'

4.6 Globalisation and Corporate Governance
    4.6.1 Key Drivers of Corporate Governance in Global Companies
    4.6.2 Governance Problems for Global Companies and Groups
    4.6.3 Other Issues Concerning Corporate Governance in Global Companies

4.7 Governance Issues in the Public Sector
   4.7.1 Historical Roots of Public Sector
   4.7.2 Changes in Public Sector
   4.7.3 Features of Indian PSUs
   4.7.4 Difficulties in Arriving at Structure of Governance in India's Public Sector
   4.7.5 Objective Function
   4.7.6 Managerial and Commercial Autonomy
   4.7.7 Board of Directors and Independent Directors
   4.7.8 Role of Investigating Agencies
   4.7.9 Other Issues
4.8 Governance Issues in the Voluntary Sector (NGO's and Charitable Organisations)
4.9 Governance Aspects: Sarbanes-Oxley Act
   4.9.1 Sarbanes-Oxley Act Section 302: CEO/CFO Certification
   4.9.2 Sarbanes-Oxley Act Section 404: Internal Control Report, Governance and Role of Auditors and Audit Committee
4.10 Case Studies on Corporate Governance
   4.10.1 Corporate Governance Failure at Satyam
   4.10.2 Corporate Governance at Infosys
   4.10.3 Corporate Governance at Tata
   4.10.4 Corporate Governance at Wipro
- Points to Remember
- Questions for Discussion
- Multiple Choice Questions
- Project Questions

Learning Objectives ...

- To understand the meaning, and purpose of OECD principles of corporate governance
- To differentiate between governance and management
- To study the potential consequences of poor corporate governance and contribution of poor governance towards business failure
- To learn the relevant theories of corporate governance including agency theory, transaction cost theory, stakeholder theory and Friedman's theory
- To be able to explain the key issues in corporate governance
- To study the application of best practices in governance
- To understand the governance issues of global companies, public sector and voluntary sector
- To learn the governance aspects of Sarbanes-Oxley Act 2002

4.1 Corporate Governance

4.1.1 Introduction

Instead of viewing corporate governance as an individual instrument it is viewed as a concept. Discussions on the appropriate management and control structures of the organisation are held. Rules relating to the relationship between the board of directors, stakeholders, management, owners and employees, suppliers, customers as well as the public are laid down.

Around the world, organisations are aware of the fact that for the sustained growth of their firm, they will need the cooperation of the stakeholders, which requires adherence to the best corporate governance practices. The Ministry of Corporate Affairs (MCA) and the Securities and Exchange Board of India (SEBI), in India, have undertaken the corporate governance initiatives. The first formal regulatory framework for listed companies specifically for corporate governance was established by the SEBI in February 2000, following the recommendations of Kumar Mangalam Birla Committee Report. In the Listing agreement, it is listed as Clause 49. There are also other laws such as the Securities Contracts (Regulation) Act, 1956; Securities and Exchange Board of India Act, 1992; and Depositories Act, 1996, that SEBI has and is maintaining.

The Naresh Chandra Committee on Corporate Audit and Governance in 2002, made recommendations in two key aspects of corporate governance: financial and non-financial disclosures: and independent auditing and board oversight of management. Through the enactment of Companies Act and its amendments, it is making all efforts to bring transparency in the structure of corporate governance.

4.1.2 Meaning and Definitions of Corporate Governance

A company is governed by a set of:
- Systems
- Principles
- Processes

which together is known as **corporate governance**.

For an organisation to fulfill its goal and objectives, in a manner that adds value to the company, and at the same time being beneficial for the stakeholders, a set of guidelines have been provided by the corporate governance. Stakeholders in this case would include everyone ranging from the board of directors, management, shareholders to customers, employees and society. The management of the company hence assumes the role of a trustee for all the others.

- **Cadbury Committee** (1992) defined corporate governance *as the system by which companies are directed and controlled*. It is a simple and concise definition that goes to the heart of the matter. It talks about a system (not individual parts), direction (by the board) and control (by shareholders) of businesses.
- The **World Bank** (1999) states that *from a corporate perspective, corporate governance is about maximising value subject to meeting the company's financial, legal and contractual obligations. From a public perspective, corporate governance is about nurturing an enterprise while ensuring accountability in the exercise of power and patronage by firms. The bank states further that the role of public policy is to provide firms with the incentives and discipline to minimise the divergence between private and social returns and to protect the interests of stakeholders.*
- As per **OECD Code on Corporate Governance (1999)**, *it is a set of relationships between a company's management, its board, its shareholders and other stakeholders. Through these relationships it provides a structure for setting the objectives of the company, the means for attaining them and monitoring performance. Good corporate governance should provide incentives to the board and management to pursue objectives which are in the interests of the company and shareholders, and it should also facilitate effective monitoring.*
- According to **Mary O'Sullivan (1998)** *corporate governance is a system comprising social institutions that influence the process of strategic investment in corporates which revolves around three major decisions viz. what types of investments or resource allocations are made, who controls this decision and how are returns from successful investments distributed.*
- **Shleifer, Vishny (1997):** *Corporate governance deals with the ways in which suppliers of finance to corporations assure themselves on getting a return on their investment.*

4.1.3 Constituents of Good Corporate Governance

For good corporate governance, the main parts are:
1. **Role and Powers of Board:** Clear classification of powers, roles, responsibilities and accountability of the CEO and the Chairman of the board has to be outlined.
2. **Code of Conduct:** It is important for the organisation to clearly communicate the code of conduct to all stakeholders, which are clearly understood by them. There should be some system in place to periodically measure and evaluate the adherence to such code of conduct by each member of the organization.
3. **Legislation:** A clear and unambiguous legislative and regulatory framework is fundamental to effective corporate governance.
4. **Board Independence:** An independent board, which is capable of assessing the performance of managers with a viewpoint, is essential for sound corporate governance. Hence, the majority of board members should be independent of both

the management team and any commercial dealings with the company. This kind of independence should be in place as it makes sure the efficiency of the board while supervising the activities of management as well as to make sure that there are no actual conflicts of interests.

5. **Board Skills:** Since the board has to perform efficiently, it should possess skills, qualities, knowledge, and experience thereby making it a quality contribution. They must also possess technical expertise, financial skills, legal skills as well as knowledge of government and regulatory requirements.

6. **Management Environment:** Under management environment issues of establishing due processes, providing for transparency and clear enunciation of responsibility and accountability, implementing sound business planning, setting up of clear objectives and appropriate ethical framework, establishing clear boundaries for acceptable behaviour, establishing performance evaluation measures, evaluating performance and sufficiently recognising individual and group contribution and encouraging business risk assessment, having right people and right skill for jobs, establishing clear boundaries for acceptable behaviour, establishing performance evaluation measures and evaluating performance and sufficiently recognizing individual and group contribution.

7. **Board Appointments:** Through extensive research, the board positions must be filled up thereby ensuring that the most proficient individuals are appointed. A well defined and open procedure must be in place for reappointments as well as for appointment of new directors.

8. **Board Induction and Training:** Induction and training is absolutely necessary so as to make sure the board stays on top of all developments, which may or will affect the corporate governance.

9. **Board Meetings:** Board meetings are the basis for board decision making. In these meetings, the directors can release some of their responsibilities. A meeting is said to be effective when planned agendas and relevant paper work, are available well in advance to the board members.

10. **Strategy Setting:** The company's objective, including the annual business plan along with the achievable and measurable performance targets and milestones must be documented well.

11. **Business and Community Obligations:** Even though the ultimate goal of the organisation is commercial, it should not forget the obligations towards the community. The proposed and ongoing initiatives taken to meet the community obligations must be informed to the stakeholders.

12. **Financial and Operational Reporting:** The board requires comprehensive, regular, reliable, timely, correct and relevant information in a form and of a quality that is appropriate to discharge its function of monitoring corporate performance.
13. **Monitoring the Board Performance:** Constant and ongoing review of the individual directors and the combined performance should be made, using the key performance indicators besides peer review.
14. **Audit Committee:** Audit committee is responsible for liaison with management, internal and statutory auditors, reviewing the adequacy of internal control and compliance with significant policies and procedures, reporting to the board on the key issues.
15. **Risk Management:** Risk analysis and management is an important functioning of the corporate governance. A well defined process of identifying, anaylsing and treating the ricks should be in place. The board has to clearly identify the major risks to the organisation and make sure that the senior management team identifies analyses and controls these risks.

Good corporate governance recognises the diverse interests of shareholders, lenders, employees, government, etc. The new concept of governance to bring about quality corporate governance is not only a necessity to serve the divergent corporate interests, but also is a key requirement in the best interests of the corporate themselves and the economy.

4.1.4 OECD Principles of Corporate Governance

The OECD principles of corporate governance can be outlined as follows:

1. **Ensuring the basis for an Effective Corporate Governance Framework:** Clear and well organised markets should be promoted in the corporate governance framework, while being consistent with the law and clearly state the responsibilities among different supervisory, regulatory and enforcement authorities.
2. **The Rights of Shareholders and key Ownership Functions:** The rights of the shareholders should be made easy and protected well.
3. **The Equitable Treatment of Shareholders:** Treatment of all shareholders, including minority and foreign shareholders should be equal. All shareholders should be heard and addressed for their rights.
4. **The role of Stakeholders in Corporate Governance:** The corporate governance framework should recognise the rights of stakeholders established by law or through mutual agreements and encourage active cooperation between corporations and stakeholders in creating wealth, jobs and the sustainability of financially sound enterprises.
5. **Disclosure and Transparency:** Timely and accurate disclosure is made on all material matters regarding the corporation, including the financial situation, performance, ownership and governance of the company should be ensured.
6. **The Responsibilities of the Board:** The strategic guidance of the company, the effective monitoring of management by the board and the board's accountability to the company and the shareholders should be in place.

4.1.5 Difference between Governance and Management

Governance	Management
Companies are directed and controlled by a system called governance.	Concentrates on the implementation of systems.
Council focuses on strategic issues in the implementation of it governance function.	The Principal and Vice Chancellor along with the management, are responsible for the operational management
Concerned with the processes and structures which are associated with management and also the control and decision making in organisations.	Must make sure that the decision making and processes are followed.
In governance the people at the top matter the most and hence activities of those having the most responsibilities for the success or failure of the institution are concentrated upon.	Make sure that the management is responsible for the operational functions of the organisation to be effective and efficient.
Good governance is the means of ensuring due and adequate control over the strategy and direction of any organisation in achieving this key objective, having due regard for the interests of all stakeholders.	Good management means the organisation is operationally effective, but it may still be ineffective in its relationships with Council, Management, employees and other stakeholders.
Concerned with the conduct of leadership.	Concerned with the operational running of the organisation.
It represents practice and rules that are effective, profitable and efficient for the running of the organisation.	Clear and unambiguous views on strategic direction from Council is expected.
Focus is on overall control. Between the Council and Executive management, the governance acts as a catalyst to make sure the firm is not subjected to governance principles, values and philosophies.	Focus is on results and performance.
Governance is described as "hands-off".	Management is "hands-on".
It is all about approving policy and goals.	Concerned with making sure that the policies are implemented and the goals are achieved.

4.1.6 Purpose of Good Corporate Governance

The Organisation for Economic Co-operation and Development defines corporate governance as *the system that is used to direct and control a corporation.* Boards of directors are elected by the company to govern the affairs and to make sure that the shareholder is satisfied. Through Corporate governance, organisations make sure the business' objectives are fulfilled.

Some of the important features of good corporate governance are:

1. Establishing Direction and Objectives

The direction and objectives of a corporation are the responsibility of the board of directors. Along with the CEO, they determine the mission of the organisation and make sure that the objectives are in line with the interests of the shareholders. The group can use feedback from senior executives, middle management, front-line employees or consultants to craft new business objectives or shift the direction in which the company is headed, even though the board has the final say.

2. Creating Policies

Management policies are to be set by the board of directors, which must be followed by the employees. The issues covered in the policy are dividend and options payouts, a code of ethics, the hiring and firing of executives and ensuring financial solvency etc. By establishing these policies, there is a transparency in the organisation and anyone can hold the board, or management employees' accountable for inappropriate behaviour.

3. Adopting Bylaws

A corporation's founders or directors will draft bylaws that fall under the business' articles of incorporation to outline the manner in which the company should be run. The foremost objective of the board is to adopt the bylaws as it spells out how directors are elected, the way meetings between shareholder and board meetings are conducted etc. Unless it is able to obtain an overwhelming majority of votes of the corporation's membership, the board does not have the power to amend the bylaws.

4. Executive Recruitment and Compensation

Corporate governance also deals with the hiring and firing of employees. Compensation packages should be approved by the board. One of the most important hiring decisions for a board is the appointment of the CEO. Appointing the correct CEO will surely inspire the confidence in the shareholders as well as attract more new investors.

4.1.7 Potential Consequences of Poor Corporate Governance

One major impact of poor corporate governance can be the failure of a business to grow in a sustainable way.

Some of the factors that point out that a company is having poor corporate governance are:

1. **Weak Management**
   - The rules of the financial control are absent or relaxed.
   - Executive decisions are made without proper review when the accountability of the board becomes vague.
   - The Board is controlled by one person. He or she may ignore advice, may not delegate as required and may push through their own plans without impartial consideration of the pros and cons of those plans.
   - The senior management team is fighting fires. They may lurch from crisis to crisis dealing with only urgent issues without any regard for future planning or solving the true causes of problems.
   - The required financial literacy required by the board to make informed decisions is absent, and even where the accounting systems generate accurate reporting, they do not have the skills or knowledge to appreciate or comprehend the nature of what is being forecast or reported.

2. **Deficient or Inadequate Accounting Systems**
   - Costing systems aren't well implemented and can result in under-pricing or unproductive recoveries.
   - There is limited or non-existent forecasting (this includes profit and loss) and cash flow planning, which means that management is not able to plan for possible shortfalls in cash.
   - The management team does not have access to the right information, as they do not have a clear picture of how the business is performing.
   - The management fails to assess the performance and also fails to plan effectively when the financial reporting systems are inadequate.

3. **Unsound Policies**
   - Increased sales without a corresponding improvement in profitability will place a burden on cash flow and could potentially lead to bulk discounting, thus corroding margins.
   - Credit control policies that are ineffective can cause a backlog of accounts receivable and affect liquidity.
   - Unnecessarily high levels of stock are held as a result of over-confident sales targets or over-production, which can tie up working capital and restrict cash flow that may bring about a liquidity crisis.

- Dependence on a small range of product or service lines or an over-reliance on a small customer base. That small customer base may then be able to dictate price and margin and/or place the business at risk should the key customer become insolvent or should their customer be lost to a competitor.

4. **Over-gearing**
   - When a business borrows more than it is able to service when it comes to the repayment of capital or interest is caused by over-gearing. This means the company can be more at risk from unexpected adverse changes in performance. This usually leads to breach of contract thereby creating an uncertainty about the future sustainability.

5. **The "one big project"**
   - Start-up businesses invest large amounts of resources to launch a product or idea and can underestimate the expense of not only developing the product but also the costs of successfully taking it to market.
   - The organisation can only depend on one big project in hand while ignoring the other smaller projects.

6. **Not Adapting to Change**
   - The most significant challenges that businesses face today is of managing change and adapting to it. When companies fail to plan and adapt, whether those changes are driven by competition, political, economic or technological issues, messy situations can result.

4.1.8 Business Failure and the Contribution of Poor Governance

The effects can be far-reaching, when a company suffers a failure due to faulty risk management, ethical or accounting violation oversight or ineffective board decision-making. Shareholders hence will get affected as the share price falls sharply and sometimes even the industry sector in which they operate can get affected. The company might ultimately fail, leading to job losses and other harmful consequences for the region where it operates.

The general implication of poor corporate governance of a company is an inability to achieve the intended purpose of the company, and its reason for being is defeated, even though it is not due to corporate governance for the corporate failures. Let us see some of the major corporate governance failures at major organisations.

Corporate Governance Failure at Enron

One can conclude from the Enron disaster that, every time one problem gets solved, another one creeps up. Not a single day passes without more things being exposed in the company and one often wonders whether there is anything that can prevent this misfortune.

It was a culture to flourish in which secrecy, rule-breaking and fraudulent behaviour was acceptable by the top management at Enron. Employees sought to generate profits at the expense of the company's stated standards of ethics and strategic goals, when the incentives were not up to the mark. It had all the good structures in place for good corporate governance along with having a CSR task force and a code of conduct of human rights, social investment, security and public engagement. The audit committee allowed suspect accounting practices and made no attempt to examine the SPE transactions. The auditors took no precaution to prevent questions on accounting. The management was openly allowed to violate the code of ethics.

The use of questionable accounting and disclosure practices, their approval by the board and their verification by the auditors arose from a variety of forces, including:

- Pressure to meet quarterly earnings projections and maintain stock prices after the expansion of the 1990s.
- Executive compensation practices.
- Outdated and rules-based accounting standards, complex corporate financial arrangements designed to minimise taxes and hide the true state of the companies, and the compromised independence of public accounting firms.

Corporate Governance Failure at Wal-Mart

Wal-Mart Stores Inc, the US supermarket group, had growing concerns from the public that it was failing to comply with its own governance policy. Some of the concerns stated were:

- Despite strong policies on paper, Wal-Mart has struggled to implement its standards across its US business.
- Over the past several years it has become increasingly concerned by signs of failure in internal controls that have led to government investigations and class action lawsuits by employees.
- Allegations include requiring employees to work during breaks and after shifts, systematic discrimination against women, and alleged questionable tactics to prevent workers from voting for union representation.
- Weaknesses in internal controls have eroded the company's reputation as an attractive employer and are adding fuel to the fires of Wal-Mart's critics.

  It got off to a promising start in 2005 with expectations of a dialogue with the independent directors on the audit committee. But this diminished over time and Wal-Mart had little choice but to bring concerns about internal controls, labour violations and the erosion of the company's reputation to fellow shareholders.

- The company was not interested in engaging in a productive discussion about how it built and supported a compliance culture and, as a result, they had joined an international group of large filers led by the New York City Employees' Retirement System to file a shareholder proposal.
- Its failure to deliver on these policy commitments is inhibiting Wal-Mart's ability to expand into new domestic markets.

4.2 Relevant Theories of Corporate Governance

4.2.1 Agency Theory

In the Agency Theory in regards to the corporate governance, there is a two-tier form of firm control:
- Owners
- Managers

The theory states that there will be some resistance and mistrust between the owners and managers. The basic structure of the corporation, therefore, is the web of contractual relations among different interest groups with a stake in the company.

In the agency theory, also known as the theory of principle, an agent comes into play when there is a parting control of the company and ownership.

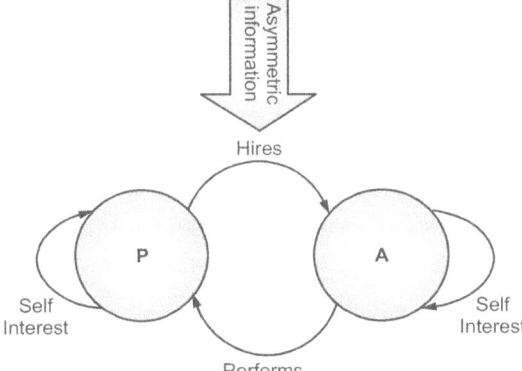

Fig. 4.1: The Principal-Agent Problem

When there are never-expanding possibilities of companies and the emergence of conflicts between stakeholders, the problem of the principle agent can be seen.

However, this problem appears to be new and is considered in Adam Smith's work called *An Inquiry into the Nature and Causes of the Wealth of Nations* (1776), which expresses doubts about the value of joint-stock companies, which reduce the financial incentives to managers in relation to the performance, if the capital is provided by the owners rather than by managers.

The problem occurs when the shareholder (principle) hires a manger (agent) to manage the company for him. Shareholders want to lead management of a company so that they maximise the value for shareholders. The management though has other plans, when they want to merge with another acquisition or build a powerful empire thereby interfering with the shareholders' interests.

Agency costs relate primarily to large publicly traded companies in particular for two reasons:

1. The biggest owner of these companies rarely own more than 50%, so the agency costs are usually absent in small family businesses.
2. In small family businesses owners are not separate from enterprise management and thus would not create any agency costs.

4.2.2 Transaction Cost Theory

Ronald Coase, an economist in the 1930s, was investigating the reasons companies exist and why they were growing so large and that's when the theory of Transaction Cost originated.

Transaction costs occur when time is spent in researching, negotiating and agreeing on a transaction. Directors would rather enter into agreements for their sources of goods and services as this reduces uncertainty as they have everything they need for the foreseeable future is the theory of transaction costs. When this is done the time and expense of sourcing materials is avoided.

Directors, on an average, would prefer to lose the flexibility of searching for inputs in order to have the certainty of predicting what would happen with their business in the future, was his theory. Whilst committing to long-term agreements and contracts avoids uncertainty and is easier to control, it could mean that better opportunities may be missed.

Coase's main concern was that directors were making their life easier at the opportunities that would improve the wealth of the shareholder. They have more time to spend on longer-term strategy issues.

Why companies are getting bigger was explained by this theory. Transaction cost theory says that in order to reduce uncertainty and to increase control, a company should tie itself up in more agreements and this therefore means more staff, more assets, more contracts and a larger company.

The board of directors may choose to buy the company that supplies them, if they are worried about the security of their supplies. This is called **vertical integration**. Supplies always coming from one company when there may be better quality or prices to be had elsewhere are the major cons of vertical integration.

This helps to explain why the agency problem is getting worse. A larger company means the gap between shareholders and directors gets bigger.

It makes their lives easier through increased control and certainty over the future when directors are likely to prefer to own things, or at least have long-term contracts in place.

This makes them establish larger organisations which may be good for them but may not result in the best decisions for the shareholders as:

1. The organisation may grow larger than is efficient.
2. By agreeing to long-term contracts, the ability to take advantage of good deals in the future may be lost.
3. Because directors will get to know the company staff, assets etc. very well (as they are internal), they may simply renew contracts without looking at outside options.

4.2.3 Stakeholder Theory

These ideas were originally developed by Ed Freeman in the 1980s, but have achieved a wider currency in the UK, in part through initiatives such as the RSA's 'Tomorrow's Company' project. The theory confronts assumptions made by the agency about the dominance of shareholder interests. It claims that the company should be managed in the interests of all the shareholders. These interests include not only those of the shareholder but also a range of other direct and indirect interests. An employee's investment in firm-specific skills means that they too should have a voice in the governance of the firm. But stakeholder theory would also insist that other groups - suppliers and customers - have strong direct interests in company performance while local communities, the environment as well as society at large have legitimate indirect interests.

It is hard to operationalise because of the difficulties of deciding what weight should be given to different stakeholder interests. Enlightened stakeholder theory therefore suggests the practical value of accountability to shareholders even if a board takes other interests into account in its conduct of a firm.

A number of key contributions have been made by the stakeholder theory in relation to the company performance. Excessive levels of executive pay and the way that these have often gone hand in hand with company downsizing and all its negative impacts on employees and local communities undermine the legitimacy of the demand for 'shareholder value'.

The most direct contribution of stakeholder ideas to company performance is to be found in Kaplan and Norton's (1992) ideas about the Balanced Scorecard and the revolution in performance measurement. They accepted the measurement of performance and potential distortions on operational effectiveness which arises from financial accounting measures like earnings per share or on the return on investment.

The Balanced Scorecard embodies key stakeholder interests in a firm-specific set of measures that link important operational drivers to financial performance. It provides managers with a way to explore the interdependencies between customers' needs, and what the company must do operationally to meet these needs and sustain competitive success. An immediate performance focus as well as pointing to key areas for continuous improvement and innovation is seen in the balanced scorecard. The focus of the balanced scorecard, they suggest, is 'strategy and vision', that establishes goals but then promotes initiative and learning - both individual, team, and across-functions - in pursuit of such goals. From this perspective the key role of senior executives and the board lies in the setting of company strategy and vision. Achieving a high performance will depend on the understanding of the key business drivers, communication and leadership skills in relation to the staff, customers and the financial markets.

4.2.4 Friedman's Theory of CSR

Mr. Friedman argues that a corporation, unlike a person, cannot have responsibility. A corporation should have legal and moral responsibilities.

There are other rules that businesses must adhere to if they wish to be successful; such as the obvious rules of the marketplace including supply and demand. In addition, as we have seen with the proliferation of 'new' technologies, the law usually follows advancements in technology and thinking. But the fundamental principle of responsibility often precedes the legal cases being decided because unless or until enough people think something should be made illegal, it won't be made illegal.

So, if one accepts that – 1) companies are in fact capable of having responsibilities and that 2) they must follow rules of the game beyond those codified into law (particularly concerns that cross borders and therefore are subject to multiple and sometimes contradictory statutes) the basic premises behind the argument Mr. Friedman made in the fall of 1970 collapse.

Companies know well that holding themselves accountable to a higher standard will keep them in good stead with their customers, employees, shareholders, suppliers, regulators and communities.

Any business, if its wants to be sustained over time, must maximise its profits but do so in a manner that meets the needs of the stakeholders that allow it to remain viable. When those need change, businesses have a responsibility to adapt their behaviours accordingly if they wish to survive. The rules of the game have changed in fundamental ways—and people today expect (and demand) more out of business than simply that they maximise their profits without coming to grief by some violation of law.

Consumers want and expect attributes from what they buy—quality, safety, value—depending of course on the price they pay.

Employees want more than a pay check. Communities want the company to be a good corporate citizen and hire from the community, provide employees with a living wage, not pollute and to pay its fair share of taxes and support the community (even if each of these things are not legally required).

Regulators may only require companies to toe the legal line, but things like sloppy paperwork and cutting it too close to the line (when it comes to things like emissions) result in more frequent and deeper investigations, costing the company time and money.

Communities often want companies to do more than what is required; leading to a host of strategic philanthropy efforts that are part of, but do not by themselves constitute a responsible corporation, especially if they are seen as compensating for a business model or culture that is less desirable.

4.3 THE STAKEHOLDER VALUE APPROACH

The stakeholder value approach, conceptualises the company as an agent who contracts with multiple stakeholders like the employees, customer, supplier, government, society and shareholder who provide different resources to the company in return for value gained by them (Ross, 1973). The figure 4.2 shows the relationship between the company and its stakeholders and Kanter had termed these relationships as alliances through concepts, competence, and connections.

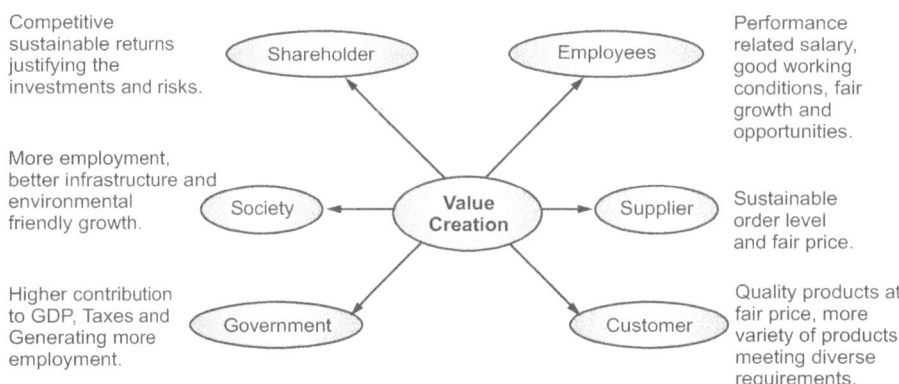

Fig. 4.2: Value Delivered by Company to different Stakeholders

It is essential to measure the value created by the company to each category of stakeholder, in order to improve the magnitude of value perpetually. The meaning of the stakeholder value components and ways for their measurement are discussed in the following section.

1. **Value to Customer**

   The financial value which is provided by the firm to the customers can be determined using the economics principle of consumer surplus. This simply means when a customer buys a product for consumption, the value created by a company to its customers is given by the excess of the price a customer is willing to pay for a product above the price actually paid by the customer.

   However, if the commodity sold is going to be used for the purpose of further business or value creation, customer value created can be measured using the Discounted Cash Flow method, i.e.

   > Value to customer = (PV of net cash flows – Amount invested)

   Where,

   PV of net cash flows represents the discounted net cash flows earned by the customer using the product. Discounting is done at a rate equal to the cost of capital of the customer.

   Amount invested = Price paid by the customer for the product.

   There are two models for the measurement of value to the customers under two circumstances. The disadvantage that the former model suffers is that it cannot be applied and quantified for all the products as the tastes and preferences of the customers can be very different, which creates different prices that the customers are willing to pay; also the same customer may pay different prices at different points of time.

   A company creates a lot of the intangible benefits to a satisfied customer like reduction in time spent for ordering, locating vendors, price negotiations etc. for future transactions thereby saving costs. The company also benefits out of creating a loyal customer and improved brand image. The value created by a company to its customers disappears if the customer can buy a similar product from another company at the same price, terms and conditions, in a product which faces a lot of perfect competition. Under such conditions, by differentiating their products, companies create value to customers.

2. **Value to Suppliers**

   The value which the company provides to the suppliers is similar to the value which it provided to the customers, with a differentiating fact that the company pays cash in return for goods.

   In simple terms, value to supplier can be expressed as:

   > Value = [Price received - Total cost]

   Under perfect competition, as the company does not create any value to the supplier, the supplier can sell his product to any other company at the same price, terms and conditions. However, if we take the macro view, all companies put together do create value for the supplier. If the supplier does not get any value added, he will discontinue his business.

3. Value to Employees

Employees contribute "human capital" to the company, which means the contribution of the employees is compared with the owners, as human skills contributed by the employees is also company specific just like the owner's capital. With this some risks are also associated with the company. The average of salary, bonus and incentives paid to the employee in addition to intangibles like skills development, reputation, experience and so on, when summed is the value created by a company. Thus, we have,

$$\boxed{\text{Value to employees} = (\text{Salary} + \text{Bonus} + \text{Other Perquisites})}$$

There is no room for companies to provide less compensation (value) to employees than others, in a competitive market condition. An employee will switch companies if the other company pays him more decently than the previous company. This shows that the values which the company was providing will fade away, as the employee gets paid better in the other company he decides to work. However, the intangible value added and personal preferences of an employee bring in the differentiation, which enable value creation to employees and help in their retention.

4. Value to Government

"Free" resources contributed by the government such as administration systems, courts, laws, education, public safety, good roads and other basic infrastructure add value. It also allows the company to function in an environment which keeps up with the current trends to work abroad. The various taxes such as income tax, sale tax, duties and excise etc. are the value contributed to the government.

A company creates value to government when:

[Value returned to government > value of free resources consumed by company].

It is difficult to calculate the size of consuming free resources and hence value them.

5. Value to Community

The firm consumes scarce resources, without paying for them but it also gives more employment opportunities, better sanitation, and contributes to social causes like health etc. and this today is known as CSR or "Corporate Social Responsibility". Value created by the company is the net result of these positive and negative contributions to the society which is part of social accounting.

6. Value to Investors

Value of a company to its investors is expressed as below:

$$\boxed{\text{Value to Investors} = [\text{PV of cash returns} - \text{Cash investments}]}$$

Where

PV of cash returns = Present Value of dividends and market value realisable on sale of stock.

It is ascertained by applying the discount rate that is equal to the cost of capital of the investor.

Cash Investments = Money paid for purchase of the security.

We can see that the minimum value created for different categories of the stakeholders can be measured. Only if stakeholders feel that they are receiving more value in return for the products given or services rendered by them, will this value creation seem adequate enough. The resource exchanges will reshape a company's perceptions of their own value to others, updating their knowledge of useful assets and capabilities, and suggesting new ways of organising and coordinating, all of which will lead to growth and value innovation.

The disadvantages of this approach are:
- It is often impossible to measure subtle values created by the company for its stakeholders such as technology know-how transfer to suppliers to improve quality of inputs, improvement in employee skills in training, etc.
- It does not provide a single objective function for value maximisation and multiple objectives is no objective. Hence, when there are conflicting interests among different stakeholders, there is no clarity on whose interests must be given priority and how decisions should be taken.
- It also does not help find the aggregate value created by a company to all its stakeholders put together. In the absence of appropriate scoring mechanism, it becomes impossible to measure the value creation by a company in a holistic manner.
- It fails to quantify the total value created by a company to each category of stakeholder, including financial and non financial value.

Adopting the stakeholder theory leaves the company with no clear cut management control or performance management and measurement system, using which the company can motivate and provide incentives for value-increasing behaviour among the employees.

4.3.1 Enlightened Stakeholder Theory

Enlightened Stakeholder Theory is also known as **Enlightened Value Maximisation**. The enlightened stakeholder approach is based on the structure of the stakeholder theory but takes the maximisation of shareholder value as the primary objective for decision makers and therefore solves the problem that arises from multiple objectives related to the stakeholder theory.

Communication with and motivation of an organisation's managers, employees, and partners is extremely difficult is seen in the enlightened value maximisation. Value maximisation is not a vision or a strategy or even a purpose; it is the scorecard for the organisation. We must give people enough structure to understand what maximising value means so that they can be guided by it and therefore have a chance to actually achieve it. They must be turned on by the vision or the strategy in the sense that it taps into some human desire or passion of their own—for example, a desire to build the world's best automobile or to create a film or play that will move people for centuries.

Indeed, it is a basic principle of enlightened value maximisation that we cannot maximise the long-term market value of an organisation if we ignore or mistreat any important constituency. We cannot create value without good relations with customers, employees, financial backers, suppliers, regulators, and communities. We can be sure using this value criterion will result in making society as well off as it can be.

Thus, **Jensen** defines "enlightened" stakeholder theory simply as *stakeholder theory with the specification that maximising the firm's total long-term market value is the right objective function.*

Enlightened stakeholder theorists can see that although stockholders are not some special constituency that ranks above all others, long-term stock value is an important determinant of total long-term firm value. They would recognise that value creation gives management a way to assess the tradeoffs that must be made among competing constituencies, and that it allows for principled decision making independent of the personal preferences of managers and directors.

4.3.2 Balancing of Conflicting Objectives

Balance between the objectives of different groups of stakeholders is essential to the long-term viability of the corporation. Fair and balanced stakeholder's perspective results in long-term shareholder maximisation value. Governance analysis must serve as a means to organise, structure and to establish an efficient prioritisation of interests.

Corporate managers are, in accordance with this view, to reconcile stakeholders and shareholders' needs and interests though strategies capable to raising both economic and social and environmental standards. If the decision making process within corporate hierarchies were captured and controlled by one set of stakeholders, other stakeholders might eventually cease to cooperate, to withhold inputs in the future, and try to withdraw inputs over which they have influence. The complex nature of modern corporations implies that shareholders' investment is better protected though the care and respect of those "external" assets. Breaches of social or environmental laws bring penalties and sanctions to corporations and diminish shareholder's revenues. Stakeholder's movement contains a prescription for corporations to pursue ends that go beyond the single interests of shareholders and means that directors and officers are to care for the interests of others involved in the company activity.

Lack of respect for social, environment issues can have disastrous consequences for the corporation's activities and profitability. Customers and clients are stakeholders whose satisfaction is a great challenge to the corporation. No company can create great wealth for its shareholders without a stable and growing revenue base, which comes from customers. As long as management invests in higher levels of customer satisfaction that earns an economic return, there is no conflict between maximising shareholder value and maximising customer satisfaction.

Suppliers are crucial to developing and implementing strategies that generate wealth. Attempts to pay prices that are below market levels may allow achieving a greater short-term profit. They are also likely to lead to supply disruptions or quality problems. Management systems are based upon cooperation with suppliers to improve quality, delivery-production schedules and inventory. Companies that pay their employees below market, or deal with their employees in ways which undermine their talents are wasting valuable assets and are not maximising wealth for shareholders. The corporation's prestige in the communities where they interact helps in achieving long-term cooperative relationship. This too is a good ground for long-term wealth maximisation.

4.4 Key Issues in Corporate Governance

Different writers and organisations define corporate governance in different ways; some define it in a narrow perspective while others want it to address the concerns of all stakeholders. Some have defined corporate governance as an instrument for a country to achieve sustainable economic development, while some others consider it as a corporate strategy to achieve a long tenure and a healthy image. Others define it as another dimension to corporate ethics. Thus corporate governance has different meanings to different people, but to all, corporate governance is a means to an end, the end being long-term shareholder, and more importantly, stakeholder value. Thus, all authorities on the subject are one in recognising the need for good corporate governance practices to achieve the end for which corporates are formed. They identify some governance issues being crucial and critical to achieve these objectives. These are:

1. Distinguishing the Roles of Board and Management: The business is to be managed by or under the direction of the board has often been stressed by companies. In such cases, the CEO is delegated the responsibility of managing the business and he in turn delegates to other senior executives. The board occupies a key position between the shareholders (owners) and the company's management.

The following functions are present in the board of a listed company:
(a) Select, decide the remuneration and evaluate on a regular basis, and when necessary, change the CEO.
(b) Render advice and counsel to top management.
(c) Review and, where necessary, approve the company's financial objectives and major corporate plans and objectives.
(d) Review the adequacy of systems to comply with all applicable laws and regulations
(e) Oversee (not directly, but indirectly) the conduct of the company's business to evaluate whether or not it is being correctly managed. Identify and recommend candidates to shareholders for electing them to the board of directors,
(f) All other functions required by law to be performed.

2. Composition of the Board and Related Issues: Shareholders elect a board of directors known as the committee, who are responsible for the policy of the company. Full-time functional directors are appointed, each being responsible for some particular branch of the firm's work.

The number of directors of different kinds that participate in the work of the board is the composition of board of directors. Over a period of time there has been a change as to the number and proportion of different types of directors in the board of a limited company.

The SEBI appointed Kumar Mangalam Birla Committee's Report defined the composition of the Board thus: "*The Board of Directors of a company shall have an optimum combination of executive and non-executive directors with not less than 50% per cent of the board of directors to be non-executive directors. The number of independent directors would depend whether the chairman is executive or non-executive. In case of a non-executive chairman, at least one-third of the board should comprise independent directors and in case of executive chairman, at least half of the board should be independent directors*".

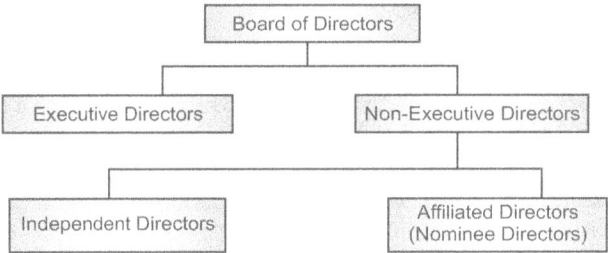

Fig. 4.3: Types of Directors

As shown in Fig. 4.3, an executive director is one who is an executive of the company and also a member of the board of directors, while a non-executive director has no separate employment relationship with the company. Independent non-executive directors are those directors on the board who are free from any business or other relationship which could materially interfere with the exercise of their independent judgement in the process of decision-making as a member of the board. An affiliated director or a nominee director is a non-executive director who has some kind of independence, impairing relationship with the company or the company's management. For example, the director may have links with a major supplier or customer of the company, or may be a partner in a professional firm that supplies services to the company, or may be a retired top management professional of the company.

3. Separation of the Roles of the CEO and Chairperson: The board acts as a link between the shareholders and the management and its decisions affect the performance of the company, hence the formation of the board is an important issue. If the role of the CEO and chairman is combined, as has been seen in many countries, it often leads to conflicts in decision-making and a lot of power is bestowed on one person, hence in some countries like the United Kingdom and Australia, the CEO is prohibited from being the chairperson of the company. The CEO leads the senior management team in managing the firm whereas the Chairperson leads the board, especially in evaluating the performance of senior executives which includes the CEO too. If the roles are combined, then the performance analysis on the CEO as well as the senior management's activities cannot be analysed. Often if the roles are combined, this brings a burden on one person and hence he has difficulty to deliver the best results.

4. Should the Board have Committees: Many committees on corporate governance have recommended in one voice the appointment of special committees for:

(i) nomination

(ii) remuneration

(iii) auditing

If these committees are formed it would remove the burden on the board to quite an extent thereby improving it efficiency. According to the **Bosch Report**, committees, apart from having written terms of reference outlining their authority and duties, *"should also have clear procedures for reporting back to the board, and agreed arrangements for staffing including access to relevant company executives and the ability to obtain external advice at the company's expense"*. If these committees have independent directors who are selected for their expertise in the chosen field, it would help the respective committees decide issues thereby promoting long-term interest in the organisation.

5. Appointments to the Board and Directors Re-election: Shareholders elect directors to the board, as per the Indian Company Law. The problem lies with the fact that the shareholders are scattered around the country and to have them come together to elect the directors is an expensive and time consuming option and therefore in most cases, special committees are appointed to select the director and then formally get the director elected by the shareholders in the Annual General Body Meeting.

Most often the shareholders vote for the director chosen by the committee, but in a rare case the shareholders may refuse the nominee of the director. Other issues in relation to the board's appointment are terms of office, duties, remuneration, appointment of a nomination committee, and re-election of directors and composition of the board on which several committees have made their own recommendations.

6. Directors' and Executives' Remuneration: This is one of the mixed and vexed issues of corporate governance that came to the centre stage during the massive corporate failures in the US between 2000 and 2002. Executive compensation has also in recent time become the most visible and politically sensitive issue relating to corporate governance.

According to the Cadbury Report: "*The over-riding principle in respect of Board remuneration is that shareholders are entitled to a full and clear statement of Directors' present and future benefits, and how they have been determined.*" There have been other committees too who have laid emphasis on issues like pay for performance, pension for non-executive directors, appointment of remuneration committee, heavy severance payments, and so on. However while controversy often surrounds the size or quantum of remuneration, this is not necessarily an issue of corporate governance - a payment that may be excessive in one context may be reasonable in another.

The key corporate governance issues are:

(i) transparency;

(ii) pay for performance (whether the payment is justified);

(iii) process for determination;

(iv) severance payment; and

(v) pensions for non-executive directors.

7. Disclosure and Audit: The OCED lays down a number of provisions for the disclosure and communication of "key facts" about the company to its shareholders. Both the Cadbury Report and the Bosch Report stressed that the board of directors has a huge responsibility to present to the shareholders an articulate and balanced assessment of the company's financial position through audited financial statements. Some of the auditing questions which have an impact on corporate governance are:

(i) Should boards establish an audit committee?

(ii) If yes, how should it be composed?

(iii) How to ensure the independence of the auditor?

(iv) What precautions are to be taken or what are the positions of the state and regulators with regard to provision of non-audit services rendered by auditors?

(v) Should individual directors have access to independent resource?

(vi) Should boards formalise performance standards?

Different committees answer these questions with different point of views which are later analysed in depth.

8. Protection of Shareholder Rights and their Expectations: The rights and expectations of shareholders have to be protected well which becomes an important governance issue to look into. Some of the questions which should be looked into are:

(i) Should companies always adhere to one-share-one-vote principle?

(ii) Should companies retain voting by a show of hands or by poll?

(iii) Can shareholder's resolutions be bundled? i.e. to place together before shareholders for approval a resolution that contains more than one discrete issue

(iv) Should shareholder approval be required for all major transactions?

These questions bring out answers from various committees with different emphasis.

9. Dialogue with Institutional Shareholders: The Cadbury Committee recommends *"that institutional investors should maintain regular and systematic contact with companies, apart from their participation in general meetings of shareholders, use their voting rights positively, take a positive interest in the composition of the board of directors of companies in which they invest, and above all, recognise their rights and responsibilities as "owners" who should act in the best interests of those whose money they have invested by influencing the standards of corporate governance and by bringing about changes in companies when necessary, rather than by selling their shares and quitting the companies."*

If institutional investors have to exercise their rights and carry out their responsibilities, companies have to provide them the required information and facilities.

10. Should Investors have a Say in making a Company a "Socially Responsible Corporate Citizen"?

There are two different thoughts doing the rounds in this question:

1. The first talks about how institutional investors should act in the financial interests of the beneficiaries. The socially responsible behaviour of corporations, for example anti-pollution measures, ecological preservation, and producing quality and environment friendly products which always enhance costs and thus reduce profits.

2. The second states environment friendliness and economic gains are not contradicting goals, but on the other hand, they benefit corporations in the long run examples being Pfizer, Dow Chemicals etc.

Though there has been much debate on both the thoughts, the ultimate point which the world wants to prefer is that corporates are committed to the overall welfare of the people who are their customers.

Internal Controls, Checks and Governance

Strategies, policies, procedures, processes and internal organisational structures that enable the insurer to operate effectively and efficiently as an operational unit and achieve strategic and operational objectives are the internal governance mechanisms.

Risk Management and Internal Control System

Insurers, should have well-defined risk management strategies, sound and comprehensive risk management systems that are integrated into their overall system of governance, making sure that risk identification, assessment, monitoring and mitigation are integrated into decision-making at all levels of the organisation which can be seen in the overall strategies, policies and business plans. To ensure proper observation and execution of board strategies and policies which is necessary and should be integrated into the risk management system, internal controls provide the processes, procedures and operating policies.

Proper risk management can be considered to rest on the following building blocks:

- **A Proper Firm-wide Risk Culture:** If a strong and all encompassing risk culture is in place, it will provide the essential foundation for risk management. This risk culture should be internalised in all the aspects of the organisation, both behavioural (including the most senior level executes and other employees) and operational, thus enabling effective risk management across the firm at all levels. On the part of the insurers, it should reflect expectations of a cautious behaviour along with fair conduct.

- **An Appropriate Risk Frame or Strategy, with due Consideration to the Interests of Policy Holders:** As noted above, an insurer should articulate its approach to risk by identifying its key risks, defining its willingness and desire to take on risk in pursuit of its objectives ("risk appetite") and assessing its capacity to absorb risk. The risk management framework or strategy should also elaborate policies for mitigating the identified risks and specify those responsible for implementation. The approach should give due attention to the interest of policyholders and should thus reflect expected prudent acceptance and management of risks.

- **A Sound Internal Control Framework:** A detailed and broad structure of internal controls which are capable of guaranteeing the proper execution of the strategies and polices should be in place. Internal control includes financial, operational and compliance controls. A good internal control structure is needed for the successful execution of compliance with the internal policies and law as well as the execution of risk management. The structure should include the segregation of duties.

- **A Strong, Comprehensive and Integrated System of Risk Management and Internal Control:** A complete and familiar approach to risk management should be adopted which brings together the categories of risk, and processes, procedures, and techniques of identifying risks and the working for assuring effective and efficient communication flows, coordination and decision-making processes. The approach should be followed so as to not lessen the governance checks and balances. Risks which arise from incentive structures as well as compensation packages should also be considered. Regular stress testing and situational analysis should be made. All parts of the organisation including business line, business support functions and control functions, as well as every level of the organisation along with key executives of the board should be involved in risk management.

It is possible that the risk management framework or strategy, as well as the internal control framework, are fully integrated into the risk management and internal control system and are thus not separately articulated. The approach taken in the guidelines advices that a separate risk management strategy will allow the board to focus on the general risk strategy, along with the key elements of risk management, leaving the execution to the management.

Prompt action by the management should be taken to correct any material control deficiencies or risk exposures which are inconsistent with the insurer's desired risk, as shown in the risk strategy. A process and management plan by the board should be in place to monitor the progress made to correct the problems. Problems may be identified through management reports, internal and external audit findings, the reports of the appointed actuary, the views and observations, of the supervisory authority and other external parties, such as credit rating agencies, and the views, solicited by the board, of the insurer's external and internal auditors, legal counsel or outside experts.

Control Functions

Control functions (also known as internal oversight functions) *should be established within an insurer to implement or ensure adherence to board policies on governance, risk management, internal controls, financial reporting and compliance, and recommend improvements where necessary.* The functions are also needed for implementing and observing the management policies. These functions should include:
- a risk management function,
- actuarial function,
- a compliance function and
- an internal audit function.

The independence of the control functions should be promoted and should have authority and status within an insurer and should be well resourced and appropriately expert, staffed by persons possessing appropriate integrity, competence, skills, expertise and relevant experience and professional qualifications. It should be kept separate from business operations or other factors that could affect the ability to perform. That said it may be beneficial for the control functions to participate as relevant in management structures (including, in a dual board system, the management board) insofar as these structures properly integrate the views of these functions to ensure sound decision-making.

Control functions should have a reporting relationship with the board and key executives, and should be able to participate in relevant board meetings.

Control functions should provide reports which consist of their findings on a regular basis. The external auditor and the heads of the control functions should meet periodically with the non-executive members of relevant board committee(s) and of the board without the management present. Procedures should be in place so as to advance identified problem areas to the board and if necessary it should be able to request a meeting of the board.

The designated person who knows the day to day working for managing the control function should head the control functions. The control function should be capable of collecting and aggregating information across the organisation, forming a comprehensive view of the activities for which the control function is responsible, identifying and undertaking any necessary actions or decisions. To fulfil their duties, the control functions should be able to obtain any data, reports or documents necessary for their findings They should be well informed and understand the regulatory and legal requirements.

The board should oversee the control functions, including their mandate, scope of activities, authority, independence and resources; organisational structure and reporting lines; the relationship among the control functions; and the selection of the heads of the control functions. The reporting feature of the control functions should be clearly documented and the authority of the control functions should be well communicated.

The control functions of the insurer should:
- assess the appropriateness of policies,
- process and carry out procedures over which they have oversight,
- identify and follow up on any identified deficiencies and propose any necessary amendments,
- any proposals to amend board policies should be communicated to the board for review and decision, and
- the heads of the control functions should consider meeting regularly to discuss control issues given the possibilities of mutual reinforcement among control functions.

Control functions may be combined as long as the integrity and authority of each function that is combined is maintained and any potential conflicts of interest arising from such combination are addressed through appropriate control procedures.

Risk Management: The risk management function should be established within all insurers to identify, assess, implement or ensure adherence to the board's risk management policy, framework, or strategy, monitor and appropriately mitigate risks lacing the insurer and develop and ensure effective application of the risk management system. The risk management function should ensure adherence to the insurer's specific risk management policies, processes, procedures and mitigation techniques and verify the appropriateness of any material risk taking, where risk management is conducted by business line functions.

The risk management function should provide regular reports to key executives and the board on the insurer's risk profile and details on the risk exposures facing the insurer and related mitigation actions as appropriate. Since it is an important function it should be headed by a non-operational key executive. It should also advice on risks relating to strategic and operational decisions, mergers and acquisitions, new product development, outsourcing and major investments.

Actuaries: A major role, in the insurance risks incurred by the insurer is played by actuaries in controlling the quality of the information the insurer discloses to its shareholders. The actuary's place and function has mainly been toward a strengthening of the powers of actuaries in both the life and non-life sectors.

Most OECD countries require life insurers to have an actuary appointed by the board.

The model of the appointed actuary is more developed in the life sector owing to the long duration of life insurance contracts and the necessity and challenge of ensuring an appropriate level of technical provisions for such contracts. However, the nature and complexity of insurance risks in the non-life sector, combined with the imperative of effective risk management, suggest the need for a proper appointed actuary or actuarial function in this sector. In a number of OECD countries, such requirement already exists. The appointment of an actuary in the life sector is therefore generally required in most OECD countries. The primary role of the actuary is to estimate the insurance risks facing an insurer, calculate policy liabilities and determine, or provide an opinion on, the appropriate technical provisions to cover these obligations.

The actuary may perform a number of other functions, such as product development and design, the determination on premium adequacy (in some jurisdictions, this may include a determination of premium reasonableness and fairness), oversight of underwriting and/or reinsurance arrangements, advice on risk management and investment policy, an assessment of the fairness or impact of transfers of insurance business and an assessment of the solvency position of the insurer and compliance with solvency requirements. In the context of mutual insurers and insurers with participating policyholders, actuaries provide determination on the fair treatment of' policyholders regarding the distribution of surplus through policy dividends and other benefits. The actuary should have access to all relevant data, accounts, and other information and relevant staff in order to carry out his/her duties. The actuary should also have a budget to engage external professional assistance when necessary.

Actuaries provide, at least annually, a statement, opinion, or report on their valuations and determinations to management, and the board. With external auditors, actuaries may, in some jurisdictions, be directed by the supervisory authority to prepare a special purpose in-depth report on the insurer's financial condition and operations.

The actuary should be free of influences that may compromise his/her ability to undertake, objectively and impartially, actuarial calculations and determine or provide advice on the technical provisions. Independence of the actuary may be understood differently depending on the jurisdiction. However, in order to a avoid conflict of interest, the actuary should, when undertaking actuarial calculations and determining or providing advice on technical provisions, be independent from business line management and decision-making. For instance, it would be inappropriate for the insurer's appointed actuary to be, at the same time, the insurer's chief executive officer or one of its key business line managers.

The actuary should be subject to strict qualification and suitability standards in order to ensure sound actuarial and financial calculations and promote proper conduct. The actuary should inform the board and the external auditor if, in the course of his/her duties, he/she becomes aware of any matter that has or is likely to have a material adverse effect on the insurer's financial condition, or aware that the insurer does not or is unlikely to comply with relevant standards. If no suitable action is taken, the actuary should inform the supervisory authority.

A potential trade-off in promoting the independence of the actuary is possible by reduced board or management responsibility and accountability for the financial statements of the insurer and determination of the insurer's solvency. The removal of the actuary may be required where the actuary fails to perform adequately the required functions and duties or no longer meets fit and proper criteria. He may resign for a variety of reasons, including possible disagreements or internal pressure.

Compliance: To monitor the insurer's adherence to general internal policies and codes, such as in relation to ethics and business conduct and to legal and regulatory requirements, a compliance function should be established. It should report material non-compliance to the board. It should also take up training efforts to ensure the employees are familiar with the internal policies. The legal and regulatory environment of applicable jurisdictions as well as evolving good practices in ethical and business conduct should be monitored. It may be responsible for managing the whistle-blowing arrangements.

Internal Audit: To monitor the insurer's implementation of, and adherence to, internal controls, assess the adequacy and effectiveness of these controls and the control environment and recommend improvements, an internal audit function needs to be established independently. Significant audit findings or material problems should be reported to the board and to the external auditor.

The internal audit function may monitor the insurer's implementation of, and adherence to governance, risk management and compliance policies, assess the adequacy and effectiveness of these policies, review and assess the risk management system and recommend improvements, as well as report material findings or problems on these matters to the board or a board committee, in the absence of independent risk management and compliance control functions.

Compensation

Compensation is an essential part of corporate governance especially in the insurer's internal governance. Compensation is the factor that binds the board members and personnel to the firm for their activities. The key component of the insurer's incentive structure is compensation and it serves to:

(a) Reinforce the alignment of the interests of the board, management and employees with the interests of the insurer (including its fundamental values and objectives) and thus, ultimately, with the insurer, be it shareholder or member policyholders.

(b) Promote good governance and risk management practices and observance of the insurer's internal controls and external compliance and thus promote a proper culture of risk and

(c) Promote fair conduct of employees with respect to consumers and policyholders.

Compensation practices may distort incentives and lead to risky or unethical behaviour of an individual and collective level that could put the insurer at risk, be it in the short term or longer term, and lead to poor treatment of consumers and policyholders. The FSF Principles for Sound Compensation Practices outline principles for appropriate compensation practices: compensation arrangements should promote long-term, firm-wide profitability, and moreover, compensation arrangements should also appropriately remunerate those belonging to the control functions to ensure that these functions attract necessary expertise, have appropriate status within the insurer and exercise independent judgement.

Finally the risk management and internal control system should consider any risks arising from compensation and incentive structures, and establish appropriate policies, processes, mechanisms and controls to manage and appropriately mitigate these risks.

Management Structures

Internal organisational structures, such as management committees, to ensure effective implementation of board policies, coordinate decision-making while avoiding over-concentration of decision-making, promote information flows across the organisation and ensure that appropriate expertise and differences of perspectives are incorporated into analysis and decision-making, need to be considered to be established by the insurers. Insurers should consider establishing, at a minimum, a management committee or similar organisational structure which is responsible for risk management so as to make sure that an enterprise-wide identification, assessment, monitoring and mitigation of risks is established and management committees dedicated to risk management, capital, investment etc may be established. These internal organisational structures may also include mechanisms to promote employee participation in certain decision-making.

Communication and Reporting

For the operation of the insurer, implementation of board strategies and policies including risk management and achievement of objectives, as well as for proper oversight of the insure effective reporting and communication is critical. Reporting should cover all aspects of the insurer's activities and processes, including its adherence to internal policies and controls and its conduct with policyholders. Reporting should include the generation, analysis, documentation and timely transmission of relevant and accurate information and appropriate escalation mechanisms so that critical new information can be elevated to appropriate levels, including the board.

By establishing appropriate reporting channels, internal controls, organisational structures such as management committees, management information systems, analytical tools, whistle-blowing arrangements (see below) and other mechanisms, effective internal reporting can be achieved. Reporting should be bi-directional, making sure that not only the top management but also all employees are informed of the internal operations, policies, decisions especially those relevant to their duties.

Whistle-blowing

With respect to inappropriate actions or behaviour, measures should be taken so that employees, stakeholders can bring matters to the attention of the board within the insurer or on the part of operators or consultants performing outsourced functions. Inappropriate actions may include illegal, unethical, or otherwise questionable conduct. Breaches of internal controls must be brought to the notice of the concerned channels but if no such action is taken then the use of whistle-blowing may be considered. Reports should be assessed in a confidential manner and should be acted upon and if there are any findings, it should be bought to the attention of the board or at least one of its committees. A person who has been given the whistle-blowing responsibility should be properly trained.

Whistleblowers should be given adequate protection and should be taken into confidence so as to ensure effectiveness of such disclosure. Protections include a strong anti-retaliation policy and appropriately tailored carve-outs in confidentiality rules applicable to employees in order to permit, in special circumstances, whistle-blowing to external parties. Keep in mind, whistle-blowing should not be used for criticism, or any misuse and an appeal method should exist for the victims. To oversee whistle-blowing arrangements and for making sure that they are effective and appropriate, a board or committee should be responsible for overseeing this.

Relations with Shareholders and other Stakeholders

The actual owners of the business are the shareholders and hence the board of directors are accountable to them. The directors are appointed by the shareholders at the AGM and the directors manage the business on behalf of the shareholders.

A number of measures have been introduced by the different reports on corporate governance, so that the directors can perform in the interest of the shareholders, such as:

- Requiring all directors to submit themselves for re-election regularly (at least once every three years).
- Requiring shareholders (particularly institutional shareholders) to actively participate in policy formation at AGMs and to use their votes to communicate with the board.

To increase the communications between shareholders in the AGM, the Hampel Report (UK) provides recommendations to do so. Shareholders must be provided sufficient notice prior to the meeting, developing a system whereby shareholders can vote on different issues separately rather than as a bundle, including a question-and-answer session for shareholders to raise any concerns, are some of recommendations made.

The OCED's (Organisation for Economic Co-operation and Development) guidelines on corporate governance gives importance to the other stakeholder groups, by stating that competitiveness and ultimate success of a corporation depends on the contributions of different stakeholders such as employees, creditors and suppliers and recommends that

"The corporate governance framework of a company should ensure that respect is given to the rights of stakeholders that are protected by law, which include rights under labour law, business law and insolvency law".

The other recommendation is to improve the participation of the stakeholder in the governance through employee representation on the board and profit sharing schemes etc.

Clause 49 of Listing Agreement and Corporate Governance Code

Clause 49, issued by SEBI was introduced in February 2000. Through Clause 49, The SEBI will monitor and regulate the corporate governance of listed companies in India. The clause which is included in the listing agreement of the stock exchange with the companies, and which makes sure that that it is compulsory for them to obey with its requirements. By the introduction of Clause 49, stock exchange tried to bring corporate governance standards among the companies, once the companies enter into a listing agreement. All Group A companies had to comply with its provisions by 31st March 2001. All other listed companies with a minimum paid-up capital of 100 million and net worth of 250 million had to comply by 31st March 2002 and the remaining listed companies with a minimum paid-up capital of 30 million or net worth of 250 million had to comply by 31st March, 2003.

The old clause was amended in to a new Clause 49 on 29th October, 2004. All the listed companies were told to obey the new clause provisions by 1 April, 2005, which many of the companies did follow.

Provisions and Requirements of Clause 49

The provisions and requirements of Clause 49 are as follows:

- **Composition of Board:** The board should be composed of in the following manner: In case of full-time chairman, 50 per cent non-executive directors and 50 per cent executive directors.
- **Constitution of the Audit Committee:** The audit committee should have three independent directors with the chairman having sound financial background. The finance director and the head of the internal audit should be special invitees and a minimum of three meetings should be convened every year.
- **Audit Committee:** The audit committee is responsible for review of financial performance on half-yearly annual basis; appointment/removal/remuneration of auditors; review of internal control systems and its adequacy.
- **Remuneration of Directors:** Remuneration of non-executive directors is to be decided by the board. Details of remuneration package, stock options and performance incentives of directors should be disclosed to the shareholders.
- **Board procedures:** The board should have at least four meetings a year. A director should not be member of more than 10 committees and chairman of more than five committees across all companies.
- **Management Discussion and Analysis Report:** This should include:
    (i) Industry structure and developments;
    (ii) Opportunities and threats;
    (iii) Segment-wise or product-wise performance;
    (iv) Outlook on the business;
    (v) Risk and concerns;
    (vi) Internal control systems and their adequacy;
    (vii) Discussion on financial performance, and
    (viii) Disclosure by directors on materials, financial and commercial transactions with the company.
- **Shareholders information:** The company should provide a brief resume of new/re-appointed directors and submit quarterly results to stock exchanges to be placed on website and presented to analysis. Shareholders/Investors Grievance Committee under the chairmanship of independent director should have a minimum of two meetings a year. The company should report on corporate governance and get certificate from auditors on compliance of provisions of corporate governance as per Clause 49 in the listing agreement.

- **Nominee Directors to be independent directors:** Nominees of institutions that have invested in or lent to the company are deemed independent directors.
- **New provisions incorporated in the new clause 49:** The board will lay down a code of conduct for all board members and senior management of the company to follow compulsorily.

The cash flow statements and financial statements will have to be certified by the CEO and CFO. At least one independent director of the holding company will be a member of the board of a material non-listed subsidiary. In case a company follows a method of preparing financial statements that is different from standard accounting standards, it should be disclosed in the financial statements and an explanation should be provided in the corporate governance report.

- **CEO is accountable for Company Risk System:** Inspired by the Sarbanes-Oxley Act, clause 49 of listing agreement was scheduled to come into effect from 1st April, 2005. However, bowing to demand from corporations. SEBI decided in the board meeting held on 23rd March, 2005, to defer the implementation of clause 49 till 31st December to provide listed entities, including public sector companies, giving time to appoint adequate number of independent directors to comply with norms. No special concession is to be extended to state owned enterprises which demanded exemption on this issue. SEBI felt that the public sector undertakings are not looked upon as a special class of companies. Under the new provisions, CEOs and CFOs in the country had been preparing for a litmus test. Beginning 31st December, 2005, all CEOs and CFOs have embarked on massive documentation to meet the requirements of Clause 49 of SEBI's listing agreement.
- **Rules of the Game:** The CEOs and CFOs are to be directly responsible for risk management (Provision 4C) and internal control systems (Section 5). Clause 49 is largely derived from the Sarbanes-Oxley Act; companies seek legal advice, they tap consultants to adopt new standards, companies want clarity on 'material' association of independent directors and fear new norms will lead to shortage of independent directors. Companies will have to spend more time and money on compliance.

CEO/CFO Certification

If according to the Companies Act, 1956, a CEO (managing director) and CFO (finance director) are appointed, or any other person who heads the finance function will have to certify to the board that:

(a) They have reviewed financial statements and the cash flow statement for the year and that to the best of their knowledge and brief:

   (i) these statements do not contain any materially untrue statement or omit any material fact or contain statements that might be misleading;

(ii) these statements together present a true and fair view of the company's affairs and are in compliance with existing accounting standards, applicable laws and regulations.

(b) There are, to the best of their knowledge and belief, no transactions entered into by the company during the year which are fraudulent, illegal or volatile of the company's code of conduct.

(c) They accept responsibility for establishing and maintaining internal controls and that they have evaluated the effectiveness of the internal control systems of the company and they have disclosed to the auditors and the audit committee, deficiencies in the design or operation of internal controls, if any, of which they are aware and the steps they have taken or propose to take to rectify these deficiencies.

(d) They have indicated to the auditors and the audit committee
 (i) significant changes in internal control during the year;
 (ii) significant changes in accounting policies during the year and that the same have been disclosed in the notes to the financial statements; and
 (iii) instances of significant fraud of which they have become aware and the involvement therein, if any, of the management or an employee having a significant role in the company's internal control system.

Role of Regulators in Corporate Governance: SEBI, IRDA, RBI, ED

(A) Role of SEBI in Corporate Governance

Established in 1992, the Securities Exchange Board of India is essential to corporate governance of India's securities market, as it serves as the central body that ensures investors are protected and the securities market is regulated.

In response to the Financial Services Assessment Programme, a program developed by the World Bank and International Monetary Fund that observes and reports on global financial systems, the Indian Parliament passed the Securities and Exchange Board of India Act, 1992 and that is how SEBI got formed. With a regulator promoting the latest in corporate governance standards, the Indian government wanted to establish a stable financial atmosphere and securities market.

Governance standards should be set by SEBI which makes sure the rights of users and investors are protected. If the markets or the players have been harmed, SEBI has the power to investigate and enforce governance standards with directives. An appeal process in place ensures accountability and transparency. Any company that does not comply with its governance standards and regulations may be terminated by SEBI in the securities list.

(B) Role of RBI in Corporate Governance

The appointment of directors and additional directors in the banks of India are controlled by the RBI.

Corporate governance requirements are intended to encourage the bank to be well managed, and is an indirect way of achieving other objectives, such as:

1. To be a body corporate (i.e. not an individual, a partnership, trust or other unincorporated entity).
2. To be incorporated locally, and/or to be incorporated under as a particular type of body corporate, rather than being incorporated in a foreign jurisdiction.
3. To have a minimum number of directors.
4. To have an organisational structure that includes various offices and officers, e.g. Corporate Secretary, Treasurer/CFO, Auditor, Asset Liability Management Committee, and Privacy Officer etc. Also the officers for those offices may need to be approved persons, or from an approved class of persons.
5. To have a constitution or articles of association that is approved, or contains or does not contain particular clauses that enable directors to act other than in the best interests of the company (e.g. in the interests of a parent company) may not be allowed.

4.5 Applying Best Practice in Governance

4.5.1 Voluntary vs. Mandatory

'**Mandatory**' *means mandated by law which results in penal consequences for noncompliance.* '**Voluntary**' *on the other hand means which does not have a legal compulsion and is purely discretionary.*

Around the world, people are arguing whether the corporate governance law should be made mandatory or should be voluntary. In countries like the United States of America, the law is mandatory but other countries like Canada, Australia and UK permit companies to make choices on certain governance practices but compel them to disclose these choices. In January 2010, the World Economic Forum held their Annual Meeting which called for stricter regulations and at the same time the United States President, Barack Obama stated that there were will be more regulations of the financial sector in the US. Many businesses, domestic as well as international, called for voluntary efforts for improved corporate behaviour, mainly through better governance practices.

The **Global Reporting Initiative** (GRI) has urged governments to ask companies to report
- on their environmental,
- social and
- governance (ESG) performance

If they fail then they have to give reasons for not doing so.

The GRI, in its Amsterdam Declaration on Transparency and Reporting, March 2009, appealed to governments to put in place policies for companies, state-owned corporations and public investment agencies to report on ESG indicators. The Chief Executive, GRI, Ernst R. Ligteringen, states that the companies should either accept the ESG reporting or should give reasons for not doing so.

Formally or informally, the regulation of corporate governance can be achieved through four primary factors

- lawmaking;
- stakeholder concentration to increase their monitoring and control capabilities;
- market discipline; and
- formal contracting between stakeholders and the company

Recent researches favour a broader approach and prefer regulation which includes voluntary sources of corporate governance standards which companies have the freedom to adopt.

Regulation which is voluntary with a 'compile or explain' clause is an equal approach between mandatory and voluntary. This has been described as 'enforced self-regulation'.

Since governance is not a 'one size fits all' or 'tick a box' approach, there can be many answers.

The pros and cons of the mandatory and voluntary systems are as follows:

1. **Minimum Standards:** The mandatory structure enables the states to establish minimum standards to which companies must adhere. Once enforced, the top management is forced to follow the standards of corporate governance leaving no scope for self interested transactions and arrangements. The state is able to achieve its investor protection objective directly as corporates are forced to comply or face penalties for non-compliance, even though the investors do not gain a lot from the mandatory standards.

   In voluntary standards, the objectives of good corporate governance may not be achieved as they may not follow such standards. Countries with mandatory standards have larger capital markets as they provide for strong legal protection to the potential investors and shield them against expropriation by entrepreneurs on the financial front.

2. **Compliance Levels:** High levels of compliance are ensured as heavy penalties for non-compliance combined with awareness about such sanctions. On the other hand, voluntary does not guarantee compliance. Voluntary systems might work in some circumstances but are unlikely to achieve the desired degree of compliance. Voluntary and self-regulation models are often misused.

3. **Costs to Investors:** Mandatory structures make the corporates accountable to their investors as the cost of obtaining information and assessing the corporates for the investors is quite less. Comparison among the corporates is relatively easier in a mandatory structure, as all corporates comply with the same law and reporting structures whereas companies are free to set their own standards and there is less certainty that they are complying with the guidelines in voluntary governance systems.

4. **Costs to Companies and to the State:** A mandatory system is very cost-effective to the investors but the same is not true for companies and the state. The company also has to bear the costs of monitoring its own practices, implementing new governance structures, producing and distributing information in accordance with the disclosure requirements. The state has to bear the costs of policy design, implementation and enforcement which include the costs of monitoring the market for compliance.

5. **Flexibility:** The mandatory regimes on the other hand are inflexible as the state lays down the objectives and prescribes the means to achieve those objectives. On the other hand voluntary regimes offer a great deal of flexibility to companies. They offer tailor-made governance structures to corporates of different sizes and cultures.

4.5.2 Rules and Principles-based Approaches

Countries such as UK and many Commonwealth countries embraced the 'principles-based' approach to the enforcement of the provisions of the corporate governance codes. This is important for publicly traded companies as the stock market had to be aware of the corporate governance provisions. Companies were able to adopt a more flexible approach to code provisions than would have been the case had compliance been underpinned by law, when they included the requirement to comply with codes within the listing rules.

The principle of 'comply or explain' emerged. If investors were dissatisfied with the explanation, the market was then able to 'punish' for the non-compliance. Some companies, especially larger ones, make 'full compliance' a prominent announcement to shareholders in the annual report, presumably in the belief that this will underpin investor confidence in management, and protect market value. Compliance in principles-based jurisdictions is not voluntary in any material sense.

Companies are asked to comply with the rules, but since it is not legally required, one should not assume that they have a free hand. Companies are not free to choose non-compliance if compliance is too much trouble.

According to the size of the business and the nature of the non-compliance, the market revaluing a company varies as a result of technical non-compliance trends. Companies which are lower down in the list in terms of market value are given more leeway than larger companies. This point is an important differentiating factor between rule-based and principles-based approaches, since the market is allowed to agree on the degree of non-compliance. This helps and is an important factor in the development of a small business where the cost of compliance is high. This approach is usually adopted in the UK.

4.5.3 Concept of 'Comply or Explain'

'Comply or explain' in governance requires trust between the corporate and stakeholders, while concerns over the regime should also be looked at head on, says Jo Iwasaki.

The major backbone of the corporate governance code is the principle of 'comply and explain'. When strategic use of comply and explain is put to good use, the result is good governance. If comply or explain is used effectively, this leads to the business to provide market-based solutions, which are often worked out between the shareholders and the company and when no regulatory intervention is needed.

Comply and explain as an approach that recognises other methods is also accepted if it achieves good governance. Departures from the code are not seen to be breaches if the accompanying explanations can provide an insight into how a company is thinking, and how they are aiming to achieve good corporate governance.

Explain Governance Choices

Choosing governance choices is difficult. Explanations that are provided are often mechanical and often fail to explain how the company's other arrangements support the principle. Companies have also criticised how non-compliance negatively affects awareness towards the market and overshadows the advantages of choosing another option that would still deliver good governance to the business.

For a period of time, this might mean regulatory intervention. It should also be recognised that in a compliance regime, regulators can achieve the benefits of 'comply or explain' by allowing long transitional arrangements and exemptions.

There needs to be an awareness of its specific advantages for better usage of 'comply and explain'. ICAEW has identified four areas where 'comply or explain' can serve businesses and investors and have advantages over other alternatives.

- **Innovation:** when introducing aspirational new ideas and changes to company governance.
- **Proportionality:** a measured application of more demanding requirements, especially for smaller businesses.
- **Avoiding box-ticking:** encourages companies to think through overarching principles before automatically complying with provisions, because they have the option to 'explain'.

- **Long-term learning:** assisting cultural change in companies that think deeply and regularly about how to meet the purpose and principles of corporate governance until it becomes part of their normal thought process.

Building Trust

People need to trust companies to demonstrate genuine commitment to good governance, and companies need to trust that their explanations will be given proper consideration, if comply or explain is to work and be sustainable.

Where this mutual trust exists, comply or explain can be seen as providing market-based solutions that are worked out between companies and their shareholders without the need for regulatory intervention.

Two conditions make the 'comply and explain' policy a success:
- shared beliefs
- institutional arrangements

In establishing the mutual trust which is essential, both are equally important. Institutional arrangements need to ensure that explanations are a credible alternative to regulatory and legal enforcement of compliance.

When the advantages of innovation, proportionality, substance over form or long-term learning are not delivered properly then doubts about 'comply and explain' arise.

4.6 Globalisation and Corporate Governance

The need for external funding is the key underlying driver of corporate governance. The organisation has to not only retain as well as attract shareholders but also obtain loans to meet funding. It has to assure the investors that the funds will not go wasted but instead will be used responsibly and will produce promising returns to the investors. Corporate governance is the substance behind such a demonstration of effectiveness and it needs to create and attach power to achieve that end. Business is driven by the exercise of power; corporate governance is driven by the need to moderate and channel that power.

4.6.1 Key Drivers of Corporate Governance in Global Companies

(A) Internal Drivers

1. Fairness

An important feature of corporate governance is "fairness". The **OECD** defines 'fairness' as *'protecting shareholder rights and ensuring contracts with resource providers are enforceable'*. This means that all the shareholders have equal and clear rights and the supply contracts are also fair. Since it has both legal and behavioural roots, fairness operates more in corporate governance. The behavioural aspects of fairness are developed in behavioural economics as a form of preferences. Fairness is the force which bonds the cooperation between the stakeholders and resists the concentration and abuse of power.

2. **Trust**

   Just like fairness, corporate governance is also driven by trust. *Trust is a relationship of reliance*. When full details are not known, trust is the only factor between humans. When corporate governance is based on principles, trust is very important as the principles will require interpretations to make judgements. Rules-based corporate governance is less open to interpretation, or even to explaining precedents, yet there has to be trust in the process of shaping the rules. One can say that trust is developed between people whereas confidence is built on facts.

   In any case, it would seem that trust has deeper roots and can cope with greater uncertainty than confidence.

3. **Risk**

   The third factor to be considered is risk. Organisations will have to identify risks as without taking risks there are no meaningful rewards. Awareness of risks is now a key dimension of corporate governance reporting, following the Turnbull Report. Managing risk is not seen still as important in organisations which should have better governance. It is perhaps significant that the ISO standard for risk management ISO 31000 was not published until 2009!

4. **Competition**

   Competition plays a crucial part of corporate governance. There are some organisations that enjoy a monopoly but this will last until the competitors would catch up.

   The Eight Core Dimensions of Corporate Governance are:

   - The identity of the organisation;
   - The purpose of the organisation;
   - Leadership;
   - The distribution of power within the organisation;
   - Inclusiveness and communication;
   - The pattern of accountability required;
   - The maximisation of effectiveness;
   - Ensuring sustainability.

   Organisations need to innovate to maintain a competitive edge. Competitive advantage is achieved by organisations which keep these dimensions in focus and updated, aware that they have to excel in all of them in order to compete successfully in the long term.

5. **Leadership**

   Leadership is equally important as it maintains a firm focus on the objective and pushes those involved to push each other to achieve the objective. It is not the only right of one person but it may change depending on the circumstances.

Leadership depends on trust and the competence to fulfill the role required at the time. In a crisis, leadership may have to be brought into an organisation in the form of a 'company doctor', in order to ride the crisis, stabilise the organisation and hand authority back to a new board.

(B) External Drivers

Some external drivers of corporate governance are present who match or motivate the internal drivers which we have seen above. Most of them operate independently, although they may operate in tandem to greater effect. These external drivers are discussed below:

1. **Media**

   Media is one of the most important external drivers that can have a major impact on the organisation. Any scandal whether small or big, the media is just waiting to publish it. Journalists love to attack and are just waiting for the news to break out; take for example Mukesh Ambani and Anil Ambani – their fallout had a major media coverage. Business and economic media, e.g. Financial Times, The Economist, etc., devote resources to the analysis of key businesses and seek the opportunity to interview key business leaders and opinion-formers (NGOs, lobby groups, business academics, etc.). Apart from such occasions mass media do not feature issues of corporate governance.

   Journalists are trying to lay their hands on some unusual angle, discord, difficulties or any weaknesses which can make news. They can also find weaknesses in press statements and probe to uncover the true situation.

   The media are not impressed by public relations; they seek a story to interest their audience. The role of the media is so great that organisations are now cautious enough to cover up the situation. Challenge from media is forcing greater openness on organisations and making them accountable for true situations rather than myths.

2. **Stakeholders**

   Stakeholders, who have always been in the background, have now started speaking up and hold a major position in the organisation's say. The Companies Act 2006 confirms their legal status in company law and the development of corporate social responsibility widens their circle from employees, customers and suppliers to encompass other constituencies which impact the organisation, e.g. the local community. Stakeholders drive corporate governance in varying ways and degrees: some, like employees, have a fundamental impact on the organisation; others, such as government, impact less directly and frequently. The shareholders are the largest potential to drive corporate governance. Though the impact is low, still, it is evident that good governance is linked to improved company performance. Shareholders seek to benefit from the wealth-creating potential of business and hence the stakeholder's involvement is increasing. NGOs and charities are laying claims to be stakeholders, and buying shares to legitimise their claims. It seems inevitable that stakeholders will seek to increase their benefits from association with companies through exploiting corporate governance and the greater wealth it produces.

3. **Activists**

   Either by having a seat on the board or by offering specialist advice, stakeholders want to be involved and take an active part in the organisation. In USA, board elections are just a formality as it is impossible for shareholders to nominate the board members. To make the elections more democratic pressure is on to change the US legislation.

4. **Regulations**

   Rules are important but inactive when there is a high degree of trust involved. Regulators act as referees to mediate between competitors. Regulation appeals to bureaucrats and is usually self-perpetuating. Regulators are expected to work with clients and avoid disruption of their activities. The 2007 Regulators' Compliance Code should encourage companies to drive for better compliance voluntarily, leaving the regulator to act as a coach rather than a policeman. With the growth of multinational companies, regulation is fragmented across different regimes and it is now common for operations to be located in low-regulation countries (following the migration of tax liabilities). This process was a major contributor to the recent financial crisis, reaction to which may facilitate moves towards better regulation.

4.6.2 Governance Problems for Global Companies and Groups

1. **Entrenched Power**

   Well-established power is one of the strongest resistors of corporate governance. This can usually be seen with well established directors (often led by a powerful CEO) or in family run businesses. Such a person is often the CEO and chairman and has all levels of powers in his hands.

   Signs that show this trend are:
   - A non-challenging finance director;
   - Complacent non-executive directors (hired by the CEO);
   - Executive directors all 'home grown' (and compliant);
   - Entrenched auditor;
   - High proportion of long service employees but above average staff turnover;
   - Low product innovation;
   - Above-average reward packages for executive directors.

   Such situations are difficult to remedy.

2. **Hidden Agendas**

The only antidote to hidden agendas is a strong culture of openness, explaining reasons for actions and documenting them in detail. Take the example of Enron, which appeared to be an exemplary company but it was consumed by hidden agendas. Hidden agendas may include insider trading, commercial espionage, favouring family or outsiders at the expense of the organisation – and just plain fraud. A good protection against fraud is to have an internal audit where the internal auditor can immediately point out any discrepancies. Decisions taken in the interest of the company cannot logically benefit individuals or cliques disproportionately.

3. **Resistance to Change**

   Change always goes hand in hand with resistance. Change cannot be kept at bay and hence it is better to welcome it with open arms instead of resisting it. Change usually happens from outside which cannot be ignored or resisted while some change occurs internally too, for example like the death of the CEO. Directors who resist the change are neglecting their duty.

4. **Secrecy**

   The standard justification for secrecy in business is to defend competitive advantage. Sophocles wrote, 'Do nothing secretly; for time sees and hears all things and discloses all.'

   Some information like technical secrets can be kept a secret but the payment methods cannot be kept a secret as they are needed at the time of recruitment. Important information can be protected by patents but the less important ones are not a secret. One area of secrecy has been private equity, created in order to avoid public accountability. Secrecy causes mistrust between people, which hinders the smooth running of corporate governance. It is usually counterproductive.

5. **Distrust/Mistrust**

   Distrust is the spirit of the relationship between rivals. Mistrust usually takes place when the organisation thinks the other party has a hidden agenda – basically caused by uncertainty. Distrust depends on a mutual belief that both parties are 'playing a game'. When this belief breaks down, mistrust takes centre stage. Distrust can said to be positive when shareholders hold directors on account.

   Most principals were found to give their agents wide discretion and to achieve better results than those seeking tight control of means employed.

4.6.3 Other Issues Concerning Corporate Governance in Global Companies

1. **Cost**

   Companies often dislike the growing cost of compliance and they see the governance as a burden. Scott McNealy of Sun Microsystems sees SOX as 'one of the most damaging buckets of sand in the gears of the market economy that were ever voted 98:0 on in Washington'. He observed that the cost incurred to most public companies was to the tune of $5 to $10 million with no benefits. Due to its effect of making reporting on management more transparent to directors and owners was the real concern of reverse SOX as suggested by Professor Cox of Duke University. With this situation, the management is held more accountable and is at a greater disadvantage. US lawyers are also protesting as they cannot afford the low legal fees which are offered by the European law firms.

   While it is salutary to recognise the growing cost of corporate governance, the benefits emerge in the increasing adoption of best practice in governance and in the pattern of improved business results achieved by serious practitioners.

2. **Whistle-blowing**

   A whistle-blower is defined as *'an employee or member of an organisation, especially a business or government agency, who reports misconduct to people or entities that have the power and presumed willingness to take corrective action. The misconduct may be a violation of a law, rule, regulation and/or a direct threat to public interest, such as fraud, health/safety violations and corruption"*. The term 'whistle-blowing' derives from the practice of English policemen to blow a whistle when they noticed a crime being committed.

   By harassment, criminal prosecution or dismissal, most whistle-blowers have suffered because of their action.

Specific benefits cited include:
- Improved disclosures, leading to greater investor confidence;
- Reduced risk of loss through fraud, protecting assets and reputation;
- Improved acquisition integration, highlighting systems incompatibilities;
- Enhanced market confidence and reputation management, avoiding earnings restatements and delayed announcements;
- Standardisation of processes and controls, reducing costs and increasing efficiency;
- Better control over management and information systems, increasing internal security.

The most effective aspects of corporate governance are
- A strong board of directors, independent of management, but with expertise to oversee management;
- Management compensation oversight;
- Strong corporation laws and regulations to protect the rights of shareholders;
- Extensive public disclosure requirements, both financial and non-financial;
- A robust independent audit function.

These aspects need to be supported by credibly strong government and market enforcement mechanisms.

If companies are given this support they can attract investors on the most favourable standards. In short the best public companies will continue to view strong corporate governance as an investment well worth making.

4.7 Governance Issues in the Public Sector

Corporate Governance as a concept is fast rising as a decisive conceptual tool to control, contain and also facilitate corporate operations across the world. Corporate governance is a means of assuring investors both individual and institutional shareholders that the corporation does not intend to misuse their money in their operations, in these times of globalisation. To make sure that corporate entities do not engage in fraud and rather grow and make profits, the structure of corporate governance is so designed. The public sector utilities with important social responsibilities to fulfill other than make profits also come under the scanner because they use the taxpayers' money for their operations. Since the non-government organisations use money given as donation for their non-profit programmes, they are often answerable to the donors if the money is well spent.

As institutional investments from financial institutions such as lending institutions, insurance companies and pension funds are growing, investors have been increasingly demanding transparency in company accounts, fair treatments and periodic updates about the company's performance. Remember, corporate governance does not protect the interests of just investors but also aims at being fair and transparent in the transactions with their customers, investors, vendors and especially the society at large.

Shareholders, in the technical sense, are the owners of a company but they mostly regard themselves as investors. Corporate governance seeks to build confidence and trust of the stakeholders by observing fairness and transparency in all company affairs. Therefore, corporate governance regulations in India promote the rights of shareholders; while at the same time ensure the interests of other stakeholders are also simultaneously protected.

4.7.1 Historical Roots of Public Sector

In India, when the state was authorised to lay a strong industrial base in the economy, that was when the public sector emerged. When India got independence the state of the economic structure was not very promising as the country was a poor country, with poor infrastructure and inadequate technological resources. The economy subjected to farming, unemployment and hunger. There was a lot of work to be done with India having to develop the infrastructure in terms of roads, power, railways etc; vast industrialisation; strong need to produce defense equipments and automobiles, railway coaches etc. Due to the above reasons setting up of vast public sector enterprises started to take place.

The reason why government had to be in business rather than encourage the private sector enterprises to grow was because such large scale industrialisation often needed huge investment outlays with low returns. In this context the private sector did not have the resources nor it could it make sacrifices of its commercial interest and that is when public sector came into the picture. The public sector can be found in:

- mining and mineral extraction,
- manufacturing of metals and other basic goods such as fertilizers, seeds, chemicals and
- heavy machinery.

In the services, public sector dominates in

- agricultural trading,
- railways,
- airlines,
- telecommunication,
- financial services,
- tourism and
- consultancies.

The public sector also played an important role in the

- achievement of constitutional goals like reducing concentration of economic power in private hands,
- increasing public control over the national economy, and
- creating a socialistic pattern of society, etc.

With all its linkages the public sector has made solid contributions to national self-reliance.

4.7.2 Changes in Public Sector

Public sector across the world, was been taken apart as people believed that government run businesses were less efficient and were not run on profit motive; it caused a huge drain on the tax payers money. India also underwent a huge resource deficiency and had to go the IMF for help. IMF demanded to restructure its economy. That is when the policy of progressive dissolution of the public sector came into play.

The private sector could even enter areas like airlines, mining etc. that were previously reserved for the public sector. The private sector could invite foreign capital and increase their capacities along with raising their investments. The monopoly of public sector thus eroded. The public sector was asked to operate like any other economic agent in a competitive market situation. In pursuit of profits, the public sector would look after its commercial interests ahead of its social duties.

4.7.3 Features of Indian PSUs

Some of the features of the Indian PSUs are:
1. Many of the public enterprises in India are publicly listed and are actively traded by individual investors owning shares alongside with the government.
2. Government ownership of assets dominates both in the manufacturing and in the banking sector.
3. When the market capitalisation is taken as a proportion of the total market capitalisation, it is most likely to be the highest in the world. Private enterprises are known not to have well diversified ownership; similarly the public enterprises also have ownership issues and control. In both cases, the structure and practice of monitoring, control, and superintendence appear to go beyond the typical corporate governance mechanisms, to direct control over management.

4.7.4 Difficulties in Arriving at Structure of Governance in India's Public Sector

Several studies (quantitative) were conducted to try to measure the efficiency of the public sector with that of the private companies.

To name a few:
1. Joshi and Little (1994) have attempted to estimate the real rates of return to investment in the public and private sectors.
2. Bhaya (1990) based his findings on the time series data from 1981-82 to 1985-86 published annually for the public and private sector by the survey of industries. He used three indicators of efficiency:
    - money,
    - workforce, and
    - material

Bhaya concluded from his findings that efficiency in the public sector is in no way inferior to the private sector.

3. Jha and Sahni (1992) use Annual Survey of Industries data for the years 1960-61 to 1982-83 for the following industries:
   - cement,
   - cotton textiles,
   - electricity, and
   - iron and steel.

   Cement and cotton textiles are primarily owned by private parties while the latter two are found mostly in the public sector. The authors have no evidence of allocative inefficiencies in general and each of them is relatively as efficient as one another.

4. Sharma and Sinha (1995) have used Cobb-Douglas production function to study productive efficiency (or economic efficiency), which mainly combines both technical and allocative efficiencies for the cement industry in India.

5. Majumdar (1995) evaluated relative performance difference between the government owned, joint sector and private sectors of Indian industry.

6. Kaur (1998) compared TFPI of 15 public and 15 private enterprises from diverse sectors, e.g. aluminium, steel, fertilizers, engineering, drugs and chemicals and consumer goods.

7. Naib (2002) compared efficiency of 26 enterprises (13 public and 13 private) for a 12 year period from 1988-89 to 1999-2000.

The results pointed out the fact that both the public as well as the private firms experienced a rise in the average annual growth rate during this period.

There are certain difficulties in arriving at a structure of governance in PSUs, even though, The Central Vigilance Commission, the Public Enterprises Selection Board, the Department of Public Enterprises, the Standing Conference of Public Enterprises as well as a few other agencies have been debating the need for the reform of corporate governance mechanisms in respect to the public enterprises.

4.7.5 Objective Function

The goal of the public enterprises have changed and become more complex, after economic liberalisation. Some of the goals of the public sector are:
- social development,
- income redistribution, and
- making profits in order to sustain itself and also ensuring services, at costs that are affordable, for a large section of the population.

Multiplicity of objectives dilutes the management's accountability.

The government should formulate a well-defined strategy for each PSU and establish the objective function based on that strategy. To protect the interest of non-government investors and to ensure effective functioning of the enterprise, clarity and transparency in communicating the objective function to all stakeholders is essential. The board of directors should use the objective function as the guide post in managing the resources of the firm.

The government should review and if necessary, revise the objective function to meet structural changes in the socio-economic environment or changes in national priorities. Frequent revisions should be avoided as they would confuse the stakeholders and will damage the credibility of the government. The government on its part should also not set multiple objectives for a particular public sector. The mission and vision statements, drafted by the government should reflect the objective function established for the particular PSU which, the board of directors should adopt.

4.7.6 Managerial and Commercial Autonomy

There is a positive and high correlation between autonomy and accountability, and autonomy and performance. Many committees were set up to study the PSU and most of them recommend autonomy. Governments have accepted autonomy but they continue to stay away from the PSUs.

While formal control by the government, as per provisions of law or the Memoranda and Articles of Association, is very extensive covering almost all areas of activities of enterprises, the informal control which consumes productive time of PSU managements, inhibits their decision making, a mockery of their autonomy and impairing their performance. Accountability not only of PSU managements, but also for bureaucracy and ministers should be defined including its content, limits, mechanics and benchmarks. Public enterprises function directly under the control of the government, even when they do not form departments in the government, there is far too much of interference in the working of the public sector enterprises, if PSUs have to become a reality. There is thus a question of autonomy of the public sector enterprise that is crucial for good performance and decision making. PSUs should be kept immune from political and bureaucratic interference.

Since we know that bureaucratic interference affects the performance of the enterprise, the government should control and monitor the PSUs without being meddlesome with the day to day management. The government should act as an informed and responsible promoter and majority shareholder of PSUs. The government policy to provide managerial and commercial autonomy to PSUs, operating in a competitive environment is much needed.

4.7.7 Board of Directors and Independent Directors

The capability and the values that the top management holds, directly depends on the enterprise. The top management must be given the freedom to put their thoughts to maximum use so as to perform well. Nominating unqualified and unsuitable persons as top management of PSUs by vested interests affects their performance.

Generally, the public sector enterprises have bureaucrats as members; and this does not qualify as independent directors. The government should appoint professionals having competence and understanding of business as board members. It may be a good idea to invite other large shareholders to nominate their representatives to the board. An independent director in a PSU board should not only be independent of the executive management, he/she should also be independent of the government and the political parties in power. The government should monitor the performance of the enterprise and the performance of its board of directors. The control and monitoring are done by government officials who are members of the board of directors. Without obstructing the authority of the directors, the government officials must communicate clearly the strategy and government views in the board meetings.

4.7.8 Role of Investigating Agencies

Effective and quick decision-making involves an element of risk which may mean occasional losses. The ultimate career decision of PSU executives seems to lie with officials of investigating agencies and not with board of management. It would be desirable to create a cadre of ombudsmen for PSUs making it imperative to refer any charges against executives to them before any disciplinary action is contemplated.

4.7.9 Other Issues

Some of the other issues faced are:

1. There is little connection between performance and pay in the public sector. This might reduce employee initiatives in the organisation. There is no adequate structure in corporate governance for the monitoring of organisational performance, since pay and performance are not related.
2. Though there are also instances of fraud in the public enterprises, yet the disclosures of the non-financial aspects in these units are not transparent.
3. An efficient risk-taking technique is often missing in PSUs. Unfortunately in PSUs, there is a positive risk aversion. Since there is a risk aversion, the boards also make them less effective and profit making is reduced greatly.
4. Ethics, morality and qualifications of political decision makers plays an important role in the performance of PSUs.
5. Memorandum of Understanding (MoU) basically covers annual plan/budget for the enterprises. Meetings are held with task forces to analyse the annual results points are allocated to the enterprises based on performance. The task force comprises of retired public/private sector senior executives and bureaucrats; it is the opinion of most of these members that these are futile exercises.

4.8 Governance Issues in the Voluntary Sector (NGO's and Charitable Organisations)

The voluntary association of people involved in collective action, around shared interests, purposes and values comprise of organisations in the third sector. These organisations are known as not-for-profit, non-governmental, civil, society, social sector organisations or developmental organisations. They are mostly known are non-governmental organisations (NGOs). NGOs provide services which are required by the market or the government. They are self-designated advocates for any concern-related matters with the public. Due to their influence they are the force everyone wants to be with, though, they are facing scrutiny from donors, regulators, and the public at large. The recent debates on governance and accountability of NGOs are all the more critical considering the growing involvements of these organisations in 'new governance' while the "traditional boundaries of governance that have relied on legal and organisational measures of answerability" are no longer adequate for our purpose.

NGO Governance

Since the NGOs are trusted and accountable for, governance needs to be in places. Some of the reasons for the increasing importance of governance in the social structure are:

1. Development begun to be looked from people-centred approach and with economic liberalisation there was change in the idea of role of the state. But in 1990s, with the growing realisation that market or state alone cannot succeed in achieving the development goals in the third world countries, northern governments and aid agencies focused on principles of 'good governance'.

2. Emphasis on development of other institutions along with the market institutions were introduced due to the failure of structural adjustment program and an increase in corruption. Other important change was pro-democracy movements across the globe that improved political and social conditions for galvanising public support for NGOs and enabled them to play a bigger role. Governance in third sector emerged due to the importance that northern donor countries and institutions gave to it and often it was also 'conditionality' for getting aid.

3. Multilateral and bilateral donors and INGOs and later governments, regional NGOs, social activists started documenting good governance practices. In this way the Millennium Development Goals (MDGs) could be met.

4. The High Development Panel appointed by the UN Secretary General to review the post-2015 MDGs when it recognised the importance of good governance for development. It recommended that a governance indicator needed to be added to the MDG framework. To quote Daniel Kaufmann, World Bank economist, *"governance matters, in the sense that there is a strong causal relationship from good governance to*

better development outcomes such as higher per capita incomes, lower infant mortality, and higher literacy." It is important for organisations in the third sector to understand the internal and external relationships among the trustees, donors, NGO management and other involved parties. Today good governance has emerged as the key area of theory, policy, and practice and seen as the foundation for a just and equitable social order.

Below we discuss the strong features of governance in relation to the different sectors we have discussed above:

1. **Independence of the Board:** Board of directors should not personally benefit from any of the actions of the organisation and hence should be unrelated with the interests of any specific stakeholders and only concerned about institutional welfare.

   Governing body or boards constitute an important governance mechanism. Independence of the board is crucial for good governance. In case of corporates and NGOs this is taken care by appointing independent directors who have no special interest or links with any stakeholders and act as trustees of the organisation.

2. **Conflict of Interest:** Honesty as reflected in transactions entered into with related parties and insider trading. Transparency in related party transactions is essential as company's executive and board of directors have conflict of interest as they represent the interest of both the parties, and hence the principle is transparency, that is 'disclose'. To avoid the issue of insider trading, wherein again there is conflict of interest, the principle is 'disclose or abstain'.

3. **Disclosure Practices related to Ownership, Board and Management Structures, Processes, and Financials:** Disclosure will help minimise the risks related to management or the board taking advantage of the shareholder's ignorance of company's operations. In case of corporates and NGOs (registered under Section 25 of Companies Act, 1956) there is a policy for mandatory disclosures (as mentioned in clause 49 of the listing agreement with the stock exchange) and in case of public governance this has come into practice with passing of Right to Information Act and by mandatory disclosures of assets and liabilities of electoral candidate. These disclosures help in making an informed decision, whether that is case of a corporate, an NGO or electing a member of assembly.

4.9 Governance Aspects: Sarbanes-Oxley Act

The Sarbanes-Oxley Act of 2002 is mandatory. All organisations, large and small, MUST comply.

The legislation came into force in 2002 and introduced major changes to the regulation of financial practice and corporate governance. Named after Senator Paul Sarbanes and Representative Michael Oxley, who were its main architects, it also set a number of deadlines for compliance.

The Sarbanes-Oxley Act is arranged into eleven titles. As far as compliance is concerned, the most important sections within these are often considered to be 302, 401, 404, 409, 802 and 906.

An overarching public company accounting board was also established by the act, which was introduced amidst a host of publicity.

Sarbanes-Oxley Compliance

Compliance with the legislation need not be a daunting task. Like every other regulatory requirement, it should be addressed methodically, via proper analysis and study.

Also like other regulatory requirements, some sections of the act are more pertinent to compliance than others. To assist those seeking to meet the demands of this act, the following pages cover the key Sarbanes-Oxley sections:

4.9.1 Sarbanes-Oxley Act Section 302: CEO/CFO Certification

(a) **Regulations Required:** The Commission shall, by rule, require, for each company filing periodic reports under Section 13(a) or 15(d) of the Securities Exchange Act of 1934, that the principal executive officer or officers and the principal financial officer or officers, or persons performing similar functions, certify in each annual or quarterly report filed or submitted under either such section of such Act that:

1. The signing officer has reviewed the report;
2. Based on the officer's knowledge, the report does not contain any untrue statement of a material fact or omit to state a material fact necessary in order to make the statements made, in light of the circumstances under which such statements were made, not misleading;
3. Based on such officer's knowledge, the financial statements, and other financial information included in the report, fairly present in all material respects the financial condition and results of operations of the issuer as of, and for, the periods presented in the report;
4. The signing officers:
   (a) Are responsible for establishing and maintaining internal controls;
   (b) Have designed such internal controls to ensure that material information relating to the issuer and its consolidated subsidiaries is made known to such officers by others within those entities, particularly during the period in which the periodic reports are being prepared;
   (c) Have evaluated the effectiveness of the issuer's internal controls as of a date within 90 days prior to the report; and
   (d) Have presented in the report their conclusions about the effectiveness of their internal controls based on their evaluation as of that date.

5. The signing officers have disclosed to the issuer's auditors and the audit committee of the board of directors (or persons fulfilling the equivalent function):

    (a) All significant deficiencies in the design or operation of internal controls which could adversely affect the issuer's ability to record, process, summarise, and report financial data and have identified for the issuer's auditors any material weaknesses in internal controls; and

    (b) Any fraud, whether or not material, that involves management or other employees who have a significant role in the issuer's internal controls; and

6. The signing officers have indicated in the report whether or not there were significant changes in internal controls or in other factors that could significantly affect internal controls subsequent to the date of their evaluation, including any corrective actions with regard to significant deficiencies and material weaknesses.

(b) Foreign Reincorporations Have No Effect: Nothing in this section 302 shall be interpreted or applied in any way to allow any issuer to lessen the legal force of the statement required under this Section 302, by an issuer having reincorporated or having engaged in any other transaction that resulted in the transfer of the corporate domicile or offices of the issuer from inside the United States to outside of the United States.

(c) Deadline: The rules required by subsection (a) shall be effective not later than 30 days after the date of enactment of this Act.

4.9.2 Sarbanes-Oxley Act Section 404: Internal Control Report, Governance and Role of Auditors and Audit Committee

Management Assessment of Internal Controls

Section 404 is the most complicated, most contested, and most expensive to implement of all the Sarbanes-Oxley Act sections for compliance. All annual financial reports must include an Internal Control Report stating that management is responsible for an "adequate" internal control structure, and an assessment by management of the effectiveness of the control structure. Any shortcomings in these controls must also be reported. In addition, registered external auditors must attest to the accuracy of the company management assertion that internal accounting controls are in place, operational and effective.

A direct excerpt from the Sarbanes-Oxley Act of 2002 report for Section 404:

(a) Rules Required: The Commission shall prescribe rules requiring each annual report required by Section 13(a) or 15(d) of the Securities Exchange Act of 1934 to contain an internal control report, which shall:

1. state the responsibility of management for establishing and maintaining an adequate internal control structure and procedures for financial reporting; and

2. contain an assessment, as of the end of the most recent fiscal year of the issuer, of the effectiveness of the internal control structure and procedures of the issuer for financial reporting.

(b) Internal Control Evaluation and Reporting: With respect to the internal control assessment required by subsection (a), each registered public accounting firm that prepares or issues the audit report for the issuer shall attest to, and report on, the assessment made by the management of the issuer. An attestation made under this subsection shall be made in accordance with standards for attestation engagements issued or adopted by the Board. Any such attestation shall not be the subject of a separate engagement.

External Auditors

- Section 404 of Sarbanes-Oxley requires an issuer's external auditors to evaluate management's assessment of internal controls and to issue a report thereon. In addition, Title 2 of Sarbanes-Oxley establishes certain independence requirements for external auditors.
- Section 201 makes it unlawful for the issuer's external auditor to provide certain types of non-audit services to an issuer concurrent with the audit.
- Section 203 requires the external auditor to rotate every five years the lead audit or coordinating partner and the reviewing partner off the engagement.
- Section 204 requires the external auditor to report to the audit committee: "(1) all critical accounting policies and practices to be used; (2) all alternative treatments of financial information within generally accepted accounting principles that have been discussed with management officials of the issuer, ramifications of the use of such alternative disclosures and treatments, and the treatment preferred by the registered public accounting firm; and (3) other material written communications between the registered public accounting firm and the management of the issuer, such as any management letter or schedule of unadjusted differences."

Recommended Role of Internal Audit

The services that can be performed by the internal audit activity in meeting the requirements of Sections 302 and 404 should not interfere with the requirement of the standards for the internal auditor's independence and objectivity. The standards provide the framework for an effective internal audit activity and the recommended role of the internal audit activity in aiding a company in meeting its Sections 302 and 404 obligations should be consistent with the standards. This section describes the internal audit activities that are considered to be consistent with the objectives of the standards.

Activities that are included in the internal auditor's recommended role in supporting the organisation in meeting the requirements of Sections 302 and 404 include:
- Project Oversight
- Consulting and Project Support
- Ongoing Monitoring and Testing
- Project Audit

Management is responsible for implementing the processes necessary to meet the regulatory requirements of Sarbanes-Oxley. The role of' the internal auditor should support the management in carrying out its responsibilities.

Audit Committee

Although Sections 302 and 404 of the Sarbanes-Oxley Act of 2002 do not assign specific responsibilities to audit committees, Sections 301 and 407 establish broad standards for and disclosures regarding audit committees.

Section 301 establishes certain general standards with which audit committee members are required to comply. These standards are:
- Except for board of director fees, audit committee members may not accept consulting, advisory or other compensatory, fees from the issuer and its subsidiaries. Audit committee members must also not be an affiliated person of' the issuer and its subsidiaries.
- Audit committees must be directly responsible for the appointment, compensation, retention, and oversight of all registered public accounting inns that prepare or issue audit reports or perform other audit, review, or attest services for the issuer.
- Audit committees must establish procedures for receiving, retaining, and addressing complaints received by the issuer related to accounting, internal controls, and auditing.
- Audit committees must have the authority to engage independent counsel, as they deem necessary.
- Issuers must provide the audit committee with appropriate funding to enable it to fulfill its responsibilities.

Section 407 requires an issuer to disclose in its annual report whether it has at least one - audit committee financial expert" serving, on its audit committee, and if so, whether the expert is independent of management. An issuer that does not have all audit committee financial expert must disclose this fact and explain why.

4.10 Case Studies on Corporate Governance

4.10.1 Corporate Governance Failure at Satyam

It is one of Corporate India's worst unfolding chapters. What could be the reason behind such a huge collapse? The top level management failed to estimate the intensity of the gangrene in the organisation. Questions also arise on the role of the auditors, and how such a magnitude of financial fraud could have gone unnoticed. Corporate governance is a field which constantly investigates how to secure and motivate efficient management of corporations. What began as a corporate governance issue back in December has now turned into a major financial scandal in India. The shares of Satyam Computer Services has plummeted more than 90% in trading at the NYSE today, a stark reminder that investors must always cover their backs or else get racked even by the big names in the industry. NYSE today halted trading in Satyam Computer at its exchanges in the US as well as in Europe after the Chairman disclosed financial bungling at the Indian IT major.

A business will always have two sides; it is not necessary to gain profits but to sustain in the market, the integrity is vital. Every day in some or the other place there is a merger or an acquisition happening, but due to the projected image the co-players in the market are dropping out their plans of taking over Satyam.

Undoubtedly there will be intense focus directed at the other Indian IT Services companies as well. The Satyam corporate governance failure may also make its competitors bolder in terms of acquiring market share created by its fallout provided the industry can regain the trust of the same investors that Satyam has deceived.

From this necessarily brief review of the evidence, and particularly of the sources of failure in financial firms, some tentative conclusions have been drawn. The conclusions are:

1. People are more important than processes. Many of the failed firms, or near failed firms which we have encountered, had Boards with the prescribed mix of executives and non-executives, with socially acceptable levels of diversity, with directors appointed through impeccably independent processes, yet where the individuals concerned were either not skilled enough for, or not temperamentally suited to, the challenges came when the business ran into difficulty.

2. There are some good practice processes worth having. Properly constituted audit committees, and Board risk committees can play an important role, as long as they are prepared to listen carefully to the sources of advice from outside the firm.

3. A regulatory regime built on senior management responsibilities is absolutely essential, which is the foundation stone of the FSA's approach. In some of the cases we have wrestled with, senior management did not consider them to be responsible for the control environment and indeed, in the old pre-FSA regime, were able to

successfully claim that they were not responsible even if the business failed. So our regulation is built on a carefully articulated set of responsibilities up and down the business. It is important that they are not unrealistic.

4. Regulators must focus attention on the top level of management in the firm. For the major firms which we regulate, we insist that our supervisors have direct access to the Board, and that they present to the Board their own unvarnished view of the risks the firm is running, and of how good the control systems are by comparison with the best of breed in their sector. Unfortunately, we find some resistance to this approach. The management of some of our firms wants to negotiate the regulators assessment, so that when it reaches the Board it is agreed on paper and sufficiently bland to cause no debate. Well-structured Board, and a confident management, should welcome an independent view, even expressed at the Board level, which they may challenge and contest if they wish. Boards should take more interest in the nature of the incentive structure within the organisation. It does not just consider the pay of the CEO but of the organisation. Most problematic cases are because of misalignment of incentives.

5. No corporate governance system will work well unless there is some engagement on the part of the shareholders. Boards are responsible to the shareholders. If these shareholders are not prepared to vote, and show little interest in the business strategy, then that accountability is somewhat notional, and unlikely to be effective.

4.10.2 Corporate Governance at Infosys

By the late 1990s, Infosys Technologies Limited (Infosys) had clearly emerged as one of the best managed companies in India. Its corporate governance practices seemed to be better than those of many other companies in India. Due to these good practices, Infosys was the recipient of many awards. In 2001, Infosys was rated India's most respected company by the Business World.

- Infosys was also ranked second in corporate governance among 495 emerging companies in a survey conducted by Credit Lyonnais Securities Asia (CLSA) Emerging Markets. It was voted India's best managed company five years in a row (1996-2000) by the Asia Money Poll. In 2000, Infosys had been awarded the "National Award for Excellence in Corporate Governance" by the Government of India. In 1999, Infosys had been selected as one of Asia's leading companies in the Far Eastern Economic Review's REVIEW 2000 Survey and voted India's most admired company by The Economic Times. Infosys had also provided all the information required by the Cadbury committee.

- Infosys had benchmarked its corporate governance practices against those of the best managed companies in the world.
- It was one of the first companies in India to publish a compliance report on corporate governance, based on the recommendations of a committee constituted by the Confederation of Indian Industries (CII).
- Infosys maintained a high degree of transparency while disclosing information to stakeholders. It had been providing consolidated financial statements under US GAAP to its global investors and financial statements under Indian GAAP to Indian shareholders.

Code of Corporate Governance

- In the late 1990s, the Confederation of Indian Industries (CII) published a code of corporate governance.
- In 1999, the Securities and Exchange Board of India (SEBI) appointed a committee under the chairmanship of Kumar Mangalam Birla to recommend a code of corporate governance. The report was submitted by the committee in November 1999 and accepted by SEBI in December 1999 (Refer Exhibit III for the highlights of the report).

Infosys took both these recommendations into account and came up the corporate governance rules as stated below.

1. Infosys had an executive chairman and chief executive officer (CEO) and a managing director, president and chief operating officer (COO).
    - The **CEO** was responsible for corporate strategy, brand equity, planning, external contacts, acquisitions, and board matters.
    - The **COO** was responsible for all day-to-day operational issues and achievement of the annual targets in client satisfaction, sales, profits, quality, productivity, and employee empowerment and employee retention.
    - The CEO, COO, executive directors and the senior management made periodic presentations to the board on their targets, responsibilities and performance.

In 2001, the board had sixteen directors. There were eight executive directors and eight non-executive directors. Infosys believed that the one thing that could help them to improve corporate governance was to bring international professionals on corporate boards.

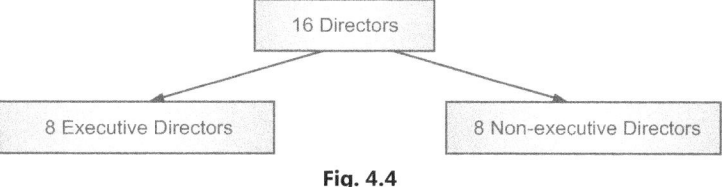

Fig. 4.4

2. The board members were expected to possess the expertise, skills and experience required to manage and guide a high growth, hi-tech software company. Expertise in strategy, technology, finance, and human resources was essential. Aged between 50–55 years, they did not serve in any executive or non-executive position in any company in direct competition with Infosys. The board members were expected to rigorously prepare for, attend, and participate in all board and relevant committee meetings.

3. Normally, the board meetings were scheduled at least a month in advance. Most of the meetings were held at the company's registered office at Electronics City, Bangalore, India.
   - The chairman of the board and the company secretary drafted the agenda for each board meeting and distributed it in advance to the board members.
   - Board members were free to suggest the inclusion of any item on the agenda.
   - Normally, the board met once a quarter to review the quarterly results and other issues.
   - The board also met on the occasion of the annual shareholders' meeting. If the need arose, additional meetings were held.
   - The non-executive directors had to attend at least four board meetings in a year. The board had access to any information that it wanted about the company.

4. In 2001, the board had three committees - the nominations committee, the compensation committee and the audit committee. To ensure independence of the board, the members of the nominations committee, the compensation committee and the audit committee were all non-executive directors.
   - The nominations committee had four non-executive directors who looked after the issue of retirement of existing members and their re-appointment, on the basis of their performance.
   - The nominations committee constantly evaluated the contribution of the members of the board and recommended to shareholders their re-appointment.
   - The executive directors were appointed by the shareholders for a maximum period of five years, but were eligible for re-appointment upon completion of their term.
   - The nominations committee adopted a retirement policy for the members of the board under which the maximum age of retirement of executive directors, including the CEO, was 60 years, which was the age of superannuation for the employees of the company. Their continuation as members of the board upon superannuation / retirement was determined by the nominations committee.

- The compensation committee, which had three non-executive directors, looked after issues relating to compensation and benefits for board members. It determined and recommended to the board, the compensation payable to the members of the board. The compensation of the executive directors consisted of a fixed component that was paid monthly, and a variable component, which was paid quarterly, based on performance. The annual compensation of the executive directors was approved by the compensation committee within the parameters set by the shareholders at the shareholders meetings. The shareholders determined the compensation of the executive directors for the entire period of their term.
- The compensation of the non-executive directors was approved at a meeting of the full board. The components were a fixed amount, and a variable amount based on their attendance of the board and committee meetings. The total compensation payable to all the non-executive directors together was limited to a fixed sum per year determined by the board.
- This sum was within the limit of 0.5% of the net profits of the company for the year calculated, as per the provisions of the Companies Act and as approved by the shareholders. The compensation payable to the non-executive directors (and the method of calculation) was disclosed in the financial statements. Since 1999, the non-executive directors were eligible for stock options.

None of the directors gained financially from any other contract of significance which the company or any of its subsidiary undertakings was party to.

5. The audit committee was responsible for effective supervision of the financial reporting process, ensuring financial and accounting controls and compliance with the financial policies of the company. The committee periodically interacted with the statutory auditors and the internal auditors to ascertain the quality of the company's transactions; to review the manner in which they were performing their responsibilities; and to discuss auditing, internal control and financial reporting issues. The committee provided overall direction on the risk management policies and also indicated the areas that internal and management audits should focus on. The committee had full access to financial data. The committee reviewed the annual and half yearly financial statements before they were submitted to the board. The committee also monitored proposed changes in the accounting policy, reviewed the internal audit functions and discussed the accounting implications of major transactions.

6. As per the recommendations of the Kumar Mangalam Committee, Infosys included a separate section on corporate governance in its annual report, which disclosed the remuneration paid to directors in all forms, including salary, benefits, bonuses, stock options.

Infosys also laid emphasis on succession planning and management development. The chairman reviewed succession planning and management development with the board from time to time. The chairman and CEO also managed all interaction with the investors, media, and the government. Where necessary, he took advice and help from the managing director, president, and COO as well as the CFO. The managing director and COO managed all interactions with the clients, taking the advice and the help of the CEO. Both the CEO and the COO handled employee communication.

Infosys - A Benchmark for Corporate Governance

Some analysts felt that Infosys' corporate governance practices offered many lessons to corporate India. Infosys had shown that increasing shareholder wealth and safeguarding the interests of other stakeholders was not incompatible. Infosys had given its non-executive directors the mandate to pass judgement on the worth of its business plans. Every non-executive director not only played an active role in decision making, but also led or served on at least one of the three (Nomination, Compensation and Audit) committees. Infosys' founders had set very high standards, in a country where malpractices by founders were rampant. The founders only took salaries and dividends and derived no other financial benefits from the company.

Commenting on the strengths and weaknesses of Infosys' corporate governance, Nandan M. Nilekani, Managing Director, Chief Operating Officer and President of Infosys, said, "The strengths are that we have been very successful in creating a value based system with a very strong focus on ethics, and strong division between personal and professional funds etc. That has translated into brand equity, shareholder value etc. Obviously, we can do things better. We believe that we can never stand still. We will keep looking at global best practices, what the world is saying on this front. We keep trying to improve the way we manage to be on par with it." It remained to be seen whether other Indian companies could emulate the Infosys form of corporate governance.

4.10.3 Corporate Governance at Tata

Founded by Jamsetji Nusserwanji Tata (J. N. Tata) in 1868, the Tata group has developed into one of India's largest business conglomerates. Tata Sons, which was established as a trading company by J. N. Tata in 1868, is the promoter of the Tata group.

Tata Industries, initially established in 1945 as a managing agency for the businesses promoted by Tata Sons, propelled the group's entry into new and high-tech industries during the early 1980s. The Tata group generated total revenues of ₹ 614.34 billion during the year 2003-04 through its various companies in seven key industry sectors. The group has 80 companies in diverse sectors, and has been moving from product-driven businesses to brand-driven businesses. The group listed its materials, chemicals, energy and engineering products as product-driven while engineering services, automotive, communications and IT, services and consumer goods have been identified as brand-driven businesses.

Corporate governance is a mechanism not only to ensure accountability but also to demonstrate responsibility. The Tata group believes corporate governance and ethics are strong pillars of excellence, and consider them as fundamental elements of its cherished heritage. As a values-driven organisation, the Tata group places importance on integrity, understanding, excellence, unity and responsibility. While the Tata Code of Conduct (TCoC) serves as a guide to employees on values, ethics and business principles they need to follow, at a professional level, Tata Quality Management Services facilitates understanding and implementation of these very values and the TCoC, with a reference manual for Management of Business Ethics (MBE).

The concept of business ethics necessitates a set of standards by which a corporate entity regulates its behaviour in terms of what is legitimate and acceptable in the pursuit of its corporate goals.

Evoking trust among stakeholders simplifies decision-making for them in the context of the business, thereby generating goodwill for the company. Globally, the realisation that goodwill is essential for the longevity of corporations has emerged only recently, as articulated in The King Report on Corporate Governance, 2002. The experience of the Tata group shows, however, that such goodwill has held Tata enterprises in good stead for over 140 years.

Tata Code of Conduct

The fountainhead of the corporate governance of the Tata Power Company is the Tata Code of Conduct. The company is committed to abide by it, in its letter and spirit. And the company has earned the Tata brand name by virtue of this commitment. It draws its strength from the five Tata values:

1. **Integrity:** Integrity refers to conducting business fairly, with honesty and transparency. Everything done must stand the test of public scrutiny.
2. **Understanding:** Understanding means caring, showing respect, compassion and humanity for colleagues and customers around the world, and always working for the benefit of India.
3. **Excellence:** Excellence refers to constantly striving to achieve the highest possible standards in day-to-day work and in the quality of the goods and services provided.
4. **Unity:** Unity refers to working cohesively with the colleagues across the group and with the customers and partners around the world, building strong relationships, based on tolerance, understanding and mutual cooperation.
5. **Responsibility:** Employees must continue to be responsible, sensitive to the countries, communities and environments in which they work, always ensuring that what comes from the people goes back to the people many times over.

4.10.4 Corporate Governance at Wipro

Founded in 1945 as Western Indian Vegetable Products by M. H. Hasham Premji, Wipro commenced operations in 1946, and set up an oil mill and a hydrogenated cooking medium plant before going public. Wipro expanded into several other businesses on its own over the years. Industries such as tin containers, crushing, soaps, wax etc. were started. Premji was succeeded by his son Azim in 1966. The first diversification happened in 1975 when Wipro set up an independent company to manufacture hydraulic cylinders (known today as Wipro Infrastructure Engineering). Wipro's tryst with information technology started in 1980, with initial focus only on computer manufacturing and R&D. When IBM was asked to leave India in 1977, due to a dispute over investment and intellectual property, Wipro made its entry. Wipro began selling through a dealer network and began assembling products made by well-known companies such as Canon, Cisco Systems, Epson, Hewlett-Packard and Sun as its name had been established by 1980.

Sustainability Governance

The centrality of sustainability to Wipro's vision and outlook is reflected in the commitment and engagement with sustainability issues by Wipro's leadership team, starting with the Chairman. The Chief Sustainability Officer (CSO) who carries overarching responsibility for sustainability charter reports to the Chairman and is part of the Corporate Executive Council, the senior most executive body in the organisation. The strength of Wipro's sustainability governance is also derived from the fact that multiple functions see themselves as key stakeholders in its success; among these, the Global Operations team, the People Function, the Investor Relations team and the Legal team play a major role in several of the programmes. The sustainability programme is reviewed on a quarterly basis by the Chairman and the Corporate Executive Council.

Code of Business Conduct

Wipro has in place a Code of Business Conduct (COBC) which provides guidelines for all business transactions as well as direction. A lot of emphasis is laid on human rights, freedom of association, elimination of child labour, advertisement and media policy, avoidance of conflict of interest, prevention of sexual harassment, prevention of fraudulent and corrupt practices, and immoveable integrity all the time. All business practices and employees, contractor employees and consultants have to follow the COBC guidelines.

The COBC is introduced to the employee right from the time induction takes place and also the employees have to annually take an online test to claim their knowledge with the system of COBC. Wipro has a zero tolerance policy for non compliance with the non-negotiable aspects of COBC e.g. child labour, anti-corruption etc.

The Ombuds-process

Wipro's Ombuds process is designed to have a robust whistle blower policy which stakeholders and employees can use without fear and which shows that Wipro is a transparent and ethical company. Any affected stakeholder can report any violations of the COBC and any other matter of reliability to the appointed Ombuds-person. The Ombuds process provides a strong framework of assurance and protection to women employees in conjunction with the Prevention of Sexual Harassment policy.

The General Counsel is also the Chief Ombuds-person who works with designated Ombuds-persons in each Business Unit. The process ensures confidential and anonymous submissions regarding:

(i) Questionable accounting or auditing matters, the conduct of which results in a violation of law by Wipro.

(ii) Substantial mismanagement of company resources.

(iii) Any instance of sexual harassment or any other form of discrimination.

(iv) Any violation of human rights as articulated in the COBC and as per the principles of the U.N. Global Compact.

Points to Remember

- **Corporate governance** refers to the set of systems, principles and processes by which a company is governed.
- **The Main Constituents of Good Corporate Governance are:**
    1. Role and Powers of Board
    2. Legislation
    3. Code of Conduct
    4. Board Independence
    5. Board Skills
    6. Management Environment
    7. Board Appointments
    8. Board Induction and Training
    9. Board Meetings
    10. Strategy Setting
    11. Business and Community Obligations
    12. Financial and Operational Reporting
    13. Monitoring the Board Performance
    14. Audit Committee
    15. Risk Management

- **OECD Principles of Corporate Governance**
    1. Ensuring the Basis for an Effective Corporate Governance Framework
    2. The Rights of Shareholders and Key Ownership Functions
    3. The Equitable Treatment of Shareholders
    4. The Role of Stakeholders in Corporate Governance
    5. Disclosure and Transparency
    6. The Responsibilities of the Board
- **Potential Consequences of Poor Corporate Governance**
    1. Weak Management
    2. Deficient or Inadequate Accounting Systems
    3. Unsound Policies
    4. Not Adapting to Change
- **Agency theory** relative to corporate governance assumes a two-tier form of firm control: managers and owners. Agency theory holds that there will be some friction and mistrust between these two groups. The basic structure of the corporation, therefore, is the web of contractual relations among different interest groups with a stake in the company.
- **Transaction cost theory** examines the theory that directors would rather enter into agreements for their sources of goods and services as this reduces uncertainty as they have everything they need for the foreseeable future. By doing this the time and expense of sourcing materials is avoided.
- Mr. Friedman argues that a corporation, unlike a person, cannot have responsibility. No one would engage in a business contract with a corporation if they thought for one minute that a corporation was not responsible to pay its bills, for example. So clearly, therefore, a corporation can have legal, but also moral responsibilities.
- The stakeholder value approach conceptualises the company as an agent who contracts with multiple stakeholders like the employees, customer, supplier, government society and shareholder who provide different resources to the company in return for value gained by them.
- **Enlightened Stakeholder Theory** is also called as Enlightened Value Maximisation. The enlightened stakeholder approach is based on the structure of the stakeholder theory but takes the maximisation of shareholder value as the primary objective for decision makers and therefore solves the problem that arises from multiple objectives related to the stakeholder theory.

Questions for Discussion

1. Define corporate governance. Discuss the purpose and OECD principles of corporate governance.
2. Differentiate between governance and management.
3. What are the potential consequences of poor corporate governance and how poor governance contributes towards business failure?
4. Discuss in detail the agency, transaction cost, stakeholder and Friedman's theories of corporate governance.
5. Explain the key issues in corporate governance.
6. Describe the application of best practices in governance.
7. Explain the governance issues of global companies, public sector and voluntary sector.
8. Elaborate the Section 302 and 404 provisions of Sarbanes-Oxley Act 2002.

Multiple Choice Questions

1. According to Cadbury (2002), corporate governance is an issue of power and:
   - (a) Rights
   - (b) Accountability
   - (c) Profit
   - (d) Appropriability
2. The OECD argues that corporate governance problems arise because:
   - (a) Ownership and control is separated
   - (b) Managers always act in their own self interest
   - (c) Profit maximisation is the main objective of organisations
   - (d) Stakeholders have differing levels of power
3. An organisation that is owned by shareholders but managed by agents on their behalf is conventionally known as the modern:
   - (a) Conglomerate
   - (b) Corporation
   - (c) Company
   - (d) Firm
4. The modern corporation has four characteristics. These are limited liability, legal personality, centralised management and:
   - (a) Fiduciary duty
   - (b) Stakeholders
   - (c) Shareholders
   - (d) Transferability
5. The view that sees profit maximisation as the main objective is known as:
   - (a) Shareholder theory
   - (b) Principal-agent problem
   - (c) Stakeholder theory
   - (d) Corporation theory
6. Which intervention resulted from the Enron scandal?
   - (a) The Hampel Committee
   - (b) The Sarbanes-Oxley Act
   - (c) The Greenbury Committee
   - (d) The Cadbury Committee

7. Where an organisation takes into account the effect its strategic decisions have on society, this is known as:
   (a) Corporate governance
   (b) Business policy
   (c) Business ethics
   (d) Corporate social responsibility
8. What makes a corporation distinct from a partnership?
   (a) If the members of a corporation die, the corporation remains in existence providing it has capital
   (b) If the members of a corporation die, the corporation ceases to exist
   (c) A corporation cannot own property
   (d) A corporation cannot be held responsible for the illegal acts of its employees
9. The term 'asymmetry of information' means information in a corporation is:
   (a) Transferable to all stakeholders
   (b) Not transferable to all stakeholders
   (c) Not equally transparent to all stakeholders
   (d) Equally transparent to all stakeholders
10. The Institute of Chartered Accountants in England and Wales consider that one particular stakeholder group should have primacy over all other groups. Which stakeholder group are they referring to?
    (a) Customers
    (b) Managers
    (c) Shareholders
    (d) Society

Answers

| 1. (b) | 2. (a) | 3. (b) | 4. (d) | 5. (a) | 6. (b) | 7. (d) | 8. (a) | 9. (c) | 10. (c) |

Project Questions

1. How is corporate governance related to corporate performance? Illustrate your answer with suitable examples from the Indian corporate sector.
2. Justify the need and relevance of corporate governance to developing countries with particular reference to India.

Chapter 5...
Corporate Ethics

Contents ...

- 5.1 Introduction
- 5.2 The Ethical Value System
  - 5.2.1 Universalism Theory
  - 5.2.2 Utilitarianism Theory
  - 5.2.3 Distributive Justice
  - 5.2.4 Social Contract
  - 5.2.5 Individual Freedom of Choice
  - 5.2.6 The Ethical Value System - Professional Codes
- 5.3 Values
  - 5.3.1 Introduction
  - 5.3.2 Meaning of Values
  - 5.3.3 Importance of Values
  - 5.3.4 Types of Values
  - 5.3.5 Sources of Value Systems
  - 5.3.6 Values Across Cultures
- 5.4 Indian Values and Ethics
  - 5.4.1 Indian Culture for the Work-life
  - 5.4.2 Indian Values for the Workplace
  - 5.4.3 Ethics in Work-life according to the Bhagavad Gita
  - 5.4.4 Attitudes and Beliefs
- 5.5 Business Ethics
  - 5.5.1 Meaning of Business Ethics
  - 5.5.2 Nature and Characteristics of Business Ethics
  - 5.5.3 Need and Importance of Business Ethics
  - 5.5.4 Ethical Practices in Management
  - 5.5.5 Ethical Values in Different Cultures
  - 5.5.6 Cultural Diversity and Business Ethics
  - 5.5.7 Culture and Individual Ethics
  - 5.5.8 Relationship between Law and Ethics
  - 5.5.9 Role of Government of India in Enforcing Ethical Behaviour
  - 5.5.10 Impact of Laws on Business Ethics

5.6　Ethics and Corporate Excellence
　　5.6.1　Corporate Mission Statement
　　5.6.2　Codes of Ethics in Business Houses
　　5.6.3　Strategies for Organisational Culture Building
　　5.6.4　Total Quality Management (TQM)
　　5.6.5　Customer Care
　　5.6.6　Care of Employees as per Statues
　　5.6.7　Objective and Optimistic Approach
- Case Studies
- Points to Remember
- Questions for Discussion
- Multiple Choice Questions
- Project Questions

Learning Objectives ...

- To understand the theories related to ethical value system
- To have a basic understanding of meaning, importance and sources of values along with values across culture
- To study the basics of Indian values and ethics
- To comprehend the meaning, nature, need and some other aspects of business ethics
- To be able to explain the relationship between ethics and corporate excellence.

5.1 Introduction

Corporate ethics are relevant to all aspects of business conduct, including board strategies; the way companies treat employees and suppliers, sales and marketing techniques and accounting practices.

Corporate ethics go beyond the legal requirements for businesses' and concerns' optional decisions and behaviour guided by values. Therefore, ethics in the business world are relevant both to the conduct of individuals and the conduct of the organisation as a whole.

Corporate, business and organisational ethics are terms that can be used interchangeably. According to O. C. Ferrell, *"organisational or corporate ethics is one of the most important and yet the most overlooked and misunderstood of concepts in business ethics"*. Usually, it is associated with the core values espoused by a given corporate or organisation. These core values are commonly written up in a code of conduct, which serves as a central guide for the day-to-day decision-making within the organisation in question.

The proper understanding of corporate ethics is essential for developing ethical leadership. This is so, since organisations want to be seen as good corporate citizens, whose behaviour and dealings are both ethical and fair. There are a number of benefits for organisations that adhere to sound ethical values, including an enhancement of executive standards of behaviour, i.e., the "tone at the top," the positive motivation of employees, the protection of the given organisation's reputation, the fostering of greater respect for laws and regulations, and improved business relationships.

"Corporate or organisational ethics" refers to the generally accepted standards that guide behaviour in business and other organisational contexts. Business ethics in the corporate area require values-based leadership from top management, purposeful actions that include, planning and implementation of standards of appropriate conduct, as well as openness and continuous effort to improve the organisation's ethical performance. Although personal values are important in ethical decision-making, they are just one of the components that guide the decisions, actions, and policies of all organisations.

The burden of ethical behaviour relates to the organisation's values and traditions, not just to the individuals who make the decisions and carry them out. A firm's ability to plan and implement ethical business standards depends in part on structuring resources and activities to achieve ethical objectives in an effective and efficient manner.

Corporate ethics apply to all aspects of business conduct, including board strategies, how companies treat employees and suppliers, sales and marketing techniques and accounting practices.

5.2 The Ethical Value System

In all organisations, values and ethics take centre stage. Values can be defined as the principles or standards of behaviour which are important or those that is valued by someone (an individual or, collectively, an organisation). Ethics are moral principles that govern a person's behaviour that help him understand the concepts of right and wrong behaviour. In other words 'what is right and what is wrong' is determined by values, and 'doing what is right or what is wrong' can be defined as ethics. The set of cultural and moral values a person or a group has is the concept of the value system. It is a standard or guide of values, which is set or adopted by the person, organisation or society which guides the behaviour in all situations.

5.2.1 Universalism Theory

Universalism refers to concepts and issues with universal application or applicability i.e. transcending any existing localising boundaries.

In particular,
- Truth may be said to be universal, as opposed to relativism conceptions;

- Rights may be said universals, for example natural rights or the 1789 Declaration of the Rights of Man and of the Citizen, heavily influenced by the philosophy of the Enlightenment and its conception of a universal human nature;
- In comparative religion, universalism is the belief that true and valuable insights are available in many of the religious traditions which have grown up in various human cultures. It posits that a spiritually aware person will respect religious traditions other than his own and will be open to learning from them. It does not deny that immersion in one tradition is a useful anchor for an individual's spiritual development.

It does not necessarily deny that some things done in the name of religion, and some religious practices, are not constructive even though it celebrates the richness and value to be found among humankind's religious traditions. The way it distinguishes itself is from the view that there is only final prophet, one faith and one chosen people superseding all others. The name **universalist** refers to certain *religious denominations of universalism, which as a core principle adhere to standards and rituals which are convergent rather than divergent, often espousing themselves as alternatives to denominations based on dogmatic or factionalised differences*;

- A **universal religion** allows anyone to join in spite of their ethnicity. Whereas ethnic religions are determined by geography, language, social boundaries as well as genealogy. Examples of universal religions are Islam and Christianity whereas Judaism and Sikhism are ethic religions. Hinduism is also typically an "ethnic" religion, but converts will be able to be re-socialised into this system.
- **Universalism** is also used as a synonym for *moral universalism*, as a compromise between moral relativism and moral absolutism.
- **Universalism** may also wish for a union among all people of the world and to create a common global institution.

5.2.2 Utilitarianism Theory

Utilitarianism, derived from the Latin word "utilis" is a theory of ethics that prescribes the quantitative maximisation of good consequences for a population. Right or wrong depend on the consequences of an act, and that the more good consequences are produced, the better the act. This is usually in the form of happiness, pleasure, or preference satisfaction. It is usually for the welfare of people and hence it is often associated with welfarist thought.

History of Utilitarianism

Utilitarianism was first proposed by the Chinese philosopher Mozi, who lived sometime between the years of 479-381 B.C. during the Warring States Period. He was the founder of the school of Mohism in ancient China and advocated a utilitarian ethical system some 1,800 years before it was promoted as a viable principle in Europe.

Jeremy Bentham proposed the European Utilitarianism. From the principle of utility, Bentham defined Utilitarianism as: *"nature has put man under the governance of two sovereign masters: pleasure and pain."* A rule of utility was developed by him *"that good is whatever brings the greatest happiness to the greatest number of people."*

Later, he talked only about "the greatest happiness principle", when he realised that the formulation recognised two different and potentially conflicting principles.

In his famous (and short) book, *Utilitarianism*, **John Stuart Mill** argued that cultural, intellectual, and spiritual pleasures are of greater value than mere physical pleasures, because the former would be valued more highly by competent judges than the latter.

The broader concept of consequentialism was further developed by other philosophers, having been motivated by Bentham and Mill's theories. Hence it is difficult to get a perfect definition for these terms - utilitarianism and consequentialism as it is not entirely clear even among the famous philosophers.

Some other famous philosophers are James Mill William Godwin, and Henry Sidgwick. Modern day advocates include R. M. Hare and Peter Singer.

Types of Utilitarianism

1. **Negative Utilitarianism**

Negative utilitarianism requires us to promote the least amount of evil or harm, or to prevent the greatest amount of harm for the greatest number. Proponents argue that this is a more effective ethical formula, since, they contend, there are many more ways to do harm than good, and the greatest harms are more consequential than the greatest goods.

Some were of the thought that negative utilitarianism would be to produce the least painful method of killing the entirety of humanity, as this ultimately would effectively minimise pain.

2. **Act Utilitarianism vs. Rule Utilitarianism**

Act utilitarianism states the principle is applied directly to the selection of particular actions under particular circumstances. For this reason AU has also been called "direct utilitarianism." A rule utilitarian, on the other hand, is the principle applied to the selection of a set of rules, which are in turn used to determine what to do in particular situations. Thus RU is sometimes called "indirect utilitarianism." If adherence to the rule produces more happiness than otherwise, it is a rule that morally must be followed at all times. Rule Utilitarianism however, focuses on general rules that everyone should follow to bring about the greatest good for that community.

Utilitarianism shouldn't be limited to a community. It should count all people. Unlike Act Utilitarianism, it establishes the best overall rule that would be pursued by the whole community. We associate this form of utilitarianism with Mill. Rule Utilitarianism, states that you must follow the rules even if it doesn't lead to the greatest pleasure for the individual at the time. Rule utilitarianism should not be confused with rules of thumb. Many Act utilitarians agree that it makes sense to formulate certain rules of thumb to follow if they find themselves in a situation in which the consequences are difficult, costly, or time-consuming to calculate exactly. If the consequences can be calculated relatively clearly and without much doubt, then the rules of thumb can be ignored.

3. Preference Utilitarianism

Like any utilitarian theory, preference utilitarianism claims that the right thing to do is that which produces the best consequences; when defined in terms of preference satisfaction, the best consequences can include things other than pure hedonism, like reputation or rationality.

Preference utilitarianism is favored by the modern utilitarian philosopher Peter Singer, who was influenced by R. M. Hare.

4. Other species

Peter Singer, along with animal rights activists, has argued that the well-being of all sentient beings (conscious beings who feel pain, including animals) deserve equal consideration with that given to human beings. Bentham made a similar argument. Even those utilitarians arguing otherwise note that suffering in animals often causes humans to suffer, thus making it often immoral to harm an animal even if the animal itself is not given a moral status.

Combinations with Other Ethical Schools

As there were certain shortcomings found in both the systems, attempts have been made to combine utilitarianism with Kant's categorical imperative. For instance, **James Cornman** proposes that in *any given situation we should treat as "means" as few people as possible, and treat as "ends" as many people as are thus then consistent with those "means". He refers to this as the "Utilitarian Kantian Principle"*.

Other consequentialists may consider happiness an important consequence, but in addition argue that consequences such as justice or equality should also be valued, regardless if they increase happiness or not.

Consequentialism says that right or wrong depend on the consequences of an act, and that the more good consequences are produced, the better the act.

Criticism of Utilitarianism

1. Utilitarianism and "Common Sense" Morality

Since Utilitarianism has lead to a number of conclusions opposing the "common sense" ethics, it has been criticised a lot. A perfect example to cite would be that it has been said that one should not sacrifice other humans for their happiness. However, utilitarians have argued that often it is the common sense that has been used to justify the positions on both the sides when dealing with controversial issues and it varies from one individual to another thereby making it a unsuitable basis for common morals.

2. Comparing Happiness

One feature with utilitarianism is of comparing happiness among a group of different people. Earlier philosophers tried to measure happiness quantitatively and compared it through calculus but it has been difficult to measure happiness.

The pleasure that a sadist gets should be as important as the pleasure an altruist gets has been criticised. While creating pleasure for an altruist simultaneously helps other people, creating pleasure for a sadist simultaneously hurts other people. Sadist pleasure is said to be superficial and temporary, which is harmful for the sadist in the long run. Hence it has been found out that the pleasure a sadist gets cannot be calculated in a utilitarian calculation.

3. Predicting Consequences

Dennett explains that the long term effects on the nuclear policy will be considered beneficial by many and might outweigh the negative consequences. He concluded that it is too early for utilitarianism to weigh all the evidence and reach a definite conclusion. It is noted that utilitarianism might be the silent principle used by critics of nuclear power.

Utilitarians need not have perfect knowledge; but some knowledge of consequences is needed as they are needed in the near future. They try to maximise their happiness and make the consequences their best estimates. If the consequences of a decision are particularly unclear, it might make sense to follow an ethical rule which has promoted the most utility in the past. They also study that people trying to further their own interests run into situations in which the consequences of their decisions are unclear. This does not mean that they are unable to make a decision.

4. The Importance of Intentions

Utilitarianism has been criticised because it has neglected the desires or intentions which motivate actions and not just at the actions, which some people consider as important. An action which was originally planned to cause harm but backfires and instead causes good results would be equal to an action that was good with good intentions. Utilitarianism applies to results, desires and dispositions, rules, institutions, punishment, desires and dispositions, argue many utilitarians. For instance, bad intentions may cause harm (to the actor and to others) even if they do not result in bad acts. Once this is recognised, supporters argue that utilitarianism becomes a much more complex, and rich, moral theory, and may align much more closely with our moral intuitions.

Morality is viewed as a personal guided rather than a form of judging actions which have already been performed. One needs to look into morality when deciding what to do, which means intentions only matter because consequences cannot be known until the decision has been made.

5. Human Rights

Utilitarianism, has been rejected as some critics say it is incompatible with human rights. It often overlooks the rights of the minority groups and also may ignore the rights of the majority.

Utilitarianism would also require the indirect impact of social acceptance of inhumane policies to be taken into consideration.

Act and rule utilitarianisms differ in how they treat human rights themselves. Under rule utilitarianism, human right is considered as a moral rule whereas in Act utilitarians, human rights are not accepted as moral principles. Act utilitarians

- Agree that acts such as enslavement and genocide always cause great unhappiness and little happiness.
- Say that human rights could be considered as rules of thumb; although torture might be acceptable under some circumstances, as a rule it is immoral.
- Often support human rights in a legal sense, because utilitarians support laws that cause more good than harm.

6. Sacrifice of an Important Individual Interest for a Greater Sum of Lesser Interests

Utilitarians judge all actions by their ability to maximise good consequences; any harm to one individual can always be justified by a gain to the other. This holds true even if one individual's loss is great and the gain for the other is minimal, as long as the individuals receive the small benefit. They deny that individuals have inviolable moral rights. Utilitarians support the legal rights but they are not considered natural to principles. This seems a bit of a problem to the utilitarians as one of them puts it as, "nothing intrinsically wrong with sacrificing an important individual interest to a greater sum of lesser interests. That assumption is retained in the foundations of the theory, and it remains a source of moral concern."

Other criticisms of utilitarianisms are based on misconceptions. The principle of "the greatest good for the greatest number", introduced by Bentham, is often mistaken as meaning that if something hurts one person and helps many, it is always moral. This is not the case, however; as noted above, Bentham dropped the misleading "greatest number" part of the principle, replacing the original formulation with the more direct "greatest happiness principle." The principle of an action is determined by the quantity of happiness produced rather than the number of people who are happy. Second, many mistakenly believe utilitarianism means individuals' interests are sacrificed for the sake of the "society" or the nation. According to utilitarianism, however, one individual's interests can only be sacrificed for the sake of the interests of other individuals. As Bentham put it, "It is vain to talk of the interest of the community, without understanding what the interest of the individual is." While it may benefit individuals to have a healthy society or a functional state, neither of these are ends in themselves.

7. **Right and Wrong Dichotomy**

Utilitarianism states that in a situation, the right act is that which produced the greatest good while all others are wrong. Therefore even charitable actions could be considered wrong under this theory. William Shaw, contemporary philosopher and utilitarian, stated that a good utilitarian would still praise the wrongdoer for their charitable donation even though it is wrong. This is because punishing such a person would likely push them to no longer make any charitable contributions, so praising the wrongdoer would better serve the greater good than punishing them.

The decision to donate to charity was lauded even if the decision to ignore the inefficiency was dishonest.

8. **Proof**

The major criticism of utilitarianism is that it has not been proved by science to be the correct ethical system. Even then, supporters say that this is common to all ethical methods and will remain until the problem of retreat argument is solved. It can be argued that almost all political arguments use an unspoken utilitarian principle, with every side claiming that their solution is the one that increases human happiness the most.

5.2.3 Distributive Justice

Distributive justice *concerns what is just or right with respect to the allocation of goods (or utility) in a society.* Distributive justice is often differentiated with procedural justice. The difference lies in the fact that distributive justice focuses on just outcomes while procedural justice focuses on just processes. A very well known philosopher of distributive justice is John Rawls.

The distribution of goods among members of society at a specific time and whether the distribution is just is the main motive of distributive justice. People, who hold equality to be important, rely on ideas of distributive justice. However, not all are concerned with equality; instead the factor that unites them is to achieve the best results and the best distribution of wealth.

5.2.4 Social Contract

Social contract theory also known as **contractarianism** is often used in political science, philosophy and sociology to denote *an implicit agreement within a state regarding the rights and responsibilities of the state and its citizens, or more generally a similar concord between a group and its members, or between individuals.* The members within the society are supposed to agree to the terms of the contract by their own choice and not to violate the contract as violating the contract would mean a problematic attempt to return to the state of nature.

Often it has been discussed that the social contract theories depended on the conception of main being either "good" or "evil". The famous theorists of contractarianism are Thomas Hobbes (1651), John Locke (1689) and Jean-Jacques Rousseau (1762).

Overview

1. State of Nature and Social Contract

The *social contract*, as a political theory, explains the justification and purpose of the state and of human rights. According to **Hobbes'** canonical theory: *Without society, we would live in a state of nature, where we each have unlimited natural freedoms. The downside of this general autonomy is that it includes the "right to all things" and thus the freedom to harm all who threaten one's own self-preservation; there are no positive rights, only laws of nature and an endless "war of all against all"* (Bellum omnium contra omnes, Hobbes 1651). An agreement was made to understand the social contract by which we each gain civil rights in return for accepting the obligation to honor the rights of others, giving up some freedoms to do so. The sovereign state is the image of the society we want to create, which represents the members and which is formed by the delegation of our power.

2. A Fictional State of Nature

The emergence of the social contract from the state of nature is explained in terms of stories showing the logical basis of rights rather than attempting at the historical accuracy. Rousseau's 1754 *Discourse on the Origin and Basis of Inequality Among Men* is more a fictional account of what has passed than a realistic description of what happened. However, ambiguity persisted, and that Hobbes' formation of the state of nature approach from the realistic description of civil war. Due to political pressures, Hobbes was unable to publish the tome until war had already broken out, and he could be protected as he had fled from the continent. Hobbes and Rousseau view the social contract as an explicit, actual agreement while Locke sees it in a more traditional fictional sense.

3. Violations of the Contract

The civil rights and the social contract are neither "natural" nor permanently fixed, rather the contract is a means towards the end and is only justified to the extent that it meets the general interest. Hence when failings are found in the contract, renegotiations take place to change the terms, by means of elections.

Since rights come from agreeing to the contract, those who simply choose not to fulfill their contractual obligations, such as by committing crimes, risk losing some of their rights and the rest of society can be expected to protect themselves against the actions of such outlaws. If one wants to be a member of the society then he must act responsibly for following its rule, along with the worry of violating them which would lead to punishment. We are comfortable with laws punishing behaviour that harm people because we are concerned about others harming us and don't plan on harming others. However, philosophers such as Michel Foucault and Gilles Deleuze have argued that this is a repressive conception, which states that we all are "potential criminals". Indeed, Foucault criticised the concept of "criminal", and pointed out the relationship between crime, class struggle and insanity which, can burst out suddenly explaining the motto "we are all virtual criminals".

Some rights are defined in term of the negative obligation they impose on others. Rights involve positive duties such as right to have stolen property returned to you, which obligates others to give you back what's yours when they find it in the hands of others Theorists argue that a combination of positive and negative rights is necessary to create an enforceable contract that protects our interests.

History

1. Classical Thought

They say that social contract ideas was started by the Greeks; Plato has Socrates make a case for social contract ideas in *Crito* but criticises them in *The Republic*. Others say that Epicurus approved the "social contract" ideas and in his *Principal Doctrines* states that justice comes from agreement not to harm each other, and in laws being made for mutual advantage (pleasure, happiness), and that laws which are no longer advantageous are no longer just. The theory of sovereignty first elaborated by Hobbes in the 17th century, in the *Leviathan*, traditionally was considered a landmark in dictatorship. Francisco Suárez (1548-1617), from the School of Salamanca, was an early philosopher in social contract. Hence looking at these points, the Greeks had little to do with contractualism as it is formulated by modern philosophy.

2. Thomas Hobbes' Leviathan (1651)

Thomas Hobbes was one of the founders of modern political philosophy. He used to travel to other European countries to study the different forms of government. Hobbes believed that humans were basically selfish creatures who would do anything to better their position. Left to themselves, he thought, people would act on their evil impulses. According to Hobbes, people therefore should not be trusted to make decisions on their own. In addition, Hobbes felt that nations, like people, were selfishly motivated. To Hobbes, each country was in a constant battle for power and wealth. To escape this people would enter into a social contract: they would give up their freedom in return for the safety and order of an organised society. Therefore, Hobbes believed that a powerful government like an absolute monarchy was best for society – it would impose order and compel obedience. It would also be able to suppress rebellion.

3. John Locke's Two Treatises of Government (1689)

John Locke (1632-1704) was a philosopher, a medical doctor, an educator, a politician, and a man of action. He was opposed to authoritarianism in matters of belief, politics, and religion in favour of individual judgement. The goal of the Second Treatise of Government was:

- To determine the origin of political power
- To determine when political power is legitimate and when it is not

- To determine when we are obligated to obey the political powers and when we may legitimately resist
- To refute political absolutism

The major historical consequence of the Second Treatise was:
- Shift of balance of political power away from Royalty and absolute rulers, and toward elected officials and divided, conditional rule
- American Revolution
- Locke advances a social contract theory, one that starts from a state of nature and works towards an explanation and justification of government
- Locke's state of nature is not nearly as bad as Hobbes's. Locke's state of nature is better than certain kinds of governments
- So on Locke's view, obedience to government is not always justified. We're better off in a state of nature than in certain kinds of government

In Locke's State of Nature we have:
- Perfect freedom
- Perfect equality

Jean-Jacques Rousseau's Du Contrat Social (1762)

Jean-Jacques Rousseau (1712-1778), in his 1762 treatise *The Social Contract, Or Principles of Political Right*, outlined a different version of the contract theory, based on the conception of popular sovereignty, defined as indivisible and inalienable - this last trait explaining Rousseau's aversion for representative democracy and his advocacy of direct democracy. As an individual, Rousseau argues, the subject can be egoist and decide that his personal interest should override the collective interest. However, as part of a collective body, the individual subject puts aside his egoism to create a "general will", which is popular sovereignty itself. Popular sovereignty thus decides only what is good for society as a whole:

The heart of the idea of the social contract may be stated simply: Each of us places his person and authority under the supreme direction of the general will, and the group receives each individual as an indivisible part of the whole...

Rousseau's version of the social contract is the one most often associated with the term "social contract" itself. His theories had an influence on both the 1789 French Revolution and the subsequent formation of the socialist movement.

4. Pierre-Joseph Proudhon's Individualist Social Contract (1851)

While Rousseau's social contract was based on sovereignty, there are some more theories adopted by other philosophers, libertarians which do not involve agreeing to anything. This is related to the non-aggression principle.

Proudhon stated that an individual does not need to surrender to sovereignty to others. He said that the social contract is not between the individuals and the state but between individuals who refrain from governing each other, each one maintaining complete sovereignty upon oneself:

"What really is the Social Contract? An agreement of the citizen with the government? No, that would mean but the continuation of [Rousseau's] idea. The social contract is an agreement of man with man; an agreement from which must result what we call society. In this, the notion of commutative justice, first brought forward by the primitive fact of exchange, is substituted for that of distributive justice. Translating these words, contract, commutative justice, which are the language of the law, into the language of business, and you have commerce, that is to say, in its highest significance, the act by which man and man declare themselves essentially producers, and abdicate all pretension to govern each other".

Pierre-Joseph Proudhon, *General Idea of the Revolution in the Nineteenth Century* (1851).

5. John Rawls' Theory of Justice (1971)

John Rawls (1921-2002) proposed a contractarian approach that has a decidedly Kantian flavour, whereby rational people in a hypothetical "original position," setting aside their individual preferences and capacities under a "veil of ignorance," would agree to certain general principles of justice.

6. Philip Pettit's Conception of Republicanism (1997)

Philip Pettit argued in the *Republicanism: A Theory of Freedom and Government* (1997), that the theory of social contract, should be modified, in order avoid dispute. Philip Pettit argues that the absence of an effective rebellion against the contract is the only legitimacy of it, in much the same way that Karl Popper argues that the criteria of scientific work is its falsifiability.

Criticism

1. Social Contract is a Violation of Contract Theory

A contract is not said to be valid unless all parties agree to it, making sure no one is pressurised or threatened to enter into it. Lysander Spooner, states that a social contract cannot be used to validate government actions such as taxation, as the government will initiate force against those who do not wish to enter a contract. He says that such an agreement is not voluntary and hence it cannot be considered a legitimate contract.

2. Implicit Social Contract Theory Presupposes its Conclusion

The theory of an implicit social contract holds that by remaining in the territory controlled by some government, people give consent to be governed. This consent is what gives legitimacy to the government. Philosopher Roderick Long argues that this is a case of begging the question, because the argument has to presuppose its conclusion:

I think that the person who makes this argument is already assuming that the government has some legitimate jurisdiction over this territory. And then they say, well, now, anyone who is in the territory is therefore agreeing to the prevailing rules. But they're assuming the very thing they're trying to prove – namely that this jurisdiction over the territory is legitimate. If it's not, then the government is just one more group of people living in this broad general geographical territory. But I've got my property, and exactly what their arrangements are I don't know, but here I am in my property and they don't own it – at least they haven't given me any argument that they do – and so, the fact that I am living in "this country" means I am living in a certain geographical region that they have certain pretensions over – but the question is whether those pretensions are legitimate. You can't assume it as a means to proving it.

3. Ronald Dworkin's Law's Empire (1986)

Ronald Dworkin in his book Law's Empire, talks on social contract theory which first distinguishes the use of social contract theory and its use in a jurisprudential sense as a basis for legitimate government.

Dworkin argues that if every citizen were a party to an actual, historical agreement to accept and obey political decisions in the way his community's political decisions are in fact taken, then the historical fact of agreement would provide at least a good prima facie case for coercion even in ordinary politics:

So some political philosophers have been tempted to say that we have in fact agreed to the social contract of that kind tacitly, by just not emigrating when we reach the age of consent. But no one can argue that very long with a straight face. Consent cannot be binding on people, in the way this argument requires, unless it is given more freely, and with more genuine alternate choice, than just by declining to build a life from nothing under a foreign flag. And even if the consent were genuine, the argument would fail as an argument for legitimacy, because a person leaves one sovereign only to join another; he has no choice to be free from sovereigns altogether.

Basically the choice is not limited to the explicit consent vs. expulsion but also includes accepting the contract, then working to alter the parts that are disagreed with, as by participating in the political process.

4. Criticisms of Natural Right

Contractualism is based on a philosophy of rights being agreed to in order to further our interests, which is a form of individualism: each individual subject is accorded individual rights, which may or may not be inalienable, and form the basis of civil rights, as in the 1789 Declaration of the Rights of Man and of the Citizen. This individualist and liberal approach has been criticised since the 19th century by thinkers such as Marx, Nietzsche or Freud, and afterward by structuralism and post-structuralism thinkers, such as Lacan, Althusser, Foucault, Deleuze or Derrida.

Several of those philosophers have attempted, in a spinozist inspiration, of thinking some sort of trans-individuality which would precede the division between individual subject and collective subject (i.e. society).

5.2.5 Individual Freedom of Choice

Choice of an individual is often influenced by education, peers, profession, family and other environmental and situational factors. A person who respects other people's space and the quality of life they enjoy is more likely to have strong ethics especially with the proper treatment of others.

Freedom of choice is expressed through education, profession, leisure time activities, dresses, food habits, and type of company.

Value based behaviour is required for the survival and development of human beings as well as the individual. The individual could be clear in his ideas and understanding of the mission statements and values, which will then help him to evaluate the work practices.

If one keeps ethical values, it will help him or her to do the right things by being honest and act in a responsible manner, thereby generating positive values such as honesty, integrity, kindness, self respect, creativity, and positive attitude.

5.2.6 The Ethical Value System - Professional Codes

The ethical values for professional codes as prescribed by the Upanishads and the Bhagavad Gita are given as under:

1. Divine values are much more powerful than physical wealth.
2. Work should be regarded as worship and one should do duty without calculation of gain and loss.
3. By cooperation and mutual help all professionals shall achieve the highest human welfare.
4. Health and character are real power; and wealth character is based on divine values and divine values are based on wisdom.
5. A professional with positive values and skills can assure harmony and progress for the society.
6. Practice of self evaluation helps to remove the weakness and enhance positive values.
7. One must develop wisdom, vision and insight for building a good personality.

5.3 Values

5.3.1 Introduction

The last two decades is known as the E-Decade – where E stands for economy, environment and ethics. In these two decades we have noticed an extraordinary industrial growth and development, thereby changing the standard of living of people.

Though we have seen a huge leap in terms of economic development, it has also given rise to unethical methods as well as the wearing-away of values, which has resulted in corruption.

An organisation in running their business should not only have good quality goods and services but should also have proper values and ethics. Organisations these days have their own code of ethics which helps them in the smooth running of the business. Employees today will become managers tomorrow and hence they need to understand the code of ethics well so that in future they can strengthen it.

The study of values and ethics provides the following benefits for the management students:

- Create awareness of social and professional values
- Inculcate integrity
- Helps to realise social responsibility
- Helps to solve ethical dilemmas
- Helps to make the organisation a better place for work and development

5.3.2 Meaning of Values

Value can be a belief, a mission, and a philosophy that is meaningful. They are qualities, characteristics or ideas about which we feel strongly. Often the values that we hold affect our decisions, goals and behaviour. Value is often a belief or feeling that someone or something is worthwhile. Values are standards to guide our actions, judgements and attitudes. According to **Milton Rokeach**, a leading researcher of values, value is *"an enduring belief that a specific mode of the conduct or end-state of existence in personality is personally or socially preferable to an opposite or converse mode of conduct or end-state of existence."*

Values give direction and consistency to behaviour and help one know what to make time for and what not to make time for. It sets the direction in an individual's life.

The value system we acquire and develop affects our attitudes, preferences, goals and aspirations. Some people value money and power and hence put all their efforts in achieving them while ignoring the social, human and ethical implications. On the other hand, some people would value kindness, justice, principles thereby declining a good lucrative career option which may require them to compromise on their values.

At the society level it is the commonly shared values of a social group which determine the quality of life in it.

5.3.3 Importance of Values

Values play a vital role in business affairs in the following ways:

1. **Corporate Culture:** An organisation needs to have a strong corporate culture for the growth of their business.

2. **Guide to Action:** Values need to be in place as they help in decision-making and the actions that need to be taken in the business. These values provide the right answer to the basic question as what is good business.

3. **Objective Standards:** Values determine the managerial functions the managers perform.

4. **Social Responsibility:** Business has social obligations. Business enterprises follow ethical norms to fulfil their responsibilities to different sections of society such as obligations towards employees, customers, society, shareholders etc.

5. **Other:**
   (a) It influences the behaviour at individual and group levels.
   (b) A manager's values affect the decision making process of the organisation.
   (c) A manager's value system plays an important role at the time of employee appraisal.
   (d) It will help managers to resolve ethical dilemmas at the work place.

5.3.4 Types of Values

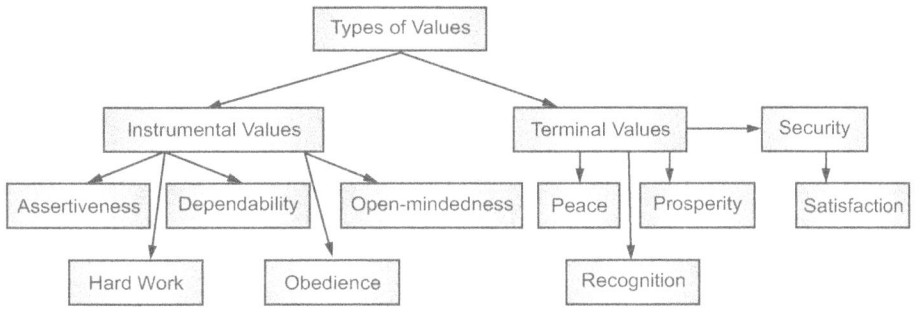

Fig. 5.1: Types of Values

1. **Instrumental Values**
   (a) **Assertiveness**: It is an important communication skill and is often linked to self-esteem.
   (b) **Dependability**: One good value quality is dependability as it is the reliability of a person that encourages others to depend on him because of his integrity, trustfulness and truthfulness.
   (c) **Hard Work:** Work with sincerity and devotion.
   (d) **Obedience:** Obedience, in human behaviour, is a form of social influence in which a person yields to explicit instructions or orders from an authority figure. Do not confuse it with conformity as conformity is behaviour which is intended to match that of others.
   (e) **Open-mindedness:** It is when a person is ready for new ideas, suggestions, opinions etc. Open-mindedness relates to the way in which people approach the views and knowledge of others, and incorporate the beliefs that others should be free to express their views and that the value of others' knowledge should be recognised.
   (f) **Truthfulness:** The quality of being authentic.
2. **Terminal Values**
   (a) **Satisfaction:** The fulfillment or gratification of a desire, need, or appetite. Pleasure or contentment derived from such gratification. A source or means of gratification.
   (b) **Peace and Harmony**: Peace is commonly understood to mean the *absence of hostilities*. Other definitions include freedom from disputes, harmonious relations and the absence of mental stress or anxiety, as the meaning of the word changes with the context. On the other hand harmony means agreement in feeling or opinion.
   (c) **Prosperity:** A state of health, happiness, and prospering.
   (d) **Recognition:** The confirmation or acknowledgment of the existence of an act performed, of an event that transpired, or of a person who is authorised by another to act in a particular manner.
   (e) **Security and Safety:** Security means the quality or state of being safe and safety means protection from harm.

Again we can classify values as follows:

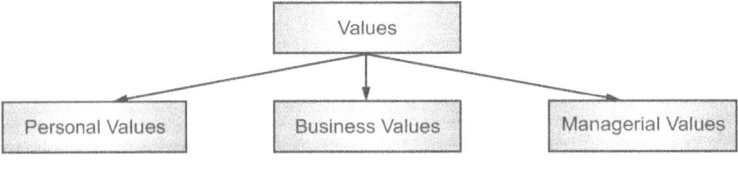

Fig. 5.2

1. **Personal Values**: A person is known by the values he believes and practices.
2. **Business Values**: An organisation is known by its quality of goods, services, customer satisfaction, growth, revenue etc.
3. **Managerial Values**: Training needs to be provided to the new entrants on value and ethics so that they can get accustomed to the environment.

5.3.5 Sources of Value Systems

The value system gets developed due to the following sources:
1. **Genetics:** Genetics plays a significant part of our value system as genes are responsible for a part of our value system, but some changes can be made by the environmental factors.
2. **Culture:** Certain values are reinforced by culture.
3. **Parents, Teachers, Friends:** Our parents, elders, teachers, gurus or even our friends establish certain values for us. What values we hold today are often derived from the views expressed by our peers.
4. **Other Value Systems:** The value systems we hold are not static and can be changed when we get exposed to other value systems.

5.3.6 Values Across Cultures

We have read many headlines involving corporate scandals which include account manipulation, corruption, cover ups etc, which leads us to believe of the decline in business ethics.

This trend is not a recent phenomenon but has been stated to start in the late 1970s. As employees look up to the top management regarding ethical and unethical behaviour in their organisations, the upper management should have a good sense of conduct regarding the ethical environment in the organisation.

In the previous section we have learnt about diversity and due to the values that differ across cultures, an understanding of these differences should be helpful in explaining and predicting behaviour of employees from other countries.

One of the most widely referenced approaches for analysing variations amongst cultures was done in the late 1970s by. A research was carried out by **Geert Hofstede** in the late 1970s, where he surveyed more than 116,000 IBM employees in 40 countries about their work-related values. He found that managers and employers varied on five value dimensions of national culture. They are listed and defined as follows:

1. **Power Distance:** The degree to which people in a country accept that power in institutions and organisations is distributed unequally. This ranges from relatively equal (low power distance) to extremely unequal (high power distance).

2. **Individualism versus Collectivism:** Individualism is the degree to which people in a country prefer to act as individuals rather than as members of a group. Collectivism is the equivalent of low individualism.
3. **Achievement versus Nurturing:** Achievement is the degree to which values such as assertiveness, the acquisition of money and material goods, and competition prevail. Nurturing is the degree to which people value relationships, and show sensitivity and concern for the welfare of others.
4. **Uncertainty Avoidance:** The degree to which people in a country prefer structured over unstructured situations. In countries that score high on uncertainty avoidance, people have an increased level of anxiety, which manifests itself in greater nervousness, stress, and aggressiveness.
5. **Long-term versus Short-term Orientation:** People who are in cultures with long-term orientations look to the future and value thrift and persistence. A short-term orientation values the past and present and emphasises respect for tradition and fulfilling social obligations.

A research study was done and here are a few highlights. China and West Africa scored high on power distance; the United States and the Netherlands scored low. Most Asian countries were more collectivist than individualistic; the United States ranked highest among all countries on individualism. Germany and Hong Kong rated high on achievement; Russia and the Netherlands rated low. On uncertainty avoidance, France and Russia were high while Hong Kong and the United States were low. China and Hong Kong had a long-term orientation, whereas France and the United States had a short-term orientation.

5.4 Indian Values and Ethics

Ethics is defined in **Indian management** as, *including all activities carried out within an organisation in order to ensure the fair and responsible behaviour of the organisation.* In India, Values and Ethics are taken from tradition, thoughts, Vedas, culture, and from the Mahabharata, Ramayana and the Arthashastra.

5.4.1 Indian Culture for the Work-life

1. **Man's Unique Inner Source:** Indian culture in simple terms states that everything is part of the divine. For example, Indians pray to the tulsi plant or to the snake during nag panchami. It states that this divine intervention in man, can lead him to perfection in wisdom, power and knowledge and due to this, man has scope for self development and improvement. With this capacity, human beings can achieve all seemingly impossible goals and overcome even monumental obstacles and difficulties. It motivates people to function, by reinforcing that he is not working alone.

2. **Holistic Relationship between Man and Nature:** The Hindu shastras have stated that there is a relationship between man and nature and also with the universe. It further states that they are interdependent and interconnected too. Indian culture places emphasis on both spirit and matter. Both these are interlinked in the holistic approach. This allows man to enjoy both the internal as well as external qualities of life. We can see that everything in this universe depends upon somebody else for their survival.

3. **Cooperation with Each Other:** Indian culture stresses upon cooperation amongst others at work and otherwise; integration, synthesis and team spirit for peaceful co-existence and mutual interdependence. Excessive competition, intra-organisation and inter-organisation, which is experienced by everybody in the workplace at present, have destroyed many a young mind and family lives, besides giving rise to stress, tension and frustration leading to alcoholism, excessive socialising, frightening loneliness, drug and sexual abuse, and even suicide. Cooperation, mutual trust and respect, joint efforts and team spirit can lead to all round prosperity and success for everyone concerned, due to the synergistic effect of combined effort. Close interdependence, interconnection and integration of human beings, society, nature and business, can only lead to the universal good of all concerned.

4. **Self Management:** The main point that Indian culture makes is that man should be able to take control of himself before he tries to manage anyone else. He should be able to analyse himself regarding his weaknesses, desires, strengths, dreams, goals etc. before being a good leader. The essence of self management lies in the proper control, harmony and integration between the body, mind, emotions, intellect and the soul. Only when one has self knowledge, can he undertake to manage himself.

5. **Yoga and Meditation:** To be a good manager one must need concentration and excellence at work. This can be achieved through yoga and meditation as yoga stands for excellence and mediation stands for concentration. When we are in a fix, we just need to sit in a quiet place to clear our mind and mediation helps us to reflect upon something deeply. Through meditation, complex problems of the firm can be solved.

6. **Dharma:** The other quality to look for in a good manager is integrity and righteousness which in our Indian culture is said to be "dharma". *Dharma stands for all those ideals, philosophies, purposes, influences, teachings and experiences that shape our character.* An organisation should inspire within itself all the essential human and ethical traits like courage, justice, self discipline etc. Dharma is different and specific for everyone in the organisation. The dharma of the chairman of the company would be different from the dharma of the office clerk. Only when an organisation keeps within its own dharma, and does not violate it, does the organisation flourish and grow.

7. **The Spirit of Renunciation (The Spirit of Sacrifice):** The spirit of renunciation of worldly goods and all material possessions is advocated by Indian philosophy and culture. The spirit of 'tyaga' is epitomised in Indian philosophy as a very great virtue. One is called upon to renounce all inner cravings and sensual enjoyment of outer objects. The tyaga philosophy is based on the belief that there is greater joy in overcoming a desire than in satisfying it.

5.4.2 Indian Values for the Workplace

1. **The Importance of Relationships in the Work Place:** Right from the time a child is born, it is exposed to warm and close relationships, along with overwhelming care and an excessive amount of love and concern from all corners which becomes a major characteristic of the Indian employee. The individual comes to the workplace with a strong need to relate to others. If this is not handled properly by the organisation, it can lead to the employee have an identity crisis which leads to poor team spirit and performance. It is up to the organisation to develop a strong relationship among the employees helping them in team building and emotional support.

2. **Respect for Elders:** Right when the Indian individual is a child, it has been put in its mind to respect, obey and admire elders. The same role is played in an organisation also where the older person offers his experience and guidance to the younger and the mistakes of the younger person gets converted into learning experiences. Such camadiere between the employees proves to be of enormous value.

3. **Respect for Hierarchy and Status:** In the Indian joint family system, a child learns very early in life, respect for hierarchical layers of people, their status within the family and their varying degree of authority. This is shown in his work life too where he adheres to the rules and regulations of the organisation, displays high support for his superiors and does not rebel. If this value of tolerance and respect for seniors is well utilised in the workplace, it then results in smooth maintenance of organisational power and mutually supports and empowers superior- subordinate relationship.

4. **Need for Security:** The Indian worker puts a very high premium on security even in the workplace, especially in his job, as in childhood all relations are protection oriented. It may make a person timid and may delay decision making, but it can also lead to the smooth functioning of the organisation. When an organisation makes employees feel safe and secure on the job, then employees are much more motivated to put in their best efforts.

5. **Need for Nonviolence:** Mahatma Gandhi had introduced the principle of 'ahimsa' or nonviolence, which was a powerful weapon against the British rulers.

The Indian value system appreciates the first ethical rule of "Do no harm". In the present context, the greatest need is the more proactive, more positive and more forceful ethical canon i.e. "practice ahimsa or nonviolence" and "do good".

6. **Need for Cooperation:** Cooperation *refers to the practice of people or greater entities working in common with commonly agreed-upon goals and possibly methods, instead of working separately in competition.*

   Cooperation is the process of groups of organisms working or acting together for their common/mutual benefit, as opposed to working in competition for selfish benefit.

   Many people support cooperation as the ideal form of management of human affairs. For cooperation to develop between two individuals, there need to be four main factors:
   - An overlap in desires
   - A chance of future encounters with the same individual
   - Memory of past encounters with that individual
   - A value associated with future outcomes

7. **Simple Living, High Thinking:** Hindu spirituality has been largely nurtured in a rural setting, and scripture recommends a simple life, free from unnecessary complication. Simple living requires the philosophical basis and inspiration provided by spiritual life. Without this higher taste, the lower self (mind and senses) erodes the desire and morality needed to develop one's relationship with Krishna. In essence, it is this pleasure of the eternal relationship with God that is being sought after even through consumerism. In the end, it is the only true pleasure. So without this higher taste, the mind eventually returns to material pleasures with the attractiveness and relevance of simple living being lost.

   Recent history provides many instances where simple living is maintained solely by the level of available technology. However, though fulfilling many of our ideals of simple living lacks the higher spiritual connection, simple living without higher thinking is also not recommended. Connection to the Supreme is the key.

8. **Rights and Duties:** Rights have no place in Indian philosophy. This however does not imply that the rights of individuals are neglected or ignored. When everyone discharges their duties as prescribed, everyone's rights get automatically fulfilled.

5.4.3 Ethics in Work-life according to the Bhagavad Gita

The Bhagavad Gita has got all the management tactics to achieve the mental equilibrium and to overcome any crisis situation. Bhagavad Gita means the song of the Spirit, the song of the Lord. The holy Gita has become a secret driving force behind the unfoldment of one's life. In the Mahabharata it is said that Arjuna got mentally depressed when he came to know the people he was fighting against were his own relatives. To motivate him, Krishna in the battle field of Kurukshetra preached the Bhagavad Gita where he motivates Arjuna to do his duty. Today, management has become a part of the office, factory, organisation or even our home. Management is a systematic way of carrying out activities in any field of human effort. In all organisations, management principles come into play through the management of resources, finance and planning, priorities, policies and practice.

Its task is to make people capable of joint performance, to make their weaknesses irrelevant, says the management guru **Peter Drucker.** It creates equilibrium in thoughts and actions, goals and achievements, plans and performance, products and markets thereby creating harmony in working together. Through maximum utilisation and with the minimum available processes to achieve the goal, it resolves situations of scarcity. Lack of management causes disorder, confusion, wastage, delay, destruction and even depression. Managing men, money and materials is the most important factor for a successful management.

Management Guidelines from the Bhagavad Gita:

There is an important distinction between effectiveness and efficiency in managing.

1. Effectiveness is doing the right things.
2. Efficiency is doing things right.

The general principles of effective management can be applied in every field, the differences being more in application than in principle. The managers' functions can be summed up as:

1. Forming a vision.
2. Planning the strategy to realise the vision.
3. Cultivating the art of leadership.
4. Establishing institutional excellence.
5. Building an innovative organisation.
6. Developing human resources.
7. Building teams and teamwork.
8. Delegation, motivation, and communication.
9. Reviewing performance and taking corrective steps when called for.

The critical question in all managers' minds is how to be effective in their job. The answer to this fundamental question is found in the Bhagavad Gita, which repeatedly proclaims that "you must try to manage yourself." The reason is that unless a manager reaches a level of excellence and effectiveness, he or she will be merely a face in the crowd.

Old Truths in a New Context

The Bhagavad Gita throws light on all the managerial issues which we face today such as conflicts, tensions, poor productivity, lack of motivation etc.

The management philosophy emanating from the West is based on the lure of materialism and on a perennial thirst for profit, irrespective of the quality of the means adopted to achieve that goal.

5.4.4 Attitudes and Beliefs

1. **Cooperation:** Cooperation is valued highly. Earlier cooperation was necessary for the survival of family and group and hence strong feelings of group solidarity, competition within the group was rare. No one is placed above or below the others and there is always a sense of security in being a member of the group. Improved behaviour and competing with one's own past performance needs to be incorporated.

2. **Group Harmony:** Always maintain harmony within the group and make sure emphasis is placed on the group. Stress is often laid on social harmony rather than task orientation. The needs of the group are considered over those of the individual.

   There may be a difference between group and individual emphasis as internal conflict may arise as those in school; an individual works for personal gain and not on group gain.

3. **Modesty:** One must remain modest even when one does well and achieves a great feat. Boasting about oneself is discouraged and often Indian children may not speak about their accomplishments and hence the outside world is not aware about their achievements.

4. **Dignity:** Value is placed on respect for an individual's dignity and personal autonomy. One is taught not to interfere in the affairs of another. People are not meant to be controlled. Unless someone asks for advice, one does not volunteer to give it.

   A conflict in these essential values is evident in circumstances in which Indians resist the involvement of outsiders in their affairs. Forcing opinions and advice on Indians on such things as careers only causes frustration.

5. **Placidity:** Feelings of discomfort are frequently masked in silence to avoid embarrassment of self or others. Placidity is valued, as is the ability to remain quiet and still. Often when Indians are ill at ease, you will notice them to be quiet pondering over what is expected of them, and they rarely show signs of anger or any

other emotions. This conflict in values often results in Indian people being incorrectly viewed as shy, slow, or backward. This value may differ sharply from that of the dominant society, which often values action over inaction.

6. **Patience:** Patience might not be valued by others who may have been taught "never to allow grass to grow under one's feet." To have the patience and ability to wait quietly is considered a good quality among Indians. Evidence of this value is apparent in delicate, time-consuming works of art, such as beadwork, quillwork, and painting.

7. **Generosity:** In India one of the most valued features is sharing and along with it come generosity. Whenever you go to someone's house, the way they treat guests is as if they were gods. It is said a valued person is not one with a large bank balance but one who gives generously. Greed is strongly discouraged.

8. **Indifference to Ownership:** Just for a status in society, mere acquirement of material goods is not important as compared to being a good human being. In the olden days those who accumulated goods were viewed with suspicion. Even today, one can see people giving away shawls, saris, money etc. to honour others and hence Indians tend not to be status conscious in terms of material goods. Non-Indians frequently have difficulty understanding and accepting the Indian's lack of interest in acquiring material goods.

9. **Indifference to Saving:** Traditionally, Indians have not sought to acquire savings accounts, life insurance policies and the like. This attitude results from the past, when nature's bounty provided one's needs. Most other needs (e.g., food, clothing, shelter, and land) were provided by nature in abundance, and little need existed to consider saving for the future. In Indian society, where sharing was a way of life, emphasis on saving for one's own benefit was unlikely to be found. This value may be at odds with the dominant culture, which teaches one to forego present use of time and money for greater satisfactions to come.

10. **Indifference to Work Ethics:** In the past, since Indians believed that nature provided their basic needs, they felt a need not to work. They used to work just to meet their immediate needs since material accumulation was not important. Observing a work schedule was not something Indians would have practiced.

11. **Careful Listening:** Being a good listener is highly valued. Since Indians have a good listening power they developed a sense of awareness which distinguishes an insincere person. As we know in the past, values and ways of life was thought through storytelling and oral recitation and hence Indians were made aware early about listening skills.

12. Careful Observation: Most Indians have sharp observational skills and note fine details. Likewise, nonverbal messages and signals, such as facial expressions, gestures, or different tones of voice, are easily perceived. Indians tend to convey and perceive ideas and feelings through behaviour.

5.5 Business Ethics

5.5.1 Meaning of Business Ethics

Business ethics is concerned with the behaviour of a businessman in doing a business. Unethical practices are creating problems to businessman and business units. The life and growth of a business unit depends upon the ethics practiced by a businessman. Business ethics are developed by the passage of time and custom. Customs differ from one business to another. If custom is adopted and accepted by businessmen and the public, that custom will become an ethic. Business ethics are applicable to every type of business. The social responsibility of a business requires the observing of business ethics. A businessman should not ignore business ethics while assuming social responsibility. Business ethics mean the behaviour of a businessman while conducting a business, by observing morality in his business activities.

- According to **Wheeler**, *"Business ethics is an art and science for maintaining harmonious relationship with society, its various groups and institutions as well as reorganising the moral responsibility for the rightness and wrongness of business conduct."*
- According to **Rogene A. Buchholz**, *"Business ethics refer to right or wrong behaviour in business decisions."*
- According to **Carter McNamara**, *"Business ethics is generally coming to know what is right or wrong in the workplace and doing what is right - this is in regard to effects of products/services and in relationship with stake holders."*
- According to **Elizabeth Vallance,** *"Business ethics attempt to apply general moral principles to business activities in order to resolve, or at least clarify, the moral issues which typically arise in business".*
- **David J. Fitzsche** states *"Business ethics is the process of evaluating decisions, either pre or post, with respect to the moral standards of the society's culture."*
- **Aristotle** defined 'virtue' as a matter of habit or the trained faculty of choice. Business ethics reflect the habits and choices managers make concerning their own activities and those of the rest of the organisation".

"The way in which the choices are framed, analysed, and either maintained or abandoned form the basic objective of the Business Ethics inquiry. The validation of Business Ethics, however, unpopular as a term, is simply a way of acknowledging that indeed, there are choices to be made concerning the means and ends which have essentially moral ingredients".

(Laura L. Nash, Good Intentions Aside – P. 5-6)

5.5.2 Nature and Characteristics of Business Ethics

1. **Provides Basic Framework:** Business ethics provide the framework within which business is to be conducted. They suggest cultural, social, legal, moral, and economic limits within which business has to be operated. Ethics suggest what is good and what is bad in business.

2. **Code of Conduct:** Business ethics are the code of conduct which businessmen should follow while conducting their normal business activities.

3. **Based on Moral and Social Values:** Business ethics are based on well-accepted moral/principal values. They recommend moral of conduct for businessmen. They include fair treatment to social groups, service to society and self-control.

4. **Needs Willing Acceptance for Enforcement:** Business ethics cannot be enforced by law or by force. They must be accepted by businessmen as self-discipline. They should come from within.

5. **Education and Guidance Required for Introduction:** Businessman should be given proper education, training and guidance to motivate them in following ethical business practices.

6. **Not Against Profit Making:** Business ethics are not against fair profit making. However, they are against making profit by cheating and exploiting consumers, employees or investors. They support expansion of business but by fair means and not through corrupt practices or illegal activities.

5.5.3 Need and Importance of Business Ethics

1. **Survival of Business:** Business ethics are mandatory for the survival of any business. Businesses with unethical practices may have short-term success, but they will fail in the long run. This is because a consumer can be cheated only once. After that, the consumer will not buy goods from that businessman. He will also inform others not to buy from that businessman. So this will defame his image and create negative publicity. This will result in failure of the business. Therefore, if businessmen do not follow ethical rules, they will fail in the market. So, it is always better for a businessman to follow an appropriate code of conduct to survive in the market.

2. **Smooth Functioning:** If the business follows all the ethical norms, then the employees, shareholders, consumers, dealers and suppliers will all be happy. And the business will get full cooperation from them. This will result in smooth functioning of the business. So, the business will grow, expand and diversify easily and quickly. It will have higher sales and higher profits.

3. **Safeguarding Consumers' Rights:** The consumer has many rights such as the right to be informed, right to choose, right to health and safety, right to be heard, right to redress, etc. But many businessmen do not respect and protect these rights. Ethical practices are essential to safeguard these rights of the consumers.
4. **Improve Customers' Confidence:** Ethical practices help in improving the customers' confidence about the quality, quantity, price, etc. of the products. The customers have more trust and confidence in the businessmen who follow ethical rules. They feel that such businessmen will not cheat them.
5. **Develop Good Relations:** Business ethics help in developing good and friendly relations between business and society. They will result in a regular supply of good quality products and services at low prices to the society. They will also result in profits for the businesses thereby resulting in the growth of the economy.
6. **Consumer Satisfaction:** In the present scenario, the consumer is the king of the market. Any business simply cannot survive without consumers. Therefore, the main aim of business is consumer satisfaction. Dissatisfaction on the part of consumers will lead to no sales and thus no profits too. Consumers will be satisfied only if the business follows all the business ethics, and hence are highly needed.
7. **Protecting Stakeholders:** Business ethics are required to protect the interest of all the stakeholders, i.e., employees, shareholders, competitors, dealers, suppliers, etc. They protect them from exploitation through unfair trade practices.
8. **Creates Good Image:** Business ethics create a good image for the business and businessmen. If the businessmen follow all ethical rules, then they will be fully accepted and not criticised by society.
9. **Consumer Movement:** Business ethics are gaining more and more importance because of the growth of the consumer movement. Today, the consumers are aware of their rights. Now they are more organised and hence cannot be cheated easily. They take actions against those businessmen who indulge in bad business practices. They boycott poor quality, harmful, high-priced and counterfeit (duplicate) goods. Therefore, the only way to survive in business is to be honest and fair.
10. **Importance of Labour:** Labour plays a crucial role in the success of any business. Therefore, while dealing with them, businessmen must use business ethics. They must be given proper wages and salaries and provided with better working conditions. There must be good relations between the employer and employees. The employees must also be given proper welfare facilities.
11. **Healthy Competition:** The business must use a code of conduct while dealing with the competitors. There must be healthy competition among the competitors. Cut-throat competition should not exist. Similarly, equal opportunities to small-scale business should be given. Monopoly must be avoided. This is because a monopoly is harmful to the consumers.

12. **Stop Business Malpractices:** Some businessmen gets involved in business malpractices by indulging in unfair trade practices like adulteration, cheating in weights and measures, artificial high pricing, black-marketing, selling of duplicate and harmful products, hoarding, etc. These business malpractices are harmful to the consumers. Business ethics help to stop these business malpractices.

5.5.4 Ethical Practices in Management

Business ethics have not only been recognised as increasingly important, but have also undergone rapid changes and developments during the past decade or so. Business ethics can be said to begin where the law ends.

As the field of business ethics is widely debated, it has been broken down into various functional areas of business itself, so that each area and each issue can be looked at individually. By grouping business ethics along with business functions, one can develop ease of understanding. Also, each individual functioning under different business areas can concentrate only on the ethics of each area, thus helping the individual grasp the business ethics code of the company.

There are different types of ethics according to the various functions of a business. These are enumerated below:

1. **Ethics of Marketing**

   Ethics of marketing are the basic principles and values that govern the business practices of those engaged in promoting products or services to consumers. Sound marketing ethics are typically those that result in or at least do not negatively impact consumer satisfaction with the goods and services being promoted or with the company producing them.

   Marketing which goes beyond the mere provision of information about (and access to) a product may seek to manipulate our values and behaviour. To some extent society regards this as acceptable, but where is the ethical line to be drawn?

   - **Pricing:** Price fixing, price discrimination, price skimming etc.
   - **Anti-competitive practices:** These include but go beyond pricing tactics to cover issues such as manipulation of loyalty and supply chains. See: anti-competitive practices, antitrust law.
   - **Specific marketing strategies:** Greenwash, bait and switch, shill, viral marketing, spam (electronic), pyramid scheme, planned obsolescence etc.
   - **Content of advertisements:** Attack ads, subliminal messages, sex in advertising.
   - **Children and marketing:** Marketing in schools.
   - Black markets, grey markets.

2. Ethics of Human Resource Management

The ethics of Human Resource Management (HRM) cover those ethical issues arising around the employer-employee relationship, such as the rights and duties owed between employer and employee. Predictably, ethics of human resource management is highly debated, just like other sub-fields of business ethics. Some argue that there are certain inalienable rights of the workplace such as a right to work, right to privacy, right to be paid in accordance with comparable worth, right not to be a victim of discrimination etc. Some others claim that these rights are negotiable. This is where the question of ethics comes in.

Ethical discourse in HRM is often reduced to the ethical behaviour of firms in relation to their employees. Many firms behave as if the basic rights mentioned above were charity rather than rights. Except in occupations where market conditions overwhelmingly favour employees, employees are treated disposable and replaceable and thus they are defenselessly trapped in extremely vulnerable positions as far as job security is considered. This expendability of employees, however, is justified in 'business morality' texts on the grounds that the employee too has the free will to leave a company midway in case another opportunity arises.

It is believed that since both employees and employers do in fact possess economic power in the free market, it would be unethical if governments or labour unions impose employment terms on the labour relationship.

Discussions of ethics in employment management practices include issues like policies and practices of Human Resource management, the roles of the Human Resource (HR) practitioners, the decline of trade unionism, issues of globalising the labour etc.

- Discrimination issues include discrimination on the bases of age (ageism), gender, race, religion, disabilities, weight and attractiveness, affirmative action, sexual harassment and so on.
- Issues surrounding the representation of employees and the democratisation of the workplace: union busting, strike breaking.
- Issues affecting the privacy of the employee: workplace surveillance, drug testing, privacy and so on.
- Issues affecting the privacy of the employer: whistle-blowing.
- Issues relating to the fairness of the employment contract and the balance of power between employer and employee: slavery, indentured servitude, employment law.
- Occupational safety and health.

3. Ethics of Purchase, Selling and Distribution:

Every day the media has reports of cases of bribery and unethical business practices that involve the purchasing of materials or services in almost every country in the world.

Although we like to think that the people who determine contracts and purchasing agreements are fair and ethical, there are some that will accept coercion that may affect the award of contracts that are worth thousands of dollars to those that are worth millions of dollars.

(a) Purchasing Standards: Every company will hold their employees to a purchasing standard that is put in place with processes, methods and rules to ensure that the procurement process is as fair as possible. However, the purchasing of materials and services is a process that involves the interaction of purchasing staff and potential vendors, which leads to personal relationships and contacts. A purchasing professional will naturally call a vendor they have personal knowledge of before they cold-call other potential suppliers. The relationship between a company and their suppliers is one that is developed over a period of time and based on personal relationships.

However, the purchasing professionals are duty bound to their employer to ascertain the best product or service at the best cost, in the timeliest fashion. Purchasing standards are in place to ensure that the needs of the company are foremost in any negotiations with potential suppliers. The first ethical standards for purchasing professionals were published by the Association of Purchasing Management in 1929.

(b) Actions of Suppliers: Although we expect purchasing professionals to be as ethical as humanly possible, most companies have a sales department whose job is sell their product and that can mean having contact with employees of potential clients, which could be purchasing or non-purchasing staff. These sales teams will have budgets to promote products with advertising souvenirs, such as pens, calendars, diaries, etc. or more tangible gifts such as lunches. In a number of studies on purchasing it has been found that almost all purchasing professionals accept something from vendors, even if it as small as an item of stationery.

Although the majority of companies will require purchasing and non-purchasing employees to sign and abide by an ethics policy, smaller companies are less likely to either have or indeed abide by a code of ethics. Small business failure is high and it is vital for companies to win business, and that can come at the expense of ethics.

(c) Non-Purchasing Employees: Although large companies insist on purchasing professionals strictly adhering to ethics codes, the same is not necessarily true for non-purchasing staff. In many companies purchasing is allowed by department heads or even line staff which bypass the purchasing department all together. This means suppliers and sales departments can target non-purchasing staff to gain sales where perhaps they have been rejected by the purchasing department. Much of this rogue procurement is never seen by the purchasing department as it either is paid for a department's cost centre or checks cut by the accounting department.

Rogue purchasing has two major drawbacks for a company. Firstly the spending is never funnelled through the purchasing department so there is no way to know if the purchaser obtained the best price for the item. Secondly, the purchaser may have been unduly influenced to make the purchase; perhaps by gifts, personal relationship or even a conflict of interest. Rogue purchases can make up as much as fifty percent of a company's overall spending for a year. If non-purchasing employees are restricted to minor or even zero purchasing, the company would be confident that the purchases were made in an ethical manner and the best product was selected based on price, quality and delivery time.

4. **Ethics of Finance and Accounting:**

   Finance is fundamentally a social science discipline. The discipline shares its border with economics, accounting and management. Finance is concerned with technical issues such as the optimal mix of debt and equity financing, dividend policy, and the evaluation of alternative investment projects, and more recently the valuation of options, futures, swaps, and other derivative securities, portfolio diversification etc. Finance is often mistaken to be a discipline free from ethical burdens. However frequent economic meltdowns that could not be explained by theories of business cycles alone have brought ethics of finance to the forefront.

   Ethics of finance is narrowly reduced to the mathematical function of shareholder wealth maximisation. In the sections devoted to 'Financial Ethics' in 'Business Ethics' books, ethics of financial markets, financial services and financial management are discussed. Fairness in trading practices, trading conditions, financial contracting, sales practices, consultancy services, tax payments, internal audit, external audit are also discussed in them.

   Below mentioned practices should be strictly avoided for following ethics in finance and accounts:

   - Creative accounting, earnings management, misleading financial analysis.
   - Insider trading, securities fraud, bucket shop, Forex scams etc. concern (criminal) manipulation of the financial markets.
   - Executive compensation concerns excessive payments made to corporate CEOs.
   - Bribery, kickbacks and facilitation payments, while these may be in the (short-term) interests of the company and its shareholders, these practices may be anti-competitive or offend against the values of society.

5. **Ethics of Production:**

   This area of business ethics deals with the duties of a company to ensure that products and production processes do not cause harm. Some of the more acute dilemmas in this area arise out of the fact that there is usually a degree of danger in any product or production process and it is difficult to define a degree of permissibility, or the degree of

permissibility may depend on the changing state of preventative technologies or changing social perceptions of acceptable risk.
- Defective, addictive and inherently dangerous products and services.
- Ethical relations between the company and the environment like pollution, environmental ethics, carbon emissions trading etc.
- Ethical problems arising out of new technologies like genetically modified food, mobile phone radiation and health etc.
- Product testing ethics like animal rights and animal testing, use of economically disadvantaged groups (such as students) as test objects.

6. **Ethics of Intellectual Property, Knowledge and Skills:**

    Knowledge and skills are valuable but not easily "ownable" objects. Nor is it obvious as to who has the greater rights to an idea – the company who trained the employee or the employee themselves, the country in which the plant grew, or the company which discovered and developed the plant's medicinal potential? As a result, attempts to assert ownership and ethical disputes over ownership arise.
    - Patent infringement, copyright infringement, trademark infringement.
    - Misuse of the intellectual property systems to stifle competition like patent misuse, copyright misuse, patent troll, submarine patent etc.
    - Even the notion of intellectual property itself has been criticised on ethical grounds: see intellectual property.
    - Employee raiding: the practice of attracting key employees away from a competitor to take unfair advantage of the knowledge or skills they may possess.
    - The practice of employing all the most talented people in a specific field, regardless of need, in order to prevent any competitors employing them.
    - Bioprospecting (ethical) and biopiracy (unethical).
    - Business intelligence and industrial espionage.

7. **International Business Ethics:**

    The issues here are grouped together because they involve a much wider, global view on business ethical matters. While business ethics emerged as a field in the 1970s, international business ethics did not emerge until the late 1990s, reflecting the international developments of that decade. Many new practical issues arose out of the international context of business. Theoretical issues such as cultural relativity of ethical values receive more emphasis in this field. Other, older issues can be grouped here as well. Issues and subfields include:
    - The search for universal values as a basis for international commercial behaviour.
    - Comparison of business ethical traditions in different countries.

- Comparison of business ethical traditions from various religious perspectives.
- Ethical issues arising out of international business transactions: e.g. bioprospecting and biopiracy in the pharmaceutical industry; the fair trade movement; transfer pricing.
- Issues such as globalisation and cultural imperialism.
- Varying global standards – e.g. the use of child labour.
- The way in which multinationals take advantage of international differences, such as outsourcing production (e.g. clothes) and services (e.g. call centres) to low-wage countries.
- The permissibility of international commerce with pariah states.

5.5.5 Ethical Values in Different Cultures

The major clash on ethical issues occurs when cultural expectations clash with those of the country one is working in. These clashes create a doubt in the minds of the individual as well as the company they are working for. The best remedy would be to understand the foreign culture and at the same time to respect one's own ethical integrity.

1. **Legal Differences:** Often the foreign country's local laws are the biggest issue one faces in the foreign land. What is considered good in your country may prove to be a violation in the foreign country. To avoid breaking the law, learn about the rules of the foreign country thoroughly. There is an international agreement on corruption. The Organisation for Economic Cooperation and the Development Anti-Bribery and Corruption Treaty has laid out a unified set of ethical practices for working abroad.

2. **Other Companies:** Sometimes, when working abroad, the problems you encounter may not be entirely because of your action, but instead could be the company you are dealing with, which maybe violating the laws. For example, if the business you're working with is in the habit of offering bribes and violating the law, you may find yourself in a difficult situation. To avoid this, outline your ethical standard and expectations and the standards of the company before venturing into the business.

3. **Working Conditions:** Educate yourself about the country you're traveling to so you know what to expect. Often the issues you face when working abroad, are due to your own company. You may encounter working and living conditions that are below your expectations. Your company may outsource work to other companies and understanding the working conditions of your company may help you avoid dealing with unethical companies.

4. **Daily Considerations:** Often, when in a foreign land, it is just not the change or issues arising in the workplace, but cultural shock. For example you may encounter gender issues in countries with strict religious beliefs that dictate a woman to cover

her head or face. Likewise, the local diet may pose an issue as you may not be used to consume certain foods such as monkey or snake or boiled chicken. Whatever you may encounter, try to be flexible and respect the foreign cultures. One of the other major concerns would be health and safety issues. Simple acts such as drinking water and using the washroom can present ethical problems. Underdeveloped countries may lack proper sewage systems, causing sewage to leak into the local water supply. Before travelling to a foreign country, always be updated on the laws and customs of the country.

5.5.6 Cultural Diversity and Business Ethics

In recent years, many employers have embraced cultural diversity initiatives with the objective of creating an all-inclusive workplace environment. Cultural diversity, or multiculturalism, is based on the idea that cultural identities should not be discarded or ignored, but rather maintained and valued. Having a diverse workforce is an excellent goal, though cultural diversity can give rise to ethical issues which are often a challenge for employees as well as managers to resolve.

1. **Religious Differences:** If an organisation has a diverse workforce, then it will include individuals with different religious beliefs. Often these religious beliefs can clash with the organisation's policies. Before an employee is hired, the HR department should address these issues and clarify that whatever the employee's beliefs are, it is important for him to respect others in the workplace.

2. **Gender Issues:** In some countries, women are legally subordinate to men. When a woman has the same opportunity for promotion as men, it can create issues as sometimes it is difficult for the man to adjust reporting to a woman and having the woman occupy the top executive positions. In some countries, it's a crime even for men and women to work together and see eye to eye socially and professionally. It is the management's duty to address these cultural sensitivities without violating antidiscrimination laws.

3. **Hiring Decisions:** When an organisation decides to hire and wants to have a culturally diverse workforce, then they must hire from a diverse pool of candidates. The HR department can advertise the job openings in employee diversity networks or non-traditional publications. However, a hiring manager must hire the person most qualified for the position, regardless of race, gender, age or national origin. Tension can be created between an organisation's diversity goals and equal employment opportunity guidelines when hiring decisions are made in an environment that values diversity.

4. **Business Practices:** A cultural conflict may occur, when a business insists that its employees follow ethical business practices. In some cultures, government agents

expect businesses to provide incentive payments to expedite approval of requests such as permit and variance applications, though these payment maybe viewed as bribes that are prohibited by laws, which may lead to civil fines and criminal culpability. The organisation needs to provide training to its employees in regard of what is acceptable and unacceptable behaviour under the law.

5.5.7 Culture and Individual Ethics

The manner in which we behave ethically is based on our values and personality. What the organisation lays down in its rule book is important but equally important is the role of our personal values which should not be ignored. Research reveals that people, who have an economic value orientation, tend to make more unethical choices. In terms of personality, employees with external focus of control were found to make more unethical choices.

The ability to interpret choices is a clear influence on whether or not we behave ethically and how we react to other people's behaviours. Often the rating we give ourselves on ethics is higher than how people actually rate us. If we tend to believe we are more ethical then we will have little scope to improve. Hence it is important to get a good understanding of ourselves.

The way we react to unethical behaviour depends on the interpretations we make. We may punish a person if we interpret responsibility to the person. The basic fact lies in how we interpret a situation at the point of moment which in turn will determine how we react to the other person's actions/behaviour.

Culture and values go hand in hand. When we look at the culture of a country we are looking at the values they portray which distinguish them from one country to another. Around the world, there is a variance in the personality and work values and this variance explains people's behaviour, attitudes, preferences, and the transferability of management practices to other cultures.

Do not generalise. Not everyone in a given country shares the same values – people differ within and across nations. Some care about relationships while some care about money. Knowing about the values held in a society will tell us what type of a workplace would satisfy and motivate employees.

Researchers found that personality traits identified in western cultures translate well to other cultures. For example, the five-factor model of personality is universal in that it explains how people differ from each other in over 79 countries. At the same time, there is variation among cultures in the dominant personality traits. In some countries, extroverts seem to be the majority, and in some countries the dominant trait is low emotional stability. For example, people from Europe and the United States are characterised by higher levels of extroversion compared to those from Asia and Africa. There are many factors explaining why some personality traits are dominant in some cultures. For example, the presence of democratic values is related to extroversion. Because democracy usually protects freedom of speech, people may feel more comfortable socialising with strangers as well as with friends, partly explaining the larger number of extroverts in democratic nations.

A research which was conducted in areas which suffered from diseases, showed people limited their social contact with strangers which led to introversion. They had to develop strict rules for hygiene to cope with the infectious diseases and hence lower levels of openness in regions that experienced infectious diseases.

People perceive other people either by the situation or by the individual themselves. For example Westerners pay more attention to the individual while Asians pay more attention to the situation. For example, in one study, when judging the emotion felt by the person, the Americans mainly looked at the face of the person in question, while the Japanese also considered the emotions of the people surrounding the focal person.

Human beings have a tendency to self-enhance. Often we see ourselves being more positive than others do, but the traits in which we self-enhance are culturally dependent. In Western cultures, people may overestimate how independent and self-reliant they are whereas in Asia, such traits are not necessarily desirable.

From the above situations we can see that there is a lot of variation in individual differences around the globe, and hence being sensitive to these differences will increase the effectiveness of the manager when managing a diverse group of people.

5.5.8 Relationship between Law and Ethics

Laws have been passed which protect employees against what the society recognises as unethical behavior in the workplace. The laws replicate the ethical standards of the society.

Between the law and ethics, there has to be an association. In some instances, law and ethics overlap and what is perceived as unethical is also illegal. Sometimes they do not overlap. Still in other instances what is seen as unethical is still legal and what is seen as illegal is seen as ethical. To one group behaviour is seen as ethical but to another group it is not seen as ethical. Further complicating this dichotomy of behavior, laws may have been legislated, effectively stating the government's position, and presumably the majority opinion, on the behavior. Remember law and ethics is not necessarily the same thing in today's diverse business environment.

Law can be defined as a consistent set of universal rules that are:
- widely published,
- generally accepted, and
- usually enforced

The rules are laid down in a manner which states the way people are required to act with others in the society. The government can use force to enforce the laws as it is the one which establishes the laws. The below points define the terms in the definition of the law.

1. **Consistent:** If two requirements contradict each other, both cannot be termed a law, because people cannot obey both.
2. **Universal:** The requirements must be applicable to everyone with similar characteristics facing the same set of circumstances.
3. **Published:** The requirements have to be published, in written form, so that they are accessible to everyone within the society.
4. **Accepted:** The requirements have to be generally obeyed.
5. **Enforced:** Members of society must be compelled to obey the law if they do not choose to do so voluntarily.

The word **ethics** is derived from the Greek word *ethos* (*character*), and from the Latin word *mores* (*customs*). When put together they define how individuals interact with one another. In philosophy, ethics defines what is good for the individual and for the society and establishes the nature of duties that people owe themselves and to one another. The following points are characteristics of ethics:

1. Ethics involve learning what is right and wrong, and then doing the right thing.
2. Most ethical decisions have extended consequences.
3. Most ethical decisions have multiple alternatives.
4. Most ethical decisions have mixed outcomes.
5. Most ethical decisions have uncertain consequences.
6. Most ethical decisions have personal implications.

One important point to keep in mind is that there is a difference between ethics and morality. Ethics includes the system of beliefs that supports a view of morality, while morality refers both to the standards of behaviour by which individuals are judged, as well as the standards of behaviour by which people in general are judged.

Ethical values and legal principles are usually closely related, but ethical obligations typically exceed legal duties. In some cases, the law mandates ethical conduct.

Law and ethics are far from being equal. The law does not prohibit acts that are termed as unethical while at the same time the law also prohibits that some may call ethical.

The following diagram shows the relationship between law and ethics.

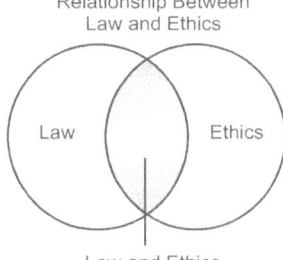

Fig. 5.3: Relationship between Law and Ethics

Establishing a set of ethical guidelines for detecting, resolving, and forestalling ethical breaches often prevents a company from getting into subsequent legal conflicts.

5.5.9 Role of Government of India in Enforcing Ethical Behaviour

In India the central or state government plays a major role on how businesses carry out their duties. The government plays a major role in most of the countries as it determines the conditions under which the person can enter a particular business by granting a license.

The government can assist the conduct of economic ventures which includes the control that merely lays down the general standards and prohibitions and those that interfere with matters that may be considered managerial. Public control may extend to the results of business operation as in the limitation of public utility profits, ceiling on dividend and imposition of excess profit taxes on business generally.

The government may sometimes take upon itself to initiate actions for the wellbeing of the public. The government also takes over private enterprises when they waste natural resources and when they fail to consider themselves as trustees of public good and abuse their power. The government takes over such enterprises so that their services continue to reach people and that their employees do not become unemployed. The government also controls the relationships between the various segments of the economy, the purpose being to settle conflicts of interests of legal rights and to prevent an undue concentration of economic power in one place.

The Indian Constitution - The preamble of the constitution states that attainment of social, economic and political justice and equality of status and of opportunity should be among the most important basic guiding principles of the functioning of the state. The constitution assures citizens of their fundamental right, the freedom to practice any profession, carry on any occupation, trade or business.

Some of the directive principles which promote ethical behaviour are cited below:

1. The state shall strive to promote the welfare of people by securing and protecting as effectively as it may, a social order in which justice, social, economic or political shall form all the institutions of national life.

2. The state shall strive to minimise the inequalities in income and endeavour to eliminate inequalities in status, facilities and opportunities, not only among the individuals but also amongst groups of people residing in different areas or engaged in different vocations.

3. The state shall in particular direct its policy towards securing -

    (a) That the citizens, men and women equally, have the right to adequate means of livelihood;

    (b) That the ownership and control of the material resources of the community are so distributed as best to serve for the common good;

    (c) That the operation of the economic system does not result in the concentration of wealth and means of production to the common detriment (loss);

    (d) That there is equal pay for equal work for both men and women;

    (e) That the health and strength of workers, men and women and the tender age of children are not abused and that citizens are not forced by economic necessity to enter a vocation unsuited to their age and strength.

4. That children are given opportunities to develop in a healthy manner and in conditions of freedom and dignity and that the children and youth are protected against exploitation and against moral and material abandonment.

5. The state shall with the limits of its economic capacity and development make effective provision for securing the right to work, to education and to public assistance in cases of unemployment, old age, sickness and disablement (Article 41).

6. The state shall make provisions for securing just and humane conditions of work and for maternity relief (Article 42).

7. The state shall endeavour to protect and improve the environment and to safeguard the forests and wild life of the country (Article 48).

8. The state shall take steps to secure participation of workers in management of undertakings, establishments of other organisations engaged in any industry (Article 43-A). The above mentioned directive principles clearly show that the government has considerable influence upon business behaviour if it has to attain the goals established by the constitution.

5.5.10 Impact of Laws on Business Ethics

The government of India has laid down various laws relating to businesses and the directive principles of the state policy of the Indian constitution provide enormous scope for government intervention in the functioning of a business.

All laws relating to business in India are classified as:

1. Business laws
2. Labour laws

(A) BUSINESS LAWS

The important business laws which regulate the business behaviour are:

1. The Industries Development and Regulation Act

This Act was passed in 1951 which gave practical effect to the industrial policy and gave the government powers to control the industry. The Act also authorises the central government to develop and control the industrial sector of India, through appropriate means. This Act however instead of benefitting the poorer section of the society has benefited the richer section.

A report on the operations of licensing under this Act by the planning commission in 1966 stated that:

1. The working of the planned economy had contributed to the growth of big companies.
2. The working of the industrial licensing system enabled the large industrial houses to obtain disproportionate large shares of the license issued.
3. The operation of the industrial licensing system was not successful in achieving the objective of regional dispersal of industries.
4. The large industrial houses were the major beneficiaries of public financial institutions. Thus this Act has not only failed to compel business to behave ethically, it has on the other hand encouraged unethical behaviour of big business houses.

Thus many controls of the government which were sought to be enforced through legislation were no doubt introduced with good intentions, but they not only failed to achieve the objectives but resulted in much unethical behaviour particularly in big business houses.

2. The Foreign Exchange Management Act, (FEMA)

This Act applies to:
- all citizens of India,
- outside India and
- to branches of companies registered in India.

The main objective of the Act is to conserve the foreign exchange resources of the country and to make proper utilisation for the economic development of the country. Foreign investments and collaborations have been sanctioned in many cases which have had no relevance to national priorities and development needs. This Act has faced severe criticisms. It is said to be the basis for corruption, black money, scams and has bought a major gap in trade. Instead of bringing in ethical behaviour, it has resulted in encouragement of unethical behaviour.

3. The Companies Act, 2013

This Act provides for a greater government control over the formation and management of companies. Some of its significant objectives which are considered ethical are:
1. Minimum standard of good behaviour and business honesty in company promotion and management.
2. Recognition of the interest of shareholders and creditors.
1. Fair and true disclosure of the affairs of the company.
2. Higher standard of accounting and auditing.
3. A provision for investigation into the affairs of any company managed in an oppressive manner to a minority of the shareholders.
4. Enforcement of the performance of duties by the management of the company.

However there exist many provisions in the Companies Act which are subject to manipulations. Companies resort to unfair trade practices while disclosing their affairs and this Act has been helpless to detect and punish such offences.

4. The Monopolies and Restrictive Trade Practices Act, 1969

The main objective of this Act is to control the restrictive and unfair trade practices.

The act stops false trade practices, advertisements that are misleading and adulteration. But some of the problems were that there was a considerable delay in disposal of cases under MRTP Act. It has been ineffective in preventing economic concentration.

5. The Essential Commodities Act, 1955

The Act was bought into force to provide keeping in mind the general public, control of production, supply and distribution of trade and commerce in certain commodities. The government had listed specific commodities as "essential commodities". Unfortunately the effects of this Act are not as expected as it has led to widespread unethical behaviour in the society.

Shortage of essential commodities has led to black marketing and the generation of considerable sums of black money has led to the creation of a parallel economy. It also led to corruption in bureaucracy which was invested with discretionary powers. This act also led to unethical behaviour and hardly proved effective in controlling essential commodities.

Some of the other laws which provide the government with sweeping powers to control business behaviour are:
1. The Capital Issues Control Act, 1956
2. The Securities Contracts Act, 1956
3. The Imports and Exports Act, 1947
4. The Indian Patents Act, 1970
5. The Partnership Act, 1932
6. The Sale of Goods Act, 1930
7. The Consumer Protection Act, 1986 and others.

(B) LABOUR LAWS

Labour laws are especially designed for the labour class. The basic attitude of labour legislation is to make sure that the regulation of employee-employer relationship is done so as to make sure social justice, labour welfare, needs of national economy and international uniformity are met as far as possible without compromising national interest and ignoring social problems.

The legislation is fundamentally based on the principle of social justice where the workmen are not exploited.

Labour legislation can be classified under the following categories:

(A) Laws relating to the weaker section (i.e. children and women):
(a) The Factories Act, 1948
(b) The Mines Act, 1952
(c) The Plantation Labour Act, 1951
(d) The Employment of Children Act, 1938
(e) Maternity Benefit Act, 1961.

(B) Laws relating to specific matters:

1. **Wages**
   (a) The Payment of Wages Act, 1963
   (b) The Minimum Wages Act, 1948
   (c) The Equal Remuneration Act, 1976

2. **Social Security**
   (a) Workmen Compensation Act, 1923
   (b) Retrenchment Benefit Act, 1947
   (c) The Payment of Bonus Act, 1965
   (d) Employee State Insurance Act, 1948
   (e) Fatal Accident Act, 1955

3. **Bonded Labour**

   Bonded Labour System (Abolition) Act, 1976

4. **Laws relating to Trade Union Act, 1926**

   (a) Industrial Dispute Act, 1947

   (b) The Workmen Compensation Act, 1923

5.6 Ethics and Corporate Excellence

Organisations operate to survive as well as to excel, in such a manner that they achieve perfection and excellence in any field and this can be termed as the basis of ethics.

Dr. M. B. Athreya: *Values like "atithi devo bhava (the customer is god) guna (quality) atmanirbharta (self-reliance) helps in surviving competition caused by globalisation and liberalisation leading to corporate excellence.*

Mr. Anil Sachdev, M.D., Eicher Consultancy Services - *It is possible to become a leading company if we excel in quality in all respect and do more with less. He also remarked "knowing our unlimited potential is the essence of Indian ethos".*

Business ethics is the source behind quality products, smooth production processes, fair employment practices, operational transparency, and concern for customers as well as shareholders and for social welfare. All these factors lead to corporate excellence.

Making mistakes or being less than excellent is certainly not unethical but individuals in the seat of authority and responsibility do have a moral obligation to perform to the best of their capacity and capability.

5.6.1 Corporate Mission Statement

An organisation mission is a generalised statement of its main purpose, often encompassing the key values which underlie those purposes and the way in which it seeks to achieve them. The mission is signified through the mission statement.

Mission is what an organisation is and why it exists. Mission is defined as an "essential purpose of the organisation, concerning philosophical questions like "what is our business, the nature of our business, and who our customers are etc. Though the mission should aim high, it should be realistic and achievable. It should be precise and have clarity. It should be unique and distinctive.

For a goal to be effective it should focus on the results instead of the activity and it should identify what the end goal of the organisation is.

For the mission statement to become more meaningful, everyone should participate in its formulation and not just its strategy planners or the top management. Only then it can be effective. If an organisation only focuses on commercial performance, it may run the risk of becoming inhuman and socially irresponsible when it has to face an ethical dilemma.

5.6.2 Codes of Ethics in Business Houses

Organisations, associations and private companies come up with their own codes of ethics which may be formally written. Sometimes if one violates these codes, it can be a ground for termination. Examples of such codes are:

- I will conduct all business dealings with fairness, honesty and integrity.
- I will protect all information and resources available to me from loss, theft, and misuse.
- I will avoid even the appearance of conflict of interest or any other impropriety.
- I will treat my fellow employees fairly and with dignity and respect.
- I will help create and sustain an atmosphere conducive to the spirit of this code.

We have seen earlier that there is a relationship between ethics and law which is important in management. Managers must take into consideration what their employees and the society consider as ethical as well, while keeping in mind the behaviours of what the customers will and will not accept.

Managers play a vital role in a company's legal and ethical performance. It is their responsibility to ensure that their employees abide by the Central, State, and Local laws, as well as any ethical codes established at the company. The policies and procedures cannot satisfy everyone but at least once these codes of ethics are in place, they can provide an outline for ethical behaviour, and allow customers to evaluate the type of company with whom they are doing business. Customers and employees must thoroughly read through these codes as well as the laws that have to be followed.

- A code of ethics is a statement of the norms and beliefs of an organisation. Norms are defined as the standard of behaviour which the organisation expects from everyone during a particular situation consisting of ethical problems. This encourages people to think in a positive attitude and to the wanted behaviour. The code of ethics generally makes an employee of the organisation aware of his or her obligation and the moral duties towards the organisation, but these codes cannot help to solve managerial dilemmas between economic and social performance.
- An organisation where its culture consists of top management's commitment to good business practices, open communication, shared values, beliefs and norms for everyone within the organisation stands to benefit from corporate excellence. The organisation culture governs people's behaviour in the direction where they strive to achieve and create excellence in corporate life.
- Values produce a sense of direction for the employees and help to guide their day to day behaviour Top management must continuously communicate these values to the lower levels in the organisation.

5.6.3 Strategies for Organisational Culture Building

Culture refers to the:
- set of values,
- dominant beliefs,
- guiding norms of behaviour for its employees,
- the climate, the atmosphere, the mental attitude shared by the members of the organisation.

A strong culture needs to be in place so as to provide a base for the productive ethos and ethical behaviour of an organisation. The organisation culture plays a dominant role in influencing employee's ethical behaviour.

Organisational culture is the tool for promoting ethical corporate behaviour. Some important strategies for organisational culture building are as follows:-

(a) Development of core values based on ethics.
(b) Focus on dominant beliefs.
(c) Corporate management's initiatives.
(d) Favourable environment.
(e) Adopt the environmental changes taking place in any organisation.

5.6.4 Total Quality Management (TQM)

Quality is no longer limited only to products and services but also measured in terms of value for customers. It is a systematic approach to guide an organisation towards excellence through superior quality products, services and processes. It is a corporate strategy.

Total quality consists of above four parameters:

(a) People
(b) Process
(c) Systems
(d) Management

Any organisation should develop and maintain this system in order to build an absolute advantage and competitive advantage from the market.

5.6.5 Customer Care

Customer is the king in the market, and hence customer care should be an utmost important factor so as to achieve success in the competitive market.

5.6.6 Care of Employees as per Statues

The corporate management's role in developing business leaders is concerned with:
1. Choice of future business leaders.
2. Career planning and development.
3. Succession planning.

The top management should decide the important employees of the organisation and decide on their development as well as to where they should be placed. There must be proper organisational structure through which one can understand the status, authority, responsibility and accountability of any employee.

5.6.7 Objective and Optimistic Approach

After the process of liberalisation, privatisation and globalisation, there appears to be a cut-throat competition and rat race among different business houses either indigenous or MNCs to win over each other.

Fulfilling short-term objectives but also fulfillment of long term objectives incorporated with ethical and, moral responsibilities by corporate houses to survive and excel in this era of intense competition and ever slippery market. Management should develop human values by setting examples so that they are perceived as role models, so as to perform corporate excellence.

If an employee is remunerated well, trained well and be overall satisfied he will be loyal to the organisation; hence Management should take care of their employees. The company will progress and the shareholders will be happy if the customers and employees have a win-win long term relationship. Shareholders since they also belong to the society will definitely influence the society, i.e., a happy shareholder will make the society happy.

The corporate management should be optimistic in approach and try to assess spirituality quotient, intelligence quotient and emotional quotient for proper balancing approach.

Case Studies

1. The Polluter's Dilemma

R. Ghosh is the environmental compliance manager for a small plastics manufacturing company. She is currently faced with the decision whether or not to spend money on new technology that will reduce the level of a particular toxin in the wastewater that flows out the back of the factory and into a lake. The factory's emission levels are already within legal limits. However, she knows that environmental regulations for this particular toxin are lagging behind scientific evidence. In fact, a scientist from the university had been quoted in the newspaper recently, saying that if emission levels stayed at this level, the fish in the lakes and rivers in the area might soon have to be declared unsafe for human consumption. Further, if companies in the region don't engage in some self regulation on this issue, there is reason to fear that the government — backed by public opinion — may force companies to begin using the new technology, and may also begin requiring monthly emission level reports (which would be both expensive and time consuming). But if the company's environmental compliance budget is tight, asking for this new technology to be installed would put her department over-budget, and could jeopardise the company's ability to show a profit this year.

Questions for Discussion:
1. What motives would the company have to install the new technology?
2. What motives would the company have to delay installing the new technology?
3. Why might the companies in this region prefer the government to impose new regulations?

2. Negligence and the Professional "Debate" over Responsibility for Design

On July 17, 1981, the Hyatt Regency Hotel in Kansas City, Missouri, held a videotaped tea-dance party in their atrium lobby. With many partygoers standing and dancing on the suspended walkways, connections supporting the ceiling rods that held up the second and fourth floor walkways across the atrium failed, and both walkways collapsed onto the crowded first floor atrium below. The fourth floor walkway collapsed onto the second floor walkway, while the offset third floor walkway remained intact. As the United States' most devastating structural failure, in terms of loss of life and injuries, the Kansas City Hyatt Regency walkways collapse left 114 dead and in excess of 200 injured. In addition, millions of dollars in costs resulted from the collapse, and thousands of lives were adversely affected.

The hotel had only been in operation for approximately one year at the time of the walkways collapse, and the ensuing investigation of the accident revealed some unsettling facts:

- During January and February, 1979, the design of the hanger rod connections was changed in a series of events and disputed communications between the fabricator (Havens Steel Company) and the engineering design team (G.C.E. International, Inc., a professional engineering firm). The fabricator changed the design from a one-rod to a two-rod system to simplify the assembly task, doubling the load on the connector, which ultimately resulted in the walkways collapse.
- The fabricator, in sworn testimony before the administrative judicial hearings after the accident, claimed that his company (Havens) telephoned the engineering firm (G.C.E.) for change approval. G.C.E. denied ever receiving such a call from Havens.

- On October 14, 1979 (more than one year before the walkways collapsed), while the hotel was still under construction, more than 2700 square feet of the atrium roof collapsed because one of the roof connections at the north end of the atrium failed. In testimony, G.C.E. stated that on three separate occasions they requested on-site project representation during the construction phase; however, these requests were not acted on by the owner (Crown Centre Redevelopment Corporation), due to additional costs of providing on-site inspection.
- Even as originally designed, the walkways were barely capable of holding up the expected load, and would have failed to meet the requirements of the Kansas City Building Code.

Due to evidence supplied at the hearings, a number of principals involved lost their engineering licenses, a number of firms went bankrupt, and many expensive legal suits were settled out of court. The case serves as an excellent example of the importance of meeting professional responsibilities, and what the consequences are for professionals who fail to meet those responsibilities. This case is particularly serviceable for use in structural design, statics and materials classes, although it is also useful as a general overview of consequences for professional actions. The Hyatt Regency Walkways Collapse provides a vivid example of the importance of accuracy and detail in engineering design and shop drawings (particularly regarding revisions), and the costly consequences of negligence in this realm.

Questions

1. Who was ultimately responsible for the fatal design flaw? Why?
2. Does the disputed telephone call matter to the outcome of the case? Why or why not?
3. What is the responsibility of a licensed professional engineer who affixes his/her seal to fabrication drawings?
4. In terms of meeting building codes, what are the responsibilities of the engineer? The fabricator? The owner?
5. What measures can professional societies take to ensure that catastrophes such as the Hyatt Regency Walkways Collapse do not occur?
6. Do you agree with the findings that the principal engineers involved should have been subject to discipline for gross negligence in the practice of engineering? Should they have lost their licenses, temporarily or permanently?
7. Was it fair that G.C.E., as a company, was held liable for gross negligence and engineering incompetence? Why or why not?

Points to Remember

- **Corporate or organisational ethics** refer to the generally accepted standards that guide behaviour in business and other organisational contexts.
- **Values** can be defined as those things that are important to or valued by someone.

- **Ethics (or moral philosophy)** involves systematising, defending, and recommending concepts of right and wrong behaviour.
- **Values** determine what is right and what is wrong, and doing what is right or wrong is what we mean by ethics.
- **Universalism** comprises concepts and issues which are said to be "universal" in appeal—i.e. transcending any existing localising boundaries.
- **Utilitarianism** (from the Latin 'utilis', useful) is a theory of ethics that prescribes the quantitative maximisation of good consequences for a population.
- **Distributive justice** concerns what is just or right with respect to the allocation of goods (or utility) in a society.
- **Social contract theory** (or contractarianism) is a concept used in philosophy, political science and sociology to denote an implicit agreement within a state regarding the rights and responsibilities of the state and its citizens, or more generally a similar concord between a group and its members, or between individuals.
- **An individual's value system** is defined as an enduring organisation of belief concerning preferable modes of conduct or end-state of existence along a continuum of relative importance.
- **Business ethics** is an art and science for maintaining harmonious relationship with society, its various groups and institutions as well as reorganising the moral responsibility for the rightness and wrongness of business conduct.

Questions for Discussion

1. Discuss in detail the theories related to ethical value system.
2. Define values. Describe the importance and sources of values.
3. How do values across cultures differ?
4. What are the lessons from Indian Ethos applicable in work-life? How are Indian values applicable at the workplace?
5. Define business ethics. Discuss the nature and need of business ethics.
6. Discuss the relationship between law and ethics. What is the impact of laws on business ethics?
7. Explain the relationship between ethics and corporate excellence.

Multiple Choice Questions

1. Which kind of theory does Utilitarianism have?
   - (a) Ethical
   - (b) Conceptual
   - (c) Behavioural
   - (d) None of the above

2. The main purpose of business ethics is to?
   (a) Understand ethical uncertainties (b) Principles And Concepts
   (c) Application of practices (d) All of the above
3. Utilitarianism suggests that it is ethical to make decisions based on:
   (a) Moral virtues (b) Common decency
   (c) What Is Best For Most People (d) None of the given
4. "Principle of Utility" as a method was the idea of:
   (a) James Mill (b) Herbert Spencer
   (c) Jeremy Bentham (d) Kant
5. Which one of the following moral judgement approaches will be used where someone has to make a decision how benefits and burdens should be distributed among the members of a group?
   (a) Utility (b) Rights
   (c) Justice (d) Caring
6. Idea of a precise quantitative method for decision-making is fully realised in:
   (a) Bentham (b) James Rachel's
   (c) Carol Gilligan (d) Henry Fayol
7. Which one of the following is a type of moral standard?
   (a) Utilitarianism (b) Rights
   (c) Justice (d) All of the above
8. Literally the word ethics stand for:
   (a) Understanding Human Nature (b) Study of morality
   (c) Properties of chemical (d) Substances
9. _____ is the philosophical study of moral values and rules.
   (a) Morality (b) Ethics
   (c) Business Ethics (d) Philosophy
10. Which one of the following is not a basic type of moral standard?
    (a) Utilitarianism (b) Rights
    (c) Justice (d) Relevant

Answers

| 1. (a) | 2. (b) | 3. (c) | 4. (c) | 5. (a) | 6. (a) | 7. (d) | 8. (a) | 9. (b) | 10. (d) |

Project Questions

1. Many social thinkers are of the opinion that morality and ethics are built on the foundation of religion. Do you subscribe to the view? Substantiate your answer.
2. Business ethics is basically a western concept. Would you agree? Substantiate your answer.

Question Paper
April 2015

Time : 2 ½ Hours												Maximum Marks: 50

Instructions to the candidates:
1. **All questions are compulsory.**
2. **All questions carry equal marks.**

Q.1 What is Social Responsibility? Explain it with respect to different stakeholders.

OR

What is the Bottom of the Pyramid opportunities? Explain economic potential of it.

Q.2 What is the concept of sustainable Development? Explain its importance.

OR

Differentiate between sustainable development and Green development.

Q.3 Write short notes (any two):
   (a) CSR report.
   (b) Understanding Ecological foot prints.
   (c) Economic dimension of sustainable development.

OR

Explain Environmental Impact Assessment (EIA). Also explain EIA in India.

Q.4 What is the concept of corporate Governance? Distinguish between Governance and Management.

OR

What is the Organisation for Economic Cooperation and Development (OECD)? Explain the OECD principles of Corporate Governance.

Q.5 Explain Business ethics with its nature and need.

OR

Write short notes on any two:
   (a) Ethical values in different cultures.
   (b) Code of Ethics.
   (c) Ethics and corporate excellence.

www.ingramcontent.com/pod-product-compliance
Lightning Source LLC
Chambersburg PA
CBHW080438230426
43662CB00015B/2318